Full Employment and Growth

To

Margie, Michael, Hugh and Roger

Full Employment and Growth

Further Keynesian Essays on Policy

James Tobin

Sterling Professor Emeritus of Economics, Yale University, US

Edward Elgar

Cheltenham, UK • Brookfield, US

Published by
Edward Elgar Publishing Limited
8 Lansdown Place
Cheltenham
Glos GL50 2HU
UK

Edward Elgar Publishing Company
Old Post Road
Brookfield
Vermont 05036
US

British Library Cataloguing in Publication Data
Tobin, James
  Full Employment and Growth: Further
  Keynesian Essays on Policy
  I. Title
  330.1

Library of Congress Cataloguing in Publication Data
Tobin, James, 1918–
    Full employment and growth: further Keynesian essays on policy /
James Tobin
    Includes bibliographical references and index.
    1. United States — Economic policy — 1993– 2. United States —
Foreign economic relations. 3. Economic Policy. 4. Monetary
policy. 5. Employment (Economic theory) 6. Keynesian economics.
I. Title.
HC106.82 T63 1996
339.5'0973—dc20   95–31937
                                                                CIP

ISBN 1 85898 372 X

Typeset by Manton Typesetters, 5–7 Eastfield Road, Louth, Lincolnshire LN11 7AJ, UK.

Printed in Great Britain at the University Press, Cambridge

Contents

PART IV INTERNATIONAL ECONOMIC RELATIONS

PART V SOCIAL POLICY

Figures

Tables

Acknowledgements

The publisher and the author wish to thank the following who have kindly given permission for the use of copyright material:

The American College for: 'Social Security, Public Debt and Economic Growth', *1990 Frank M. Engle Lecture on Economic Security*, 1990.

American Economics Association for: Review of 'Stabilizing an Unstable Economy' by Hyman P. Minsky, *Journal of Economic Literature*, Vol. XXVII, March 1989, pp. 105–7.

Eastern Economics Association for: 'An Old Keynesian Counterattacks', *Eastern Economic Journal*, Vol. 18, No. 4, Fall 1992, pp. 387–400.

Elsevier Science Publishers B.V. for: 'One or Two Cheers for the Invisible Hand', in S. Ghon Rhee and Rosita P. Chang (eds), *Pacific-Basin Capital Markets Research*, 1990, pp. 55–64.

Federal Reserve Bank of Kansas City for: 'The Case for Preserving Regulatory Distinctions', in *Restructuring the Financial System*, 1987, pp. 167–83.

Federal Reserve Bank of New York for: 'Remarks on International Considerations for US Monetary Policy in the Near Term', *Colloquium on International Financial Integration and the US Monetary Policy*, 1989, pp. 184–7.

Harvard Graduate Society Newsletter for: 'Current Controversy in Macroeconomics: The Four Schools', *Harvard Graduate Society Newsletter*, Fall 1990, pp. 5–9.

Harvard International Review for: 'Legacies of Reaganomics', *Harvard International Review*, Vol. XVI, No. 4, Summer 1992, pp. 10–13.

Harvard University Press for: 'Poverty in Relation to Macroeconomic Trends, Cycles and Policies', in Danziger *et al.* (eds) *Confronting Poverty*, 1994, pp. 147–67.

Industrial Relations Center, University of Minnesota for: 'Health Care Reform as Seen by a General Economist', George Seltzer Distinguished Lecture, April 1994.

Macmillan for: 'The International Monetary System: Pluralism and Interdependence', in Steinherr and Weiserbs (eds), *Evolution of the International and Regional Monetary Systems*, 1991, pp. 3–9.

M.E. Sharpe Inc. for: 'Thinking Straight about Fiscal Stimulus and Deficit Reduction', *Challenge*, March–April 1993, pp. 15–17.

M.E. Sharpe Inc. and William Brainard for: 'On Crotty's Critique of q-theory', *Journal of Post Keynesian Economics*, Vol. 12, No. 4, Summer 1990, pp. 543–9.

MIT Press and Robert Solow for: Introduction to James Tobin and Murray Weidenbaum (eds), *Two Revolutions in Economic Policy: The First Economic Reports of Presidents Kennedy and Reagan*, 1988, pp. 3–16.

National Association of Business Economics for: 'The Adam Smith Address: On Living and Trading with Japan: United States Commercial and Macroeconomic Policies', *Business Economics*, January 1991, pp. 4–16.

National Bureau of Economic Research for: 'Monetary Policy in the 1980s' in Martin Feldstein (ed.), *American Economic Policy in the 1980's*, 1990, pp. 151–6.

New York Times Company for: 'Bring the Dollar Down', *The New York Times*, Sunday 24 March 1991.

Routledge for: 'The Invisible Hand in Modern Macroeconomics', in Michael Fry (ed.), *Adam Smith's Legacy*, 1992, pp. 117–29.

Time-Warner for: 'Monetary Policy', in David R. Henderson (ed.), *Fortune Encyclopedia of Economics*, 1993, pp. 272–9.

Every effort has been made to trace all the copyright holders but if any have been inadvertently overlooked the publisher will be pleased to make the necessary arrangements at the first opportunity.

Preface

In *Policies for Prosperity: Essays in a Keynesian Mode* (Wheatsheaf Books, 1987) I published a collection of policy-oriented essays written between 1973 and 1986. The economic events that dominated those years were the two big shocks to oil supplies and prices, the resulting stagflations and recessions, the slowdown in growth and productivity in Europe, North America, and Japan, and the incomplete recoveries of the 1980s. Accompanying these events were important developments and controversies in government policies, notably Thatcherism, Reaganomics, monetarism and supply-side fiscalism. Parallel movements and debates occurred in the economics profession, with 'new classical' doctrines challenging the mainstream Keynesian teachings of the 1960s. My essays of those years defended Keynesian theories and policies against these attacks.

Those issues did not go away, but new political and economic events brought new challenges to economic policy and to economics in the years following. I did not go away either, and 26 policy-oriented writings – accessible, I hope, to students and general readers – are collected in this book. I am still a Keynesian – a columnist once referred to me as a 'Keynesian who won't quit'. I continue to fight for Keynesian policies and against the extreme revivals of classical economics within my profession. But many of these essays respond to other recent developments, notably the 'globalization' of markets for goods and for finance, the difficulties of transition to capitalism in the former communist economies, and the persistent rise in poverty and inequality in the United States.

Peter Jackson, who encouraged and helped me prepare the 1987 collection, has again earned my gratitude for the same services. Only I am culpable for errors and defects. As always, Yale University, its Department of Economics and its Cowles Foundation for Research in Economics have been generously supportive of my work, despite my formal retirement in 1988. My intellectual debts to my colleagues and students are too numerous to list. During the preparation of this book and the writing of most of its contents, the secretaries who faithfully assisted were Arlene Gianforte, Lois Jason and Marian Daly. They deserve my thanks, as do my stellar undergraduate assistants Greg Back, Andrew Metrick, Austan Goolsbee, Mitchell Tobin (no relation), Vassil Konstantinov and Serkan Savasoglu.

PART I

Macroeconomic Policy

Part I   Macroeconomic policy

This book begins with an essay prepared for a symposium in Edinburgh in 1986 to celebrate the 200th birthday of Adam Smith's *The Wealth of Nations*. His famous 'invisible hand' has recently been stretched to imply a complacent view of business cycles as healthy natural phenomena that require no interventions by central banks and governments. My dissent from this Panglossian view is, in different ways, the theme of the first five chapters. The sixth is an explanation of 'Tobin's q.', intended to clear up some misunderstandings. Incidentally, in the United States 'q', the ratio between the aggregate market value of corporate equity plus debt and the replacement cost of corporate productive capital assets, reached post-war highs in 1993, 1994 and 1995. The boom in corporate securities values both reflected and supported recovery and prosperity. Chapters 6 and 7 are, for a change, defences of my brand of mainstream Keynesian theory against attacks from the left.

1. The invisible hand in modern macroeconomics*

THE INVISIBLE HAND AND THE KEYNESIAN DICHOTOMY

The 'invisible hand', one of the great ideas of history and one of the most influential, is Adam Smith's most important legacy to macroeconomics, as to all economics. It is particularly important today as the ultimate inspiration for the new classical macroeconomics and the real business cycle theory. These are intellectual movements that engage many of the best brains in the profession, especially among younger cohorts and especially in the United States. They dominate the agenda even of theorists and econometricians who are sceptical or hostile to their methods and conclusions.

These movements are revolutions counter to Keynesian economics, itself a revolution against invisible hand orthodoxy. Keynes claimed to have detected a massive market failure. Workers were involuntarily unemployed, workers who were willing to work at real wages not exceeding their marginal productivities. Employers did not hire them, because of insufficient *effective* demand for what they would produce. The employment and output of the idle workers would enhance social welfare. Yet the market mechanism could neither prevent this failure nor correct it – could not correct it, that is, in good time and without government assistance. Keynes alleged this market failure to be an endemic flaw in capitalism.

The Great Depression lent credibility to Keynesian theory. So did the post-war prosperity of the advanced capitalist economies, which was widely attributed to the use of Keynesian stabilization policies. In the profession something of a reconciliation was achieved between Keynesian macroeconomics and classical or neoclassical microeconomics. Paul Samuelson called it the 'neoclassical synthesis'. At least it was coexistence, with each tradition assigned its domain, its textbook chapters, and its semester of the introductory course. The new terms with prefixes 'micro' and 'macro' signalled the division of the subject. Here is the Keynesian dichotomy in Keynes's own words.

*First published in Michael Fry (ed.), *Adam Smith's Legacy*, London: Routledge, 1992.

> I see no reason to suppose that the existing system seriously misemploys the
> factors of production which are in use.... It is in determining the volume, not the
> direction, of actual employment that the existing system has broken down.... Thus
> I agree with [Silvio] Gesell that the result of filling in the gaps in the classical
> theory is not to dispose of the 'Manchester System', but to indicate the nature of
> the environment which the free play of economic forces requires if it is to realise
> the full potentialities of production (Keynes, 1936: 379).

In other words, the invisible hand does just fine, with one giant exception.
Once this failing is remedied, once full employment is restored, and maintained, classical economics comes into its own, telling how resources are
allocated, how relative prices are determined, and how private and social
utilities are maximized. And Keynesian economics tells how to restore and
maintain full employment.

Keynes, it is true, was also critical of the inequalities of income and wealth
generated by free market capitalism. In this, however, he was not out of the
mainstream of his classical opponents, notably including Professor A.C. Pigou.
Moreover, Keynes asserted that the high propensity of wealthy countries to
save, which might be a source of unemployment and stagnation if left to
itself, could if channelled into accumulation of capital so reduce its rate of
return as to bring about 'the euthanasia of the rentier'.

As the domain of economics was divided, business fluctuations or 'cycles'
were macro phenomena, to be understood by theories of aggregate demand
set forth by Keynes and his successors. This was also initially the viewpoint
of monetarists, notably Milton Friedman, who differed from Keynesians with
regard to the determinants of aggregate demand, the sources of disturbances
in it, and the proper instruments and strategies of stabilization of demand.
Aggregate demand theories were, and still are, the rationales of the equations
of most econometric models – academic, proprietary and governmental.

THE CLASSICAL COUNTER-REVOLUTION

There were always true believers in the invisible hand who were uncomfort-
able with the macro/micro partition and with the rationale for it offered by
the neoclassical synthesis. Many of them were general equilibrium theorists,
or at any rate economists who took seriously its market-clearing paradigm.
They balked at describing as 'equilibrium' any situation with excess supplies
or demands in any markets, let alone in whole economies. Direct or indirect
disciples of Adam Smith, they believed that movements of prices – including
wages and interest rates – would quickly or instantaneously eliminate excess
supplies or demands. They understood how governmental or monopolistic
restrictions of competition might delay or prevent market clearings. If so, the

remedies would be removal of the restrictions; in any case Keynesian fiscal and monetary operations would be futile or worse. They saw Keynesian macroeconomic theory as dependent on an arbitrary and gratuitous assumption, endogenous inflexibility of money wage rates, which apparently attributed irrationality, even 'money illusion', to private agents.

In the 1970s unrest of this kind exploded into outright rebellion. There were reasons for this explosion outside of the profession, as there always are for major developments in economics, as there were in the times of Smith and Ricardo and Marx as well as those of Keynes. Just as the Great Depression of the 1930s was an environment favourable to the Keynesian revolution, the 'Great Stagflation' of the 1970s inclined both economists and the general public to welcome the counter-revolution. The sociology of our discipline is fascinating, but I am concerned here rather with its internal dialectics.

The new classical economics is, as the name applies, a revival of the major macroeconomic propositions of Smith, Say, Ricardo and Mill.[1] These propositions were less explicit and conscious in Smith than in his followers, but they were there nonetheless and served to inspire Say and other successors. They are implications of his central anti-mercantilist themes: that national wealth consists in the capacity to produce useful commodities, or goods that can be traded for them, rather than in the accumulation of gold and silver money, and that free competitive markets yield optimal results while government regulations are counter-productive. The two main macroeconomic propositions are Say's Law, that is, the impossibility of generalized excess supply, and the neutrality of money, that 'veil' which obscures the true and real economic phenomena to near-sighted observers.[2]

Real business cycle theory is a logical spin-off of new classical macroeconomics.[3] The business fluctuations we observe, this theory alleges, are sequential equilibria moving in response to basic exogenous shocks. These shocks are changes in tastes (as among work and leisure, consumption now and consumption later), in technology and productivity, in resource availabilities, and in external supplies, demands and prices. There can be no Keynesian shocks to effective aggregate demand, because markets clear so that there are never any excess supplies or demands. That disposes of the 'Keynesian dichotomy', the view that business cycles are disequilibrium phenomena, fluctuations of demand around a fairly smoothly growing capacity to produce. Real business cycle theory erases the common distinction between long-term growth trends and short-period cycles. They are one and the same. Supply and demand move together, not necessarily smoothly. All the shocks, all the outcomes that matter, are real. Nominal prices, money supplies, indeed all variables measured in the monetary unit of account, are irrelevant sideshows. Money is neutral not just in the long run but in the short run too. (Of course, gold and silver and other commodities of intrinsic non-monetary value may double as money. Changes in their supplies and demands and values in terms of labour and other goods and services will have real consequences.)

MACROECONOMICS IN *THE WEALTH OF NATIONS*

Adam Smith would feel at home with most of the content of his self-anointed modern disciples, it not with their language, style and methodology. His theory of economic progress in Book III focused on the growth of 'stock', accumulated savings as purchasing power over labour, at the disposition of business entrepreneurs. Continuously oriented to the most profitable uses and embodied in the most productive forms, stock is deployed to exploit opportunities for applying new technologies and for extending the division of labour. Smith emphasized stock as circulating capital. He appears to have assumed a one-period lag between inputs of labour and materials and outputs of saleable goods, in the manner of Piero Sraffa's 20th century classical model of production and prices. This assumption enabled Smith to speak of profits on stock interchangeably as mark-ups and as rates of return over time (I, vi, 6).

Smith would not be surprised that rates of growth fluctuate and are sometimes negative. He never found reason for such fluctuations in generalized shortages or excesses of demand. Nor did he find them in monetary expansions and contractions, even of gold and silver, nor in the commodity export or import surpluses that bring money into the nation or drive it out. In contrast, Hume expected monetary expansions and contractions to have at least temporary real effects, which indeed are part of the classical specie flow mechanisms of balance-of-payments adjustment (Dillard, 1988: 303; Smith, 1776: 308–9).

Smith said little about the determinants of saving and of the size and pace of accumulations of stock, but he regarded these as constraints on growth. He correctly saw holdings of gold and silver as diverting stock from productive employment, and therefore he welcomed prudent substitution of paper money for these precious metals. He was talking of banknotes, in modern terms 'inside money', liabilities that enable banks to make productive business loans, real bills. He seemed unworried about the possible inflationary dangers of this process, expecting rather that over-issue would depress the exchange values of the notes of errant banks (1776: 270–313).

Smith evidently believed in purchasing power parity for tradeable goods, even in the short run. He anticipated a theory that returned to fashion about 20 years ago as 'the monetary theory of the balance of payments', Smith, 1776: 284–8, 308–9, 403–6; Kindleberger, 1984: 8; Frenkel and Johnson, 1975). It concerns a system of fixed exchange rates, for example the gold standard. According to this model, the stock of money in any one country is just what is needed and desired to handle the economy's real transactions at given international nominal prices. The country is presumed to be too small to affect those prices by itself. Anything that creates in the one country an excess demand for real money balances, for example, productivity gains that increase output and transactions at existing prices, will suck gold into the country, entailing temporarily an export surplus. And vice versa, an expansion in domestic credit and banknote issue could create an excess supply of money. It would be worked off by export of gold (or by incurring gold debt to foreigners) and import of goods. The world-wide aggregate of nominal money supplies determines world-wide nominal prices.

Adam Smith's specific macroeconomic ideas are not an important part of his legacy to modern 'new classicals'. The invisible hand is their true inspirations. They reject the Keynesian dichotomy and expect competitive markets to transmute self-interest into public interest in macroeconomic as well as microeconomic outcomes. I turn now to an examination of the legitimacy of this application of Smith's great idea.

THE INVISIBLE HAND AND GENERAL EQUILIBRIUM THEORY

In *The Wealth of Nations* the invisible hand is a conjecture, an audacious and powerful idea to be sure, but an unproved assertion. It is a long way and almost two centuries from Smith to Arrow–Debreu, from the invisible hand to the twin fundamental theorems of welfare economics (Arrow, 1953; Debreu, 1959). These maintain that: 1) a competitive equilibrium is Pareto-optimal; and 2) any Pareto-optimal allocation is a competitive equilibrium for some distribution of endowments. Of course, Pareto-optimality is a very weak criterion. Smith (1776: 423) identifies 'public interest' with maximum 'annual revenue of the society', which I take to be real net national income. Two roads were travelled: the Anglo-Saxon line of economic theory through Marshall and Pigou; and the continental European road via Léon Walras, Vilfredo Pareto and Maurice Allais. Thanks to Irving Fisher, John R. Hicks and Paul Samuelson, the two strands came together earlier in this century.

Smith's conjecture was eventually rigorously proved by Arrow and Debreu, but at considerable cost to its generality. Let me remind you of some of the possible violations of the restrictive but necessary assumptions, stressing particularly those of macroeconomic significance.

Non-Convexities

The fundamental theorems cannot survive non-convexities in tastes or technology. Smith himself eloquently and realistically stressed specialization and division of labour as sources of efficiency and progress. But general equilibrium theory cannot cope with economies of scale and scope. For one thing, if these non-convexities can be internalized in single firms, they are inconsistent with perfect competition.

Imperfect Competition

The fundamental theorems require that all agents treat market prices as parameters beyond their control. This is the meaning of perfect competition. However, because of non-convexities or other factors, many prices are not impersonal data but decisions of firms and individuals or outcomes of negotiations. Smith was, understandably, imprecise on this point. The 'market' was a vague metaphor for many varieties of institutions for the purchase and sale of commodities, not a rigorous concept. The same is true for many uses of the term today, indeed for almost all lay discussions.

Externalities

Third-party effects not considered by firms and households are a well-known source of market failures. Deals among the parties, even if conceivable, entail transactions costs. Competitive markets do not naturally exist for by-product goods and bads. Externalities are often treated as exceptional *curiosa* (orchards and beehives) in older welfare economics literature. But the spate of environmental hazards now tells us that externalities are no joke.

Time and Uncertainty

Saving, investment and other intertemporal choices are not easy to introduce into general equilibrium models. Choices involving uncertainty are harder still. Irving Fisher and J.R. Hicks made important contributions. Arrow and Debreu 'solved' these problems simply by multiplying the list of commodities and distinguishing them by the time and 'state of nature' prescribed for delivery. The states of nature exhaust all possible contingencies. Competitive markets determine simultaneously prices for all these commodities. The market opens only once; the rest of economic history is just the deliveries then contracted. Lo and behold, the fundamental theorems apply! One difficulty is that the number of 'commodities' would be so numerous relative to the number of transactors that competitive markets could not exist for most commodities. This is true even though it suffices to have a number of markets equal to the sum of the number of states of nature and the number of basic goods and services rather than to their product.

'Sequence Economies' and Incomplete Markets

In actual economies spot markets are open continuously or repeatedly, few futures contracts are traded and few contingencies are insurable. As a result, there are plenty of opportunities for market failures. Rational expectations methodology, the theoretical rage of the last 20 years, can be seen as an attempt to compensate for missing markets. It attributes to agents a great deal of global knowledge of the structures of the economies and markets in which they are operating. However, it has not been shown how agents can acquire this knowledge from sequential observations generated by incompletely in-formed market participants. Those observations are distorted by the mis-informations that guided the agents. Note, by the way, that Smith's invisible hand alleged that every individual need respond only to local information and incentive. That conjecture certainly remains unproved.

Instabilities

Prices set in multiple interrelated markets might not clear all the markets of excess supplies and demands all the time. 'False' trading may occur at wrong prices. Presumably prices and quantities will then move in response to excess supplies and demands. Will these movements converge to the equilibrium? It is not certain without additional restrictive assumptions, for example that traded commodities are 'gross substitutes' in collective excess demand func-tions. A particular example of instability, related to the incompleteness of markets and the difficulty of forming rational expectations, concerns the responses of competitors to a profitable opportunity for investment. If a margin of price above cost opens up, the opportunity for each firm appears large, maybe indefinitely large if constant returns to scale apply. Each firm knows the market will absorb only a finite expansion of capacity in aggre-gate, but is ignorant of its competitors' plans. This situation can lead to over-building and to cobweb cycles, familiar in office space and ships.

Money

There is no room for money, especially paper money but also the fiat compo-nent of commodity money, in these general equilibrium models. Attempts to introduce it have foundered on the economies of scale and externalities that are intrinsic virtues of money. In consequence of these virtues, markets –

whether perfectly or imperfectly competitive – generate prices in money rather than in Smith's labour hours or any other commodity numéraire. Since money useful as a means of exchange is necessarily also a store of value, decisions to hold it over time are intertwined with other saving and investment decisions and are not necessarily neutral.

KEYNES'S REVOLT AGAINST THE PREMISES OF CLASSICAL MACROECONOMICS

Keynes was quite clear about the theoretical foundations of his rebellion against classical – he could have said neoclassical – macroeconomics. Markets or other processes set nominal wages, not real wages, and nominal prices, not relative prices. These nominal wages and prices are sticky, if only because there is not continuous and instantaneous market-clearing. Perceiving, as did Smith, that money is a store of value competitive in savers' portfolios with other assets, including real capital, Keynes rejected, as Smith did not, money neutrality.

Shocks to aggregate real demand frequently occur, possibly because business firms change their views of the future profitability of capital investments and of the acceptability of the risks, possibly because consumers decide to shift consumption between present and future. Keynes was quite explicit about missing markets, particularly the absence of futures markets. When a consumer decides not to eat lunch today, he conveys a negative demand signal to his customary restaurant but no signal of when in the future and where he intends to spend the amount saved. No investment is undertaken to prepare for his future demands (Keynes, 1936: 210–13). Absent such signals or Arrow–Debreu contracts, businesses and other investors who buy long-lived durable assets are exposing themselves to incalculable risks (Keynes, 1936: Chapter 12). Keynes also envisaged monetary shocks, changes in money supplies or velocities, which may become real demand shocks because nominal prices are sticky. But it is a vulgar fallacy, all too epidemic nowadays, to describe these as the only sources of Keynesian aggregate demand fluctuations.

Keynes questioned the capacity of the economy, once displaced from full employment equilibrium, to return to that equilibrium on its own. The normal price responses to excess supply would not, he said, be reliable adjustment mechanisms for nominal wages and prices all over the economy. He did not believe that increased flexibility of nominal wages and prices would reduce the volatility of real output and employment in response to real demand or monetary shocks. Price reductions would not occur instantaneously, fast enough to forestall even temporary declines in output and employment. Price reductions would take real time. The process of deflation itself – the argument also applies to disinflation – would discourage demand, quite possibly aggravating the disequilibrium instead of correcting it (Keynes, 1936: Chapter 19, especially p. 265).

Keynes's multiplier comes on stage as soon as it is admitted that even part of the adjustment to changes in aggregate demand takes place in quantities. The multiplier reinforces the changes in quantities. This is an implication of the point that Keynes regarded as his most important innovation, the principle of effective demand. Agents' purchases are constrained by the amounts they actually realize from selling their endowments (of labour, for example), regardless of how much they would buy if they could sell all they wanted to sell at prevailing prices. This point was rediscovered by the mathematically formal 'general disequilibrium theory' of recent years (Barro and Grossman, 1976; Malinvaud, 1977).

In situations of excess supply of labour and of capital capacity, there are positive 'multiplier' externalities to individual increases in expenditure on goods and services, for example business capital investments. These give the government a role in economic stabilization, not only via expenditures, taxes and monetary measures but possibly also via indicative planning in the style of Jean Monnet.

Keynes's departures from the assumptions of general equilibrium theory are all, I submit, legitimate and reasonable. They do not reflect vulgar ignorance or casual neglect of the standard paradigm of economic theory, but rather a recognition of its shortcomings in application to real-world macroeconomics. Neither Keynes nor the architects of the subsequent 'neoclassical synthesis' solved all the theoretical problems involved, including the specification of suitable equations for macroeconometric models. Younger generations of theorists will find a challenging and fruitful agenda here if they overcome the temptations of the new classicals.

ROBINSON CRUSOE MACROECONOMICS

New classical macroeconomics begins with the position that the invisible hand, in the form of modern general equilibrium theory, deserves the benefit of the doubt. That is, the burden of proof is on anyone who contends that market failures occur and that there is room or need for government macroeconomic policy. Of course, these latter-day disciples of Adam Smith know that today's economies are not like those described in *The Wealth of Nations*, much less like those described in Arrow–Debreu. Following Milton Friedman's 'methodology of positive economies', they hypothesize that actual economies function 'as if' the general equilibrium model applied.

Real business cycle models simulate a simple economy with classical properties, subjected to a random process of technological shocks, and compare the variances and covariances of the simulations with those from actual economies. The tests have little power. If the hypothesis that they are the same cannot be rejected by the comparisons, it is accepted, even though simulations of many other models could survive similar comparisons.

Even weak tests reject new classical explanations of cyclical fluctuations of employment and unemployment as voluntary intertemporal choices. According to these explanations, periods of high unemployment reflect choices of leisure now in anticipation that work will yield higher real wages later. No reasonable empirical estimates of responses of leisure–work–consumption choices to real wages are anywhere near large enough to explain fluctuations of the magnitude of post-war business cycles, let alone those of the 1930s. Moreover, the unemployed themselves say they are searching for work and are not out of the labour force. In times of high unemployment, disproportionately large numbers of unemployed result from lay-offs rather than voluntary quits. The Keynesian story fits the facts much better.

Real business cycle models are Robinson Crusoe economies. A single representative individual is making choices for the whole economy. This simplification enables the model-builder to derive behaviour explicitly from rational optimization subject only to constraints of resource availabilities and technology. Obviously this is not a money economy. It is not even the barter economy Smith and the classicals perceived through the veil of money. It is not even a market economy, because no transactions need occur. Any prices generated are just the shadow prices of the optimal allocations chosen by Robinson Crusoe.

In Keynes's view the essential task of macroeconomics was to explain how markets do and do not coordinate the behaviours of diverse agents: households and firms, savers and investors, workers and employers, creditors and debtors, bulls and bears, citizens and governments. To assume away this diversity is to default the responsibilities of the profession to maintain seriousness and relevance.

Adam Smith is not responsible for excesses committed in his name. His main purpose was to oppose protectionism and other regulations favouring special interests at the expense of the general public. His important message was that the accumulation of precious metals by contriving foreign trade surpluses was contrary to the national interest, for the true wealth of a nation lay in its capacity to deliver useful goods and services to its citizens. Modern macroeconomists of all shades could agree, and usually do.

Who knows what Smith would have thought of Walras, Arrow and Debreu, or of Lucas, Sargent and Barro? *The Wealth of Nations* is a very down-to-earth book, with a simple thematic moral, a rudimentary theoretical model, an imaginative intuition, a vast collection of historical and institutional material, and a great deal of wisdom and common sense. Perhaps looser claims for the invisible hand, less sweeping, less rigorous and less abstract than general equilibrium models, would be more congenial to Smith. Second-best claims that admit market failures but say governments are worse? Schumpeter's argument for the substantial but uneven progress due to the innovations of temporary monopolies? Perhaps Smith would not be altogether unfriendly to Keynes's activism against mass unemployment and to Keynes's contention that such macroeconomic activism would enable the principles of the 'Manchester School' to achieve their full potential.

NOTES

1. The major figures are Robert Lucas, Thomas Sargent and Robert Barro. See Lucas, 1981; Sargent, 1976; Lucas and Sargent, 1978; Barro, 1974. 'Rational expectations' is the important theoretical and methodological innovation. But the neoclassical assumption of market-clearing is essential for the strong macroeconomic propositions.
2. Dillard (1988) refers to the 'veil' proposition as the 'barter illusion' of classical economists, who of course scorned vulgar 'money illusion'. Like Keynes, Dillard contests the view that a money economy is a supremely efficient system of multilateral barter. The efficiencies of money as a medium of exchange come at a cost, namely that Say's Law is not assured.
3. For exposition of this theory of business cycles see Plosser (1989).

REFERENCES

Arrow, Kenneth (1953), 'Le Rôle de Valeurs Boursieres pour la Repartition la Meilleure des Risques', *Econométrie*, Paris: Centre National de la Recherche Scientifique, 41–8.
Barro, Robert (1974), 'Are Government Bonds Net Wealth?', *Journal of Political Economy*, **82**, November–December, 109–17.
Barro, Robert and Herschel Grossman (1976), *Money, Employment and Inflation*, Cambridge: Cambridge University Press, 82–93.
Debreu, Gerard (1959), *Theory of Value*, New York: Wiley.
Dillard, Dudley (1988), 'The Barter Illusion in Classical and Neoclassical Economics', *Eastern Economic Journal*, **XIV** (4), October–December, 299–318.
Frenkel, Jacob and Harry G. Johnson (1975), *The Monetary Approach to the Balance of Payments*, London: George Allen & Unwin.
Keynes, John Maynard (1936), *The General Theory of Employment, Interest and Money*, New York: Harcourt Brace & Co.
Kindleberger, Charles P. (1984), 'Was Adam Smith a Monetarist or a Keynesian?', *Business Economics*, January, 5–12.
Lucas, Robert E. Jr (1981), *Studies in Business Cycle Theory*, Cambridge, Mass.: Massachusetts Institute of Technology Press.
Lucas, Robert E. Jr and Thomas J. Sargent (1978), 'After Keynesian Macroeconomics', in *After the Phillips Curve*, Conference Series No. 19, Boston: Federal Reserve Bank, 49–72.

Malinvaud, Edmond (1977), *The Theory of Unemployment Reconsidered*, Oxford: Basil Blackwell.

Plosser, Charles I. (1989), 'Understanding Real Business Cycles', *Journal of Economic Perspectives*, **3**, Summer, 51–77.

Sargent, Thomas J. (1976), 'A Classical Macroeconomic Model for the United States', *Journal of Political Economy*, **84**, April, 207–38.

Smith, Adam (1776), *An Inquiry into the Nature and Causes of the Wealth of Nations*, ed. Edwin Cannan, New York: Modern Library, 1937.

2.   An old Keynesian counterattacks*

THE CENTRAL MACROECONOMIC ISSUE

The crucial issue of macroeconomic theory today is the same as it was 60 years ago when John Maynard Keynes revolted against what he called the 'classical' orthodoxy of his day. It is a shame that there are still 'schools' of economic doctrine, but perhaps controversies are inevitable when the issues involve policy, politics and ideology, and elude decisive controlled experiments. As a lifelong Keynesian, I am quite dismayed by the prevalence in my profession today, in a particularly virulent form, of the macroeconomic doctrines against which I as a student enlisted in the Keynesian revolution. Their high priests call themselves 'new classicals' and refer to their explanation of fluctuations in economic activity as 'real business cycle theory'. I guess 'real' is intended to mean 'not monetary' rather than 'not false', but maybe both.

I am going to discuss the issues of theory, Keynesian versus classical, both then and now. Since the main purpose and preoccupation of macroeconomic theory is to guide fiscal and monetary policies, the theoretical differences imply important differences in policy. Moreover, prevailing doctrines seep gradually into the ways the world is viewed not only by economists but also by students, pundits, politicians and the general public. It is in this sense, but only in this sense, that I shall be talking about current events.

The doctrinal differences stand out most clearly in opposing diagnoses of the fluctuations in output and employment to which democratic capitalist societies like our own are subject, and in what remedies, if any, are prescribed. Keynesian theory regards recessions as lapses from full-employment equilibrium, massive economy-wide market failures resulting from shortages of aggregate demand for goods and services and for the labour to produce them. Modern 'real business cycle theory' interprets fluctuations as moving equilibrium, individually and socially rational responses to unavoidable exogenous shocks. The Keynesian logic leads its adherents to advocate active fiscal and monetary policies to restore and maintain full employment. From real business cycle models, and other theories in the new classical spirit, the logical implication is that no policy interventions are necessary or desirable.

*Eastern Economic Journal, **18** (4), Fall 1992.

Should we describe the macro economy by two regimes or one? The old Keynesian view favours two regimes. In one, the Keynesian regime, aggregate economic activity is constrained by demand but not by supply. If there were additional effective demands for goods and services, they could be and would be satisfied. 'Demand creates its own supply.' The necessary inputs of labour, capital capacity and other factors are available, ready to be employed at prices, wages and rents that their productivity would earn. Only customers are missing.

The second regime, which Keynes called 'classical', is supply-constrained. Extra demand could not be satisfied at the economy's existing capacity to produce. The needed workers or other inputs are not available at affordable wages and rents. The supply limits bring about prices and incomes that restrict aggregate demand to capacity output. Should capacity increase, those prices and incomes will automatically generate just enough additional purchasing power to buy the extra output. 'Supply creates its own demand.'

Keynesians believe that the economy is sometimes in one regime, sometimes in the other. New classicals model the economy as always supply-constrained and in supply-equals-demand equilibrium. In their real business cycle models, the shocks that move economic activity up and down are essentially supply shocks, changes in technology and productivity or in the bounty of nature or in the costs and supplies of imported products. Although external forces of those kinds, for example weather, harvests and natural catastrophes, have been the main sources of fluctuating fortunes for most of human history, and although events continually remind us that they still occur, Keynesians do not agree that they are the main source of fluctuations in business activity in modern capitalist societies.

The distinction between the two views can be concretely illustrated by reference to Figures 2.1 and 2.2. Charts of this kind were originated by President Kennedy's Council of Economic Advisers in 1961. They were meant to depict a Keynesian view of the US economy. In Figure 2.1 the wiggly track is the reported real (that is, inflation-corrected, measured in 1987 prices) gross national product (GNP). The smooth track is potential GNP (PGNP), a hypothetical estimate of the growing capacity of the economy to produce goods and services. PGNP approximates the supply constraint on GNP. This cannot, of course, be taken literally. 'Capacity' means what can be produced by the normal peacetime operations of a market economy, not what can be done in an emergency mobilization like that of World War II. Sometimes, Figure 2.1 shows, actual GNP exceeds PGNP. These are situations of unsustainably low unemployment and labour shortage; the economy is overheated and inflation is increasing.

Conceptually PGNP is meant to correspond to full employment, indicated by the balance between unemployment and vacancies and by stable rates of

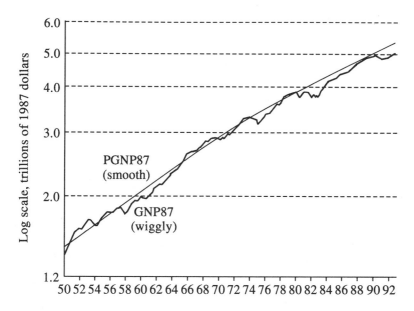

Figure 2.1   Real GNP: actual and potential, quarterly 1950–92

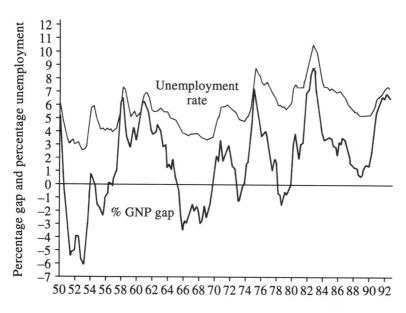

Figure 2.2   GNP gap and unemployment rate, quarterly 1950–92

change of money wages and prices. In practice, in Figure 2.1 when GNP coincides with PGNP, the unemployment rates rise gradually from 4 to 5.5 per cent. The proximate determinants of the growth of PGNP are the growth of employment – which is, since the unemployment rate is held constant, essentially that of the labour force – and the growth of the productivity of labour. Both of these growth rates slowed down around 1973; in Figure 2.1 the slope of PGNP on the logarithmic scale is reduced from 3.5 to 2.5 per cent in that year.

The sources of PGNP growth are *supply* phenomena. They are the consequences of demographic and technological trends, which by their very nature change slowly. Actual GNP wanders around PGNP. The Keynesian interpretation of the volatile gap between the two series is that it reflects fluctuations in *demand*. Spending can and does go up and down more quickly than capacity. When actual GNP falls below PGNP, the economy is in the Keynesian demand-constrained regime. When it is above or equal – or even, say, 1 or 2 per cent below – PGNP, the economy could be viewed as supply-constrained.

Figure 2.2 charts the percentage gap between PGNP and GNP, together with the overall unemployment rates. Clearly the two series go up and down synchronously. However, the amplitude of the gap is much the greater. A one point increase or decrease in the unemployment rate is associated with a $2^1/_2$ or 3 per cent change in the same direction in the gap. This phenomenon is one of the most important and reliable empirical regularities of macroeconomics. It is known to economists as Okun's Law, because the late Arthur Okun quantified the gap and its relationship to unemployment for the Council of Economic Advisers to President Kennedy in 1961. The Council wanted to demonstrate to the President and Congress that the economic pay-offs of fiscal and monetary stimuli to reduce unemployment went far beyond the direct benefits to the unemployed themselves.

It may seem paradoxical that a one percentage point reduction of unemployment, which might be expected to mean approximately a 1 per cent increase in employment, would raise output by more than 1 per cent, indeed a great deal more. The answer is that the same spending that reduces unemployment rates raises labour inputs to production in other ways: increased hours of work, movement of discouraged workers into the labour force, and more efficient use of overhead workers and of other redundant workers kept on payrolls in hard times.

Apostles of new classical macroeconomics and real business cycle theory reject the Keynesian interpretation. For them, there is no PGNP path distinct from actual GNP. The fluctuations of actual GNP are also fluctuations of PGNP, caused by shocks to the economy's productive capacity. One could of course draw a trend, a moving average, through the GNP path. However, it would be purely descriptive. It would have no macroeconomic significance.

There is only one regime. The economy is always against its supply constraint. It is never demand-constrained in the sense that demand falls short of the normal capacity of a market economy. The economy is continuously at full employment, but the unemployment rate corresponding to full employment fluctuates from one quarter to the next.

Keynesians interpret the quarter-to-quarter and year-to-year fluctuations of unemployment as largely involuntary: workers whose marginal productivities are no less than existing real wages are willing to take such jobs, but the jobs don't exist. New classicals, in contrast, regard all unemployment as voluntary; workers choose to withdraw from or enter or re-enter the labour force as the advantages of employment change relative to other uses of time. The supply shocks that drive the economy also change those advantages and those choices.

Practical people – forecasters of business conditions, business managers, politicians, workers, even bankers and central bankers – are instinctively Keynesians, especially during recessions. They realize that companies lay off workers and even shut down when their sales fall off. They blame cutbacks in defence for unemployment in Groton, Connecticut, where submarines are built, and blame declines in air travel for hard times in St Louis and Seattle, where aircraft are made. But the dominant theory in academic macroeconomics today has no room for economy-wide demand shocks and demand-side recessions.

How come? It all has to do with *market-clearing*, specifically the role of prices in clearing markets, that is, in equating demand and supply. The favourite assumption of orthodox economic theory, classical or neoclassical or new classical, is that the price in any market is determined by the condition that supply equal demand. That is pictured in economists' favourite diagram for beginning students, and it is the unquestioned assumption of PhDs. Figure 2.3 is such a diagram, for a single commodity and its market. If the demand curve is D_0 and the supply curve is s_0, the price is p_0 and the quantity is x_0. Should demand shift to D_1 while supply remains at S_0 price moves to clear the market at p_1, x_1.

Does such a price adjustment occur instantaneously, so that there is no real time during which the markets fail to clear? Is there no real time during which price stays at p_0 and sellers are able to sell only x_{01} even though they would like to sell x_0, so that there is excess supply of *ES*? The arrow pointing downwards reflects what we tell our introductory students. If there is excess supply in a market, the price falls. The question is 'how fast?'. Should we model the whole economy as if all markets, labour markets as well as product markets, are cleared by price adjustments at every moment of time? If so we are altogether ruling out excess demands and excess supplies – in particular, involuntary unemployment – and assuming that all the prices and quantities

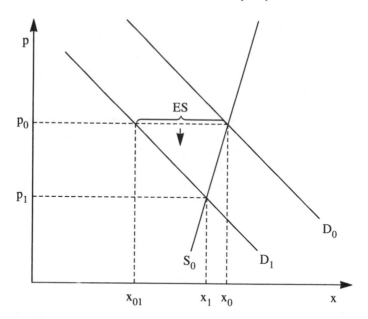

Figure 2.3   Supply, demand, market-clearing

we observe reflect demand/supply equalities: in other words that no non-price rationing of sales among buyers or sellers occurs. This is the essence of the Keynesian–new classical dispute.

DEJA VU: THE SAME MACROECONOMIC CONTROVERSY 60 YEARS AGO

It's nothing new. The same controversy occurred in the 1930s. It was pretty hard to maintain classical orthodoxy during the Great Depression. But in the absence of any intellectually respectable alternative, the classical supply-constrained, market-clearing model was used by economists in diagnosing, misdiagnosing, the Depression and by policy-makers in resisting demand-creating remedies. What came to be known as the 'Treasury View' in Britain was echoed in the United States by the Hoover Administration, the Federal Reserve and initially by the Roosevelt Administration too, and in Germany by the Bruening Government, the last government of the Weimar Republic before Hitler.

John Maynard Keynes started revolting against orthodox theories and policies in 1925, when the Depression was beginning in Britain. But it was not until he wrote *The General Theory of Employment, Interest and Money* (1936) that he could present a coherent theoretical alternative. The intention of the word 'General' in the title was precisely to distinguish his theory from the 'classical' supply-constrained market-clearing model. He did so by arguing that economies like those of the UK, Western Europe and the US are usually in demand-constrained regimes. Over the next 20 or 25 years, the Keynesian revolution swept the profession and became generally accepted mainstream wisdom. Twenty years later a classical counter-revolution had reopened the debate of the 1930s and put Keynesian economics on the defensive.

According to the synthesis of classical and Keynesian macroeconomics reached by 1960, Keynesian macroeconomics is short run. It does not pretend to apply to long-run growth and development. It does not tell poor countries how to lift themselves out of poverty or rich countries how to be richer 50 years hence. In the long run – perhaps with the help of Keynesian policies – markets will somehow clear, new workers will get jobs and the fruits of technological progress will be realized.

In the 1930s Keynes suspected that involuntary unemployment was not just a transient cyclical phenomenon but a chronic defect of advanced capitalism. In New England's Cambridge, Alvin Hansen (1938) warned of secular stagnation. These views were natural enough in the 1930s. Both Keynes and Hansen were depicting outcomes to be feared in the absence of the remedial policies and institutions of demand stabilization they were recommending. It can be argued that habitual application of those remedies after World War II, reinforced by the expectation that they would be used, moderated the severity of cyclical departures from the full-employment path.

The most important innovation of the *General Theory*, according to its author, is what he called *the principle of effective demand*. This is his term for the demand constraint I described above. The word 'effective' captures the idea that workers can spend on goods and services only the wages they actually earn from employment, not the amounts they would spend if they had all the jobs they would like to have at existing wages. Likewise, employers can hire workers only to the extent they are needed to produce the goods and services they can sell. During the recent recession this impasse was nicely captured by a cartoonist with economic intuition (Figure 2.4).

Keynes's 'classical' opponents in the 1930s were much more moderate than their descendants today. In the *General Theory*, Keynes's foil was his long-time friend and Cambridge colleague, Professor A.C. Pigou. Neither Pigou nor other orthodox economists of the day were arguing that a model in which prices cleared all markets at every instant of time was a reliable approximation to actual economies or a practical guide to government policies. The debate was about the efficacy and speed of the economy's natural recuperative mechanisms. If shocks occur that bring about unemployment, will they set in motion corrective adjustments that restore full-employment

Tom Toles
The Buffalo News
October 1991

Figure 2.4   Keynes's macroeconomic impasse: the principle of effective demand

equilibrium? Specifically, will deflation (or disinflation), the wage and price declines that naturally result from excess supplies (like *ES* in Figure 2.3), do the job? Will they do it without help from countercyclical fiscal and monetary policies? Keynes said, 'No, or anyway not always, and if ever, not soon enough'. Pigou said 'Yes, surely yes, eventually anyway'. As a theorist, his main concern was to deny that Keynes's demand-constrained outcomes deserved the status of *equilibria* in the sense that they would repeat themselves indefinitely in the absence of external shocks. Pigou resented that word 'General'. But as a practical matter he agreed with Keynes on public works spending as a means of reducing unemployment.

In contrast, new classical theorists today do not allow excess supplies or demands ever to arise in the first place. Thus they finesse the Keynes–Pigou issue, the speed and efficacy of natural adjustment mechanisms in eliminating discrepancies between demand and supply.

THE PRICE FLEXIBILITY CONTROVERSY

What young theorists today describe as Keynesian economics is a caricature of the true thing. Here is a description by authors who, by labelling themselves 'new Keynesians', evidently intend to convey sympathy:

> According to the Keynesian view, fluctuations in output arise largely from fluctuations in *nominal* aggregate demand. These fluctuations have real effects because nominal wages and prices are rigid... [T]he crucial nominal rigidities were assumed rather than explained, [although] it was clearly in the interests of agents to eliminate the rigidities they were assumed to create... Thus the 1970s saw many economists turn away from Keynesian theories and toward new classical models with flexible wages and prices (Ball, Mankiw and Romer, 1988, 1; emphasis added).

Those new classical models are market-clearing models, and they have not just flexible prices but *perfectly* and *instantaneously* flexible prices, an assumption that is surely more extreme, more arbitrary and more devoid of foundations in individual rational behaviour than the imperfect flexibility assumed in Keynesian models. There is a great deal of semantic double-talk in the assertion that the macroeconomic market failures described by Keynesian models vanish if money wages and prices are assumed flexible rather than rigid.

Price flexibility is not a yes-or-no circumstance. Consider instead a spectrum of the degree of price flexibility, from complete flexibility at one extreme to complete rigidity at the other. Complete flexibility means instantaneous adjustment, so that prices are always clearing markets, jumping sufficiently to absorb all demand or supply shocks. Complete rigidity means that nominal prices do not change at all during the period of analysis. In between are various speeds of price adjustment, various lengths of time during which markets are not clearing.

Who owns the middle ground? We Keynesians do, despite common beliefs to the contrary. Keynes and Keynesian economists did not assume complete rigidity, nor did they need to. It is not true that only an arbitrary and gratuitous assumption of complete rigidity, converting nominal demand shocks into real demand shocks, brings into play Keynes's multipliers and other demand-determining processes (including the IS/LM curves taught to generations of college students). Any degree of stickiness that prevents complete instantaneous price adjustment has the same qualitative implications.

In the quotation above, 'nominal aggregate demand' means aggregate dollar spending on goods and services. This is not what Keynes meant by 'effective demand'. He was referring to demands for quantities of goods and services, measured in constant prices, not in current dollars. He stressed changes in these real demands, not mindless changes in total dollar spending irrespective of what dollars could buy, as the sources of depressions and prosperities. Only people who formed their opinions of Keynesian economics without reading Keynes could make this mistake.

What is true is that Keynes stressed that we live in a monetary economy, as opposed to a frictionless market-clearing barter economy. Prices, including wages and salaries, are quoted in dollars. It is dollar prices that initially respond to excess supplies and demands, not real or relative prices, which value each commodity or service in terms of other commodities. In insisting on this fact, Keynes was deviating from a cherished principle of classical theory, the proposition that 'money is a veil' behind which everything works out as it would in a miraculously efficient barter economy. Money is neutral. It affects nominal prices but not real variables. According to this proposition, which Don Patinkin (1956) called 'the classical dichotomy', people do not value money for its own sake, and therefore they behave in ways that produce the same real outcomes regardless of how much money is circulating. Real prices, the terms of trade between commodities, are the same whether dollar prices are high or low and whether they are inflating, deflating or stable. Dudley Dillard (1988) called this the 'barter illusion' of classical economics.

In any single small market of a large economy, the distinction between money price and real price may be negligible. If a fall in the demand for bagels leads to a decline in their prices in dollars, that is also a decline relative to prices of gasoline, videotapes, plumbers, and everything else. If Figure 2.3 applies to bagels, we would not have to specify whether the price on the vertical axis is cents per bagel or fractions of a standard shopping-cart package per bagel, and we could assume that the demand and supply curves stay in place as the bagel price moves.

In attacking the classical assumption that markets are continuously cleared by price adjustments, Keynes stressed labour markets in particular, asserting that wages do not move fast enough to avoid excess supplies of labour – involuntary unemployment – at prevailing wages. The difference between money price and real price, negligible for a local bagels market, is crucial for an economy-wide labour market. It is the real wage – the value of wages in goods produced and consumed – that should equate employers' demands for labour with workers' willing supplies. When shocks throw this market out of equilibrium, these real-wage demand and supply schedules may well stay put as wages and other prices adjust. But if in Figure 2.3 the money wage is the price on the vertical axis, we cannot assume that the demand and supply schedules stay in place as the money wage declines. The demand for labour will certainly depend on the wages that the workers are paid and spend on the products they themselves make, as the intuitive cartoonist–economist understood.

Therefore, if an economy-wide excess supply of labour arises and leads to a fall in money wages throughout the economy, it is by no means obvious that *real* wages fall as much – or at all. Quite possibly, employers just reduce proportionately the dollar prices of the goods they produce. Keynes argued that workers could be quite willing to take jobs at lower real wages but have no way to communicate this willingness.

The question boils down to whether proportionate deflation of all nominal prices, both money wages and product prices, will or will not increase aggregate effective real demand. This is a complicated matter, and I cannot do it justice here. Two issues in this debate need to be distinguished. The first concerns the relation of real aggregate demand to the nominal *price level*. The second concerns its relation to the expected *rate of change* of nominal prices.

Keynes, in Book I of *The General Theory*, denied that real aggregate demand was related at all to the price and money wage level. In effect, he turned the classical neutrality proposition against the classicals. If all money wages and prices are lowered in the same proportion, how can real quantities demanded be any different? Thus if real demand is deficient, how can a purely nominal price adjustment undo the damage?

Actually Keynes himself provided an answer in a later chapter. If the nominal quantity of money remains the same, its real quantity increases, interest rates fall and real demand increases. This mechanism, often called the 'Keynes effect', would fail if demand for money became perfectly elastic with respect to interest rates – the 'liquidity trap' – or if demand for goods for consumption and investment were perfectly inelastic.

Pigou (1943, 1947), Patinkin (1948) and other authors provided another scenario, the 'Pigou effect' or 'real balance effect', which alleges a direct positive effect on spending resulting from households' increased wealth, in the case at hand taking the form of the increased real value of their holdings of dollar-denominated assets. This effect does not depend on reduction of interest rates.

To an astonishing degree, the theoretical fraternity has taken the real balance effect to be a conclusive refutation of Keynes. Yet this effect is of dubious strength, and even of uncertain sign. Most nominal assets in a modern economy are 'inside' assets, that is the debts of private agents to other private agents. They wash out in accounting aggregation, leaving only the government's nominal debt to the private sector as net wealth. Some, though probably not all, of the interest-bearing debt is internalized by taxpayers who feel poorer because of the taxes they expect they or their heirs to have to pay to finance the interest payments. The base of the real balance effect is therefore quite small relative to the economy. In the United States today the monetary base, the non-interest-bearing federal debt, is only 6 per cent of GNP.

While Don Patinkin (1948) stressed the theoretical importance of the real balance effect, he disclaimed belief in its practical significance. In the Great Depression, he pointed out, the real value of net private balances rose 46 per cent from 1929 to 1932, but real national income *fell* 40 per cent.

That inside assets and debts wash out in accounting aggregation does not mean that the consequences of price changes on their real values wash out. Price declines make creditors better off and debtors poorer. Their marginal propensities to spend from wealth need not be the same. Common sense suggests that debtors have the higher spending propensities – that is why they are in debt! Even a small differential could easily swamp the Pigou effect – gross dollar-denominated assets are 200 per cent of United States GNP.

Irving Fisher (1933) emphasized the increased burden of debt resulting from unanticipated deflation as a major factor in depressions in general and in the Great Depression in particular. Fisher's wealth redistribution effect is quite possibly stronger than the Pigou and Keynes effects combined, particularly when output and employment are low relative to capacity. This may be one reason for the weakness of demand in world economies over the past four years.

An even more important argument refers to *rates of change* of nominal prices. The process of change works on aggregate demand in just the wrong direction. Greater expected deflation, or expected disinflation, makes people want to hold money rather than buy goods. It is an increase in the real rate of interest, necessarily so when nominal interest rates are constrained by the zero floor of the interest on money. This is another factor Fisher stressed in his explanation of the Great Depression. Keynes stressed it too, as a pragmatic reinforcement of his overall argument.

The process of price change matters when the change takes place in real time, because during the transition it tends to move the demand/supply balance in the wrong direction. After a negative demand shock, an increase in demand associated with a lower price level is required to restore equilibrium; a falling price actually diminishes demand.

Not surprisingly, the new classicals, and evidently some self-styled new Keynesians too, take the easy way out. The possible instability of the price-adjustment process is an embarrassment. They tacitly avoid it by assuming perfect flexibility, so that after surprise shocks, prices jump to their new equilibria without passage of time.

The problematic stability of real-time price adjustment is evident in Figure 2.5. Here the horizontal axis represents expected price deflation or inflation,

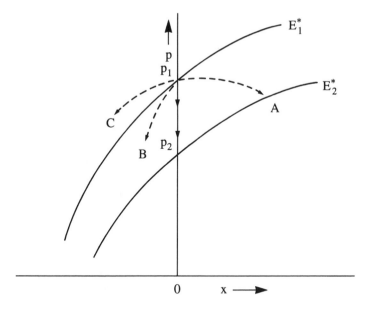

Figure 2.5   Aggregate demand related to price level and price change: the questionable stability of price adjustment

x. The vertical axis represents p, the log of the price level. An upward sloping curve like E_1^* plots combinations (x,p) of expected price change and price level that generate the same aggregate real demand, E. The slope reflects the assumptions that demand is related negatively to the price level and positively to its expected rate of change. In given circumstances, a higher curve refers to a lower demand E and a lower curve to higher demand. The curvature of the E^* loci reflects the assumption that the 'Keynes effect' of increases in real money balances in lowering interest rates declines as those balances rise and interest rates fall.

Suppose that initially the 'isoquant', E_1^*, makes demand equal to full-employment equilibrium output, Y_1^*, here taken to be constant. Points above or left of that isoquant are positions where E is lower than Y_1^*, characterized by Keynesian unemployment. Points below or right of E_1^* are positions of macroeconomic excess demand. In Figure 2.5, the equilibrium inflation rate (expected and actual) and price are $(0, p_1)$. Suppose now that a discrete one-time negative shock to real demand shifts the isoquant for $E = Y^*$ down to E_2^* so that the new equilibrium inflation rate and price are $(0, p_2)$. The old isoquant E_1^* now implies an E lower than Y^*. To restore equilibrium the price level must fall from p_1 to p_2. How is the price decline to be accomplished? One scenario is the new classical miracle, an instantaneous precipitous vertical descent, so that there is no time interval during which actual or expected price changes are other than zero. If jumps of that kind in p are excluded, there is no path of actual price changes and rationally expected prices that avoids departure from $E = Y^*$ during the transition. It would take a burst of positive inflation, actual and expected, to offset the negative demand shock, as at point A. But this would move the price level in the wrong direction.

The likely scenario is a path like B or C in Figure 2.5. The excess supply that now characterizes the initial equilibrium point $(0, p_1)$ and the first isoquant induces prices to decline, and the anticipation of their decline is bad for aggregate demand. Along B the real balance effect is strong enough to overcome the negative effects of the deflation; aggregate demand E is increasing as the path hits lower isoquants. The new equilibrium may be attained, though probably by a damped cyclical process. Along C, however, the price level effect is too weak to win out, and the gap of E and Y below Y^* is increasing.

Fisher and Keynes both thought that output and employment would be less volatile if money wages and prices were fairly stable, rather than flexible. They were right. Earlier, (Tobin, 1975), I exhibited a simple formal macroeconomic system, classical in the sense that it has only one equilibrium, which is characterized by full employment and a constant price level. It is easy to specify plausible dynamics that make the equilibrium unstable because the price-change effects outweigh the price-level effects. Moreover, the system could be stable locally but unstable for large displacements.

The question of whether price flexibility (in any sense short of the perfect-flexibility fairy tale) is stabilizing has begun to receive considerable attention. Delong and Summers (1986) have investigated this question using the Fischer–Taylor staggered-contract model (Fischer, 1977; Taylor, 1980), amended to allow both price-level and price-change effects on demand. Their most interesting simulation has the intuitively desirable property that close to the limit of perfect price flexibility, greater price flexibility means greater output stability, while further away from it, the reverse is true. Similar results are obtained by Caskey and Fazzari (1988) and Chadha (1989).

EMPIRICAL EVIDENCE

We do not need fancy econometrics to mobilize evidence against the 'real business cycle' view that observed fluctuations in output and employment are movements in price-cleared equilibrium. Here are a number of regularities of US business cycles that falsify the implications of the new classical hypothesis (Okun, 1980).

1. **Unemployment itself**. If people are voluntarily choosing not to work at prevailing wages, why do they report themselves as unemployed, rather than as 'not in labor force'? Real business cycle theory explains fluctuations of unemployment as intertemporal choices between work and leisure. Workers drop out when real wages, the opportunity costs of leisure, are temporarily low relative to what they expect later. This might be an explanation of cyclical movements in employment if real wages were strongly pro-cyclical, but there is no such systematic regularity. Nor is there empirical evidence of high sensitivity of labor supply to current and expected real wages.

2. **Unemployment and vacancies**. New Classicals ask us to believe that the labor market is in equilibrium at 9 percent unemployment, the same as it is at 5 percent. If so, there would be no reason to expect the balance between unemployment and job vacancies to be any different in the two cases. *Both* unemployment and vacancies would be higher in recession. However, a strong negative association between unemployment and vacancies – as would be expected in Keynesian theory – is obvious in the US and other market capitalist economies.

3. **Quits and layoffs**. If recessions and prosperities are both equilibria, there is no reason to expect the relative frequency of voluntary quits from jobs and involuntary 'separations' to be any different. But of course there are many more layoffs, relative to quits, when unemployment is high and vacancies are scarce. There are many more 'job losers' relative to 'job leavers' in recessions.

4. **Excess capacity.** The utilization of plant and equipment varies cyclically parallel to the utilization of labor. Presumably machines are not choosing leisure voluntarily.

5. **Unfilled orders and delivery delays**. These move pro-cyclically, again suggesting strongly that demand is much higher relative to supply in prosperities than in recessions.

6. **Monetary effects on output**. According to the 'classical dichotomy', monetary events and policies should affect only nominal prices. Real outcomes should be independent of them. The evidence that this is not true is overwhelming.

The list could go on. Why do so many talented economic theorists believe and teach elegant fantasies so obviously refutable by plainly evident facts? Trying to answer that question would take us into a speculative excursion on the sociology of the economics profession, beyond the scope of this paper.

NOTE

This paper is a written version of my lecture at the 1992 annual meetings of the Eastern Economic Association in New York City. The lecture and this paper draw on a longer paper with a similar message (Tobin, 1993). I would like to express my gratitude for the faithful and valuable research assistance of Mitchell Tobin, Yale College 1992 (no relation).

REFERENCES

Ball, L., N.G. Mankiw and D. Romer (1988), 'The New Keynesian Economics and the Output–Inflation Tradeoff', *Brookings Papers on Economic Activity*, 1–65.

Caskey, J. and S. Fazzari (1987), 'Aggregate Demand Contractions with Nominal Debt Commitments', *Economic Inquiry*, October, 583–97.

Caskey, J. and S. Fazzari (1988), 'Price Flexibility and Macroeconomic Stability: An Empirical Simulation Analysis', Washington University Department of Economics, Working Paper 118, January.

Chadha, B. (1989), 'Is Increased Price Inflexibility Stabilizing?', *Journal of Money Credit and Banking*, November, 481–97.

Delong, J.B. and L.H. Summers (1986), 'Is Increasing Price Flexibility Stabilizing?', *American Economic Review*, December, 1031–44.

Dillard, D. (1988), 'The Barter Illusion in Classical and Neoclassical Economics', *Eastern Economic Journal*, October–December, 299–318.

Fischer, S. (1977), 'Long-term Contracts, Rational Expectations, and the Optimal Money Supply Rule', *Journal of Political Economy*, February, 191–205.

Fisher, I. (1933), 'The Debt-Deflation Theory of Great Depressions', *Econometrica*, October, 337–57.

Hansen, A.H. (1938), *Full Recovery or Stagnation*, New York: W.W. Norton.

Keynes, J.M. (1936), *The General Theory of Employment, Interest and Money*, New York: Harcourt Brace.

Okun, A.M. (1980), 'Rational-Expectations-with-Misperceptions As a Theory of the Business Cycle', *Journal of Money, Credit and Banking*, November, Part 2, 817–25.

Patinkin, D. (1948), 'Price Flexibility and Full Employment', *American Economic Review*, September, 543–64.

Patinkin, D. (1956), *Money, Interest and Prices*, New York: Harper and Row, 2nd ed., 1965.

Pigou, A.C. (1943), 'The Classical Stationary State', *Economic Journal*, December, 343–51.

Pigou, A.C. (1947), 'Economic Progress in a Stable Environment', *Economica*, August, 180–90.

Taylor, J. (1980), 'Aggregate Dynamics and Staggered Contracts', *Journal of Political Economy*, February, 1–23.

Tobin, J. (1975), 'Keynesian Models of Recession and Depression', *American Economic Review*, May, 195–202.

Tobin, J. (1993), 'Price Flexibility and Output Stability: An Old Keynesian View', *Journal of Economic Perspectives*, Spring.

3. Current controversy in macroeconomics: the four schools*

THEORY, IDEOLOGY AND POLICY

Economics is a scholarly discipline, one would like to say a science. But because of its subject matter it is close to policy, politics and ideology. It's a two-way relationship. As the great economist Joseph Schumpeter told us graduate students here at Harvard, economics draws its energy and inspiration from real-world concerns and from ideological enthusiasm and challenges. Otherwise it would be a dry and sterile study.

The stimulus of public policy and controversy, along with healthy scholarly curiosity, brought forth Adam Smith's *Wealth of Nations* in 1776. It is, among other things, a tract against mercantilism – in modern lingo, against protectionism, industrial policy and inordinate ambition for balance-of-trade surpluses. Likewise David Ricardo's immense contributions to economic science were triggered by the financing of the Napoleonic wars, the free trade debates between British manufacturers and landed aristocracy, and other controversies and practical problems of his day. A century later the inability of orthodox economics to explain or remedy the Great Depression of the 1930s led John Maynard Keynes to revolutionize economics. Generally speaking, it takes big events and their interpretations to discredit old ideas and replace them with new ones – the Industrial Revolution, the Corn Laws, the Great Depression, the stagflation of the 1970s, perhaps the Reaganomics experiments of the 1980s.

That is one direction of causation. The other direction is the influence of economic doctrines themselves on public opinion and public policy. Certainly the 'free market' theories of Smith and Ricardo and a host of successors have been extremely powerful unto this very day. They withstood the challenge of Marxism and triumphed over it, first intellectually and now practically. Keynes's ideas became the accepted wisdom of the policy-makers in most advanced capitalist democracies in the first three decades after World War II. On a more prosaic plane, Presidents and would-be Presidents have

*Lecture at Clayton State College, Georgia, January 31, 1990, and at Harvard University, April 21, 1990. First published in Harvard Graduate Society Newsletter, Fall 1990.

economic advisers, bureaucracies rely heavily on economists, many economists participate in policy debates in Congressional hearings and in the
media, and pundits and politicians echo – imperfectly and perhaps uncon-
sciously – fashionable ideas in economics.

THE KEYNESIAN REVOLUTION

These relationships, in both directions, have been particularly important and
interesting in the last 25 years and remain so today. I want to tell you that
story this morning, specifically the part of it that has to do with *macro*economics, that is, economy-wide developments and policies: fluctuations and
trends in GNP, unemployment and price inflation, and government fiscal and
monetary policies.

These 25 years have been turbulent times for economies and for macroeconomics. Let me describe first the turbulence in the profession. I have to start
further back. In the 1930s Keynes challenged the complacency of the orthodox (classical) tradition of Smith and Ricardo. That tradition expected markets to 'clear', because prices would be adjusted so as to eliminate excess
demands or excess supplies. It was hard to explain mass unemployment in
these terms. Why didn't labour markets provide jobs for all who were willing
to work at prevailing wages? Why didn't the labour market clear?

Keynes contended that there was an endemic flaw in market capitalism, a
flaw he attributed to inadequate aggregate demand for goods and services –
with a shortage of demand there would be a shortage of jobs. His opponents
found this to be nonsense; according to them, there could be shortages of
demands for particular products (Chevrolets, Coca Colas, cucumbers) but not
for all products taken together, not for the whole GNP.

These differences in theory were mirrored in differences of view about
policy. Keynes thought the deficiencies in effective aggregate demand could
be remedied by government spending or by tax cuts and monetary expansions
to induce additional private spending. His classical opponents warned that
such measures would fail of their objectives and would simply be inflationary. Keynesian ideas looked good to economics students like myself in the
1930s. We could see the unemployment all around us, and we hadn't been
brainwashed. Keynesian remedies seemed to work when and where they
were tried, and the onset of war was an experiment that caused them to be
applied without the restraints of peacetime.

After the war the profession synthesized the old and the new, and a mainstream consensus in macroeconomics had been achieved by the early 1960s.
The synthesis recognized the relevance of orthodox (neoclassical)
*micro*economics, and also stressed that Keynesian demand measures some-

times, perhaps frequently, needed to be applied in reverse, to prevent or contain excess demand and inflation. In what follows I shall use the word 'Keynesian' to refer to this synthesis rather than to the literal contents of Keynes's great book *The General Theory of Employment Interest and Money* (1936).

The unparalleled success of Western economies in the 20 years after the war was attributed in part at least to the readiness of most governments to use Keynesian tools of demand management. Business fluctuations were moderate, unemployment was low, inflation likewise. A good bit of right-wing suspicion of Keynesian economics in the profession and in the public arena was overcome or neutralized. In the United States perhaps the peak of Keynesian consensus was reached in the first Kennedy–Johnson Administration, where Keynesian theories and policies were openly espoused and applied. Otherwise Congress would never have passed in 1964 a deficit-increasing tax cut, not to arrest or reverse a recession but to keep an ongoing recovery from petering out.

THE SOURCES OF COUNTER-REVOLUTION

In the heyday of Keynesian theory and policy there was considerable confidence that wise government policies could steer the economy – some said 'fine tune' it – and tame the business cycle. Subsequent events shook this confidence and disrupted the consensus, both within the economics profession and in the wider arenas of public opinion and politics. The Vietnam War overheated the economy, reduced unemployment to an untenably low rate (3 per cent instead of the 4 per cent that had been the Administration's objective), and raised the inflation rate from 2 per cent in 1964–65 to about 5 per cent in 1969–70). These outcomes were probably avoidable. President Johnson did not follow the advice of his Keynesian economists, who wanted a tax increase in 1966. The tax increase finally enacted was too little and too late. The Federal Reserve did not restrict credit severely enough to check the wartime boom until 1969. And of course Vietnam, quickly followed by Watergate, damaged in a very generic sense public confidence in the integrity and efficacy of government.

The stagflation of the 1970s was even more damaging to the old synthesis and consensus in macroeconomic analysis and policy. The main proximate causes were the two OPEC oil and energy price hikes in 1974–75 and 1979–80. In magnitude and influence they are probably without precedent or parallel in the modern peacetime economic history of developed capitalist economies. The inflations, and the severe recessions that followed when central banks tried to control the inflations, were widely blamed on Keynesian economics. Its protagonists hadn't contemplated stagflation – high inflation and high unemployment at the same time. Hadn't their favourite policies over-heated the economy, necessitating the most severe recession since the 1930s to bring prices under control? And not once but twice! Both the country and the profession were ready for counter-revolution. The 1970s stagflation was to Keynesian economics what the 1930s Depression was to classical ortho-doxy.

Within the economics profession there have been three counter-revolution-ary movements, monetarism, new classical macroeconomics and supply-side economics. Let me try to explain each 'School' in turn.

Monetarism

Monetarism is the oldest. Indeed its main ideas go way back to David Hume. The principal proposition is the Quantity Theory of Money, namely that average prices are proportional to the quantity of money in circulation. Its modern revival is due mainly to Milton Friedman, who kept the tradition alive and well during the heyday of Keynesianism. He and monetarism were waiting in the wings as Keynesian theory and policy appeared to falter.

Friedman opposed fine-tuning and all activist policy and advocated an outcome-blind monetary rule: just keep the money supply growing at a steady non-inflationary rate, irrespective of what is happening month by month in the economy. In this regime, he alleged, unemployment would gravitate to its 'natural rate', a rate that government policy is helpless to reduce. Monetary policy that attempts to aim at unnaturally low unemployment may succeed temporarily but its main and lasting effect is simply to cause inflation. As for fiscal policy, which Keynesians had stressed, Friedman dismissed it as of no macroeconomic importance.

It happens, of course, that in microeconomics, too, Friedman has been a crusader for free markets, deregulation and minimal government. In his faith that the economy will do just fine without government macroeconomic activ-ism, he adheres to the doctrines of the classical tradition that Keynes chal-lenged. Friedman's own monetarist explanation of the Great Depression of the 1930s was to blame it on inept Federal Reserve policy. Friedman's mon-etarist explanation of the great stagflation of the 1970s was also to blame it on the Fed: OPEC puts up oil prices but it takes printing money by the central bank to put prices up all over the economy.

Monetarism has had great influence on the central banks of the world, particularly in Western Europe, North America and Japan. Beginning around 1970, Congress required the Federal Reserve to state targets for growth of monetary aggregates twice a year. And in 1979 the Fed took monetarist policies very seriously, announcing that it would restrict money supplies until inflation was conquered regardless of the side effects on business activity and unemployment. Since 1982, however, the Fed has reverted to pragmatic fine-tuning. Monetarism remains strong in the governments and central banks of West Germany, Britain and Japan.

New Classical Macroeconomics

New classical macroeconomics is, as the name suggests, a revival of the old classical orthodoxy that Keynes challenged more than half a century ago. It also embraces the essentials of monetarism, asserting strongly that monetary policies have no real effects and just determine the purchasing power of money. The young theorists who are the apostles of the revival bring more powerful ammunition to the fray, the new methodology of rational expectations. They are also more purist than their forebears 60 years ago and than Friedman in their adherence to the view that prices clear all markets continuously.

One implication is that there can never be any involuntary unemployment. If employment and unemployment fluctuate from year to year, it is because workers voluntarily choose, for example, to take more leisure now and do more work later, when real wages may be higher. Although some new classicals have even tried to interpret the unemployment of the 1930s (up to 25 per cent of the labour force in the United States) in these terms, others are content to regard the Great Depression as an inexplicable aberration which has already had too much effect on theory and policy.

Whereas Keynesians – and even some old-fashioned monetarists – interpret business cycles as fluctuations in demand around the economy's smoothly growing supply capacity, new classicals interpret business cycles as movements in supply/demand equilibrium. They do not regard the cycles as problems, but rather as society's optimal adjustments to its ever changing external environment, for example the oil shocks of the 1970s. These laboured interpretations, called 'real business cycle theory' to emphasize the irrelevance of monetary and financial sideshows, are in high fashion right now.

Obviously, new classicals see no point in macroeconomic policies. Monetary policies and inflations have no real effects at all, whether good or bad. Deficit spending is also both ineffectual and innocuous, because rational people will know that it just postpones taxes. They will therefore spend no more when the government borrows than when it taxes; in effect they will buy the government bonds to provide for the future taxes they or their progeny will have to pay.

New classical macroeconomics has been very popular within the profession, where its methodology and logical purity have great attractions to young theorists. However, its evident failure to explain many obvious empirical facts is undermining its appeal. Many macroeconomists find themselves torn between a Keynesian paradigm that fits many facts but is theoretically unsatisfying and a new classical paradigm that is theoretically attractive but empirically suspect.

The new classical movement has not had a public crusader of the force and skill of Milton Friedman. Its leaders, Robert Lucas, Thomas Sargent, Robert Barro and Edwin Prescott, are not household names, TV personalities or frequent writers of Op-ed pieces. Their influence in the wider arena is more indirect and diffuse, arising from their considerable effect on the way professional economists think about the economic world. New classical macroeconomics strongly reinforces the trained instincts of economists to support generally *laissez-faire* positions. Markets work just fine. All is for the best in the best of all possible worlds. There are obvious and important echoes of this faith in Reaganomics, in Thatcher economics in Britain, and in West Germany.

Supply-Side Economics

Supply-side economics has been a strong intellectual influence on the conservative counter-revolution in the politics of economic policy throughout the developed world, especially in the United States. Here an extreme form of the supply-side movement became the heart of Reaganomics and rationalized the radical federal budget policies of the 1980s.

A central supply-side claim is that high tax rates on the fruits of economic activities deter the taxed activities. No economist is likely to dissent from this general proposition. For decades, even centuries, economists have been asserting it, teaching it and trying to give it empirical content in their research. What was new about supply-side economics? Several related empirical contentions about recent history: that actual economic policies in the post-war era neglected the truths about incentives, that over-taxation was the source of the stagflation of the 1970s, that Keynesian demand-side policies caused inflation and retarded real economic progress.

The moral was that cuts in tax rates would dramatically increase the economy's rate of growth. Workers and managers would work harder and longer. Households would save more. Businesses would invest more in new capital plant and equipment and in research and development projects. Entrepreneurs and venture capitalists would assume more risks. Arthur Laffer drew his famous curve on a cocktail napkin, purporting to show that the cuts in tax rates would actually raise the government's revenues, so large would be the increases in the economy's capacity to produce resulting from enhanced incentives.

In 1980 as a candidate and in 1981 as President, Ronald Reagan persuaded voters and legislators to take these claims very seriously. That is one big reason for the radical experiment in fiscal policy in the United States over the last nine years – an example not followed by other conservative governments in Europe and Japan.

I would like to interject a commercial for a book, *Two Revolutions in Economic Policy: The Kennedy and Reagan Economic Reports*. This book reprints the initial Council of Economic Advisers reports stating the economic philosophies of these two Administrations, one a Keynesian manifesto in 1962, the other an anti-Keynesian manifesto in 1982 with supply-side, new classical and monetarist elements. It exemplifies very well the thesis of my lecture today – the close two-way connections between economic theories and the economic policies of governments. The Editors are Murray Weidenbaum, the Chairman of Reagan's first Council, and myself, the surviving member of Kennedy's initial Council. We get no royalties; we persuaded the MIT Press to publish the book as a public service, for one reason because the 1962 Report was out of print at the Government Printing Office but mainly because their juxtaposition teaches a lot about economics. Chapter 4 of this collection is an essay introducing the Kennedy reports reprinted in *Two Revolutions*.

The recent 1990 Report, written by the three distinguished academics who make up President Bush's Council, is interesting for the same reasons. It also repudiates 1962 vintage activism in fiscal and monetary policies, and it opposes tax increases on supply-side grounds. But it is more moderate in tone and substance than the Reagan manifesto.

Within the economics profession, supply-side is not a School in the same sense as the other three approaches I have been outlining to you. Many mainstream economists have been 'supply-siders', long before the label was coined. They were studying the incentive and disincentive effects of government taxes, transfers and expenditures. Their quantitative estimates of these effects were much smaller than those of the supply-side enthusiasts like Laffer.

Some sober supply-siders were particularly concerned about the effects of taxation on saving and capital investment. Martin Feldstein at Harvard was a leader of this group. He became Chairman of the Council of Economic Advisers for Reagan, but left because of his basic disagreements with the Administration about budget deficits. People like Feldstein were tackling a much harder problem than the ideological supply-siders. That problem is the following: the government has to have revenues to finance its activities. All taxes have some disincentive and distortionary effects. You can't avoid these effects altogether and still collect revenues. And you have to worry about fairness. So what mixture of taxes would be the least harmful way of collecting revenues? Supply-siders simply finessed those intellectually difficult problems.

LESSONS OF THE 1980s

The magnitudes of the federal deficits in the 1980s were beyond all previous peacetime experience, not just in dollars but in relation to the size of the economy. During Reagan's Presidencies the federal debt rose to 43 per cent of Gross National Product (GNP), even higher if the debt held by the social security trust fund was included. The deficits absorbed more than half the net savings of American households, businesses and state and local governments.

In macroeconomics, experiments as dramatic as the radical fiscal policy of the Reagan Administration are rare. What happened? Can we learn anything that helps us choose among the various schools? The Reagan tax cuts and the buildup of defence spending came on line just as the deep recession of 1979–82 was hitting bottom. Unemployment was nearly 11 per cent, compared to 5.8 per cent in 1978–79. Excess industrial capacity was 32 per cent, compared to a norm of 13 to 15 per cent. Beginning with 1983, the economy enjoyed seven years of expansion, during which real (inflation-corrected) GNP grew on average more than 4 per cent annually, jobs were created at 2.4 per cent per year, unemployment fell almost to 5 per cent and excess capacity narrowed to 17 per cent. The Administration and the supply-siders brag about this recovery; naturally they say it vindicates their policies and their theories. A Harvard economist now in Washington has argued this case in a recently published book, Lawrence Lindsey's *The Growth Experiment: How the New Tax Policy is Transforming the US Economy*. For the better, he says.

But wait just a minute! Here is the conventional Keynesian interpretation of the same events: I submit that it fits the facts of the experiment better.

The United States experienced six or seven earlier business cycle recoveries since World War II. There is nothing extraordinary about the expansion of the 1980s, except its length. Indeed the expansion of the 1960s was just as long, and by many measures of performance superior. Anyway, recoveries are demand-side phenomena. This one was no exception. The tax cuts gave a big boost to consumption spending, and the defence build-up was a big addition to demand as well. The Federal Reserve, having abandoned its monetarist stance in 1982, managed the expansion of aggregate demand, and 'fine-tuned' very skilfully. In fact, the Fed could have generated the whole recovery without the help of the big fiscal deficits – one could say without the embarrassment of the big fiscal deficits, which compelled the Fed to keep interest rates (corrected for inflation) much higher than in any of the previous six recoveries, in order to keep the economic engine from overheating.

The 1980s expansion was not a supply-side victory. There has been no remarkable growth in the supply capacity of the economy. Trend productivity growth for the economy as a whole collapsed at the time of the first oil shock. It has recovered very little in the 1980s. The rapid growth in 1983–87 took place mainly by putting back to work idle resources of labour and capacity, not by making such resources produce more. In 1988–89 the catch-up phase of this cyclical expansion came to an end, and the economy can now grow only at the trend rate permitted by the growth in labour force and in labour productivity, totalling together only 2 to 2.5 per cent per year, compared to nearly 4 per cent in the 1960s.

Worse yet, the fiscal and monetary policies of the 1980s are having very negative supply-side by-products. The tax cuts caused a consumption boom, not a saving boom. The government's deficits were negative savings that more than offset any positive incentive effects of the tax cuts on private saving. Capital investment, the source of future productivity gains, was held back by the high interest rates resulting from the fiscal deficits. Half the net capital investment that did occur was, in effect, financed by borrowing from foreigners. High American interest rates attracted funds into dollar assets, appreciating our currency and making our products uncompetitive in foreign markets and in our own markets. We are now a large debtor nation, with a trade deficit that probably will be with us for the rest of the century.

Britain and continental Western Europe also performed an experiment for us economists in the 1980s. Influenced by monetarism and new classical macroeconomics, especially by their interpretations of the macroeconomic disappointments of the 1970s, the governments and central banks of those countries have as a matter of principle eschewed any demand-expanding policies, fiscal or monetary, since the recession of 1979–82. The principle is that those policies always fail in their objectives and generate inflation, no matter what the initial conditions, high unemployment or low. In this respect European policy-makers differ not only from their own practices in the past but also from the United States in the 1980s. According to the theories they were following, markets would generate recovery on their own. But the United States recovered from the recession, and those European economies did not. Their unemployment rates remain chronically higher than before the recession. The real growth of Western Europe since the recession is very little higher than the sustainable growth of labour force and productivity; there has been very little 'catch-up' from recession, indeed from the last two recessions.

The evidence supports a demand-side Keynesian interpretation of the events of the past decade. Yes, I think I already perceive some of the natural repercussions in my profession. Keynesian ideas are regaining some respectability, relative to the competition of the other schools. Theorists are back at the modelling boards, trying to repair the flaws in Keynesian theory that made it vulnerable to the counter-revolutionary attacks.

There are young macroeconomists, some right here in this university, who style themselves New Keynesians. They seek to explain the failures of prices to clear markets as rational behaviour by price-setters who incur costs every time they change prices. I guess I should welcome any lifelines they may throw to us 'Old Keynesians', but I'm suspicious of this one. Keynes himself rejected the idea that the source of the problems he observed and analysed was inflexibility of prices. He doubted that falling prices and wages would cure demand deficiencies, because the process of deflation itself has negative effects on propensities to spend. This was even more strongly emphasized by the great American economist, Irving Fisher of Yale, a contemporary of Keynes.

In time we will see, I feel confident, a new synthesis and perhaps a new consensus around it. And that in turn will influence the informal and implicit models that reporters, politicians and men and women of Wall Street and Main Street carry in their heads and use to form opinions on economic issues and policies. From such cycles, I have to believe and do believe, comes progress, but it certainly does not come in steady linear progression.

And though the logic and discipline internal to the profession have much to do with its evolution, so do big events in the outside world. We are living through another such event, the collapse of communist central planning in theory, practice and ideology. That too will leave its mark on economics, but in what way it's too early to tell.

4. Introduction to the Kennedy reports*

This Introduction was planned to be the work of three veterans of the first year of the New Frontier. Walter Heller was taking the lead, as he did in 1961 as Chairman of the Council of Economic Advisers, the post he held throughout the first Kennedy–Johnson term. He was enthusiastic about this republication of the Council's work. Alas, Walter died suddenly on 16 June 1987. We had already lost two other comrades, Kermit Gordon, Council member 1961–62 (Budget Director 1962–64), and Arthur Okun, staff member 1961–64 (later Council member and Chairman). We miss all three, most acutely when a project like this recalls the happy excitement of our work together a quarter-century ago. To their memory we dedicate our part of this book.

THE PREPARATION OF THE REPORTS

The first weeks after the 20 January inauguration of a new Administration are hectic. Not yet fully organized or staffed, Kennedy's new Council was immediately assigned major responsibility for drafting the President's first economic message to Congress, transmitted on 2 February 1961. A message to Congress states the President's policies and legislative recommendations, reflecting advice from his own White House staff and from interested agencies throughout the Executive branch. Kennedy's second economic message to Congress appears over his signature as the first part of the 1962 *Economic Report of the President*.

The Council's 6 March 1961 statement, *The American Economy in 1961: Problems and Policies*, was its other immediate task – Heller, boasting that it was accomplished in 44 days, naturally counted Saturdays and Sundays. This statement was prepared for the regular hearings of the Joint Economic Committee on the annual Economic Report, which in 1961 had been submitted in January by the outgoing President and Council. In addition to receiving our statement, the Committee took extensive further testimony, oral and written, from the three Council members.[1]

---

*First published in J. Tobin and M. Weidenbaum (eds), *Two Revolutions in Economic Policy: The First Economic Report of Presidents Kennedy and Reagan*, Cambridge, MA: MIT Press, 1988. (Written with Robert M. Solow.)

A major purpose of the testimony was to explain and elaborate the programme the President set forth in his 2 February message. More broadly, the Council's statement and testimony were its own analytical exposition of the Administration's general approach to economic policy and its application to the circumstances of the day. In this respect it is analogous to our *magnum opus*, the second part of the 1962 *Economic Report of the President*, the annual Economic Report of the Council.

In preparing the 1962 Economic Report, the Council saw the opportunity not only to meet the statutory requirements of the Employment Act as we interpreted them, but also to offer a careful and thorough exposition of the theoretical and empirical foundations of macroeconomic policies. Like *The American Economy in 1961*, the 1962 Economic Report was a team effort. The Council attracted a staff remarkable for its talents and its enthusiastic dedication. Two staff members, Robert Solow and Arthur Okun, had become in all but name additional members of the Council. The Council decided the architecture of the Report, and staff members submitted drafts in their fields of expertise. Gordon, Okun, Solow and Tobin synthesized these materials and drafted the four chapters. After receiving comments from the staff, other federal agencies and the White House, Walter Heller and the four principal authors of the draft chapters prepared the final version.

Besides Solow and Okun, staff economists contributing to the 1962 Economic Report were Richard Attiyeh, Barbara Berman (Now Bergmann), Charles Cooper, Richard Cooper, Rashi Fein, Marshall Kaplan, David Lusher, Richard R. Nelson, George Perry, Lee Preston, Vernon Ruttan, Walter Stettner, Lloyd Ulman, Leroy Wehrle and Sidney Winter. The Council also relied heavily on outside economists. Joseph Pechman and Paul Samuelson were constantly consulted. Others who gave help on the report included Kenneth Arrow (who later joined the staff), Otto Eckstein, Peter Kenen, Robert Lampman, Charles Schultz and Robert Triffin. Knowledgeable readers will recognize many persons of professional distinction among these names; some were already distinguished in 1961 and others were young then but destined to become leaders in the profession.

Frances James was the conscience of the agency from its inception in 1946 to her retirement in 1977. She would not allow any factual allegation or statistic to appear in print without assuring herself of its accuracy. She was invaluable to our Council. So was her assistant, Catherine Furlong, who succeeded Frances and continues her tradition to this day.

THE ECONOMICS OF KENNEDY'S ECONOMISTS

The authors of these 1961 and 1962 Reports were all, despite individual differences of interest and emphasis, exponents of the synthesis of Keynesian and neoclassical economics developed over the previous 15 years. American economists, notably Samuelson, played leading roles in this intellectual development. By 1961 it was becoming the mainstream of macroeconomics. The Council sought to set forth its principles and to apply them to the United States of the 1960s, in language accessible not just to economists but to all earnest readers.

Journalists on the Washington economics beat dubbed our approach the 'new economics', but they exaggerated its novelty. The Council was following well-trodden Keynesian paths in its analyses of fiscal policies: the utility of the budget as an instrument, automatic or discretionary, of economic stabilization; the priority of macroeconomic performance over the traditional convention of annual budget balance; the distinction between deficits and surpluses resulting from business cycles and those resulting from budget programmes and tax laws; the possibility of unintended 'fiscal drag' on the economy. In these respects, the Kennedy Council was reviving, in its own way, themes of the Truman Council.

Commentators seeking simple labels called the 'new' economists of the Council 'fiscalists', conveniently contrasting them to the 'monetarists' led by Milton Friedman, who stressed the central macroeconomic role of money and Federal Reserve policy. The dichotomy was quite inaccurate. Long before 1960 the neo-Keynesian neoclassical synthesis recognized monetary measures as coequal to fiscal measures in stabilization of aggregate demand. Council economists understood that the same short-run outcomes, aggregate employment and output, could be achieved by various combinations of fiscal and monetary policies. To chose among these 'policy mixes', they suggested other criteria – in particular, the long-run growth of the economy.

Two of the authors of the 1962 Economic Report, Solow and Tobin, had contributed to neoclassical growth theory in the 1950s, and Chapter 2 was devoted to long-run growth. Taming the business cycle and maintaining full employment were the first priorities of macroeconomic policy. But this should be done in ways that promote more rapid growth in the economy's capacity to produce. We were not one-eyed demand-siders. Demand calls the tune in the short run, but advances in supply determine long-run progress. For this reason, we saw the desirability of policy mixes that emphasized private and public investment for the future, relative to current consumption. These mixes would usually entail low interest rates and tight government budgets.

The principles are very relevant today; the Reagan Administration has ignored them, at considerable danger to the country.

EDUCATING THE PRESIDENT AND OTHERS

The Council's Reports were educational documents, aimed at readers within the federal government as well as outside. Congress needed to be persuaded, and so did the Federal Reserve, the Treasury, the Commerce and Labour Departments, and other executive agencies. Our most important reader was the President himself.

John F. Kennedy, unlike Ronald Reagan, came to the White House without a settled economic agenda or ideology. As Senator and candidate, he sought advice from academics in his home state of Massachusetts, notably J.K. Galbraith and Paul Samuelson, who differed on many issues. His speeches during the campaign of 1960 did not present a coherent programme. He attacked the Eisenhower Administration for the economy's sluggish performance under its stewardship and promised to 'get the country moving again'. The fact that he entered the White House without deep personal understanding of economic issues or firm convictions on policies suggested to us that he could be persuaded by cogent argument.

Kennedy's instincts and politics were generally liberal. But as he assumed the Presidency, he was keenly aware that financial markets' suspicions of a liberal Democratic President could cause him trouble. Moreover, again unlike Reagan, Kennedy had just barely won the election. Although his party controlled both houses of Congress, conservatives senior to the former Massachusetts Senator held most of the positions of power.

Throughout Kennedy's Presidency, Walter Heller taught him economics; we others helped, but no one could match Heller's knack of making points in concise readable colourful language. The President was an apt pupil, intrigued by the subject intellectually as well as pragmatically. His 1962 Yale Commencement Address showed that he had found his own political economy.

The caution and ambivalence of Kennedy and his close advisers were evident during the transition from election to inauguration. Samuelson chaired a Task Force on economic conditions. Among the members were Heller and Tobin, until their selection for the Council in December 1960. Early in the group's deliberations, the Florida 'White House' passed the word that the President-elect was not prepared to take anti-recession measures that would significantly increase the budget deficit.

Samuelson's Report of 6 January 1961 made only modest proposals for immediate action. However, in his diagnosis of the state of the economy and his precepts for future fiscal and monetary policy, Samuelson anticipated most of the themes of the Council Reports yet to come.

A parallel Task Force on economic policy chaired by Alan Sproul, retired President of the New York Federal Reserve Bank, paid special attention to the country's international financial problems and the constraints they placed on domestic expansion. One motivation in organizing the Sproul group was to reassure the financial community at home and abroad that liberal academics, Galbraith, Samuelson *et al.*, were not the only sources of economic advice to the new President. Robert Roosa of Sproul's Bank was a key member of this Task Force and became an Undersecretary of the Treasury.

The new Secretary of the Treasury, Douglas Dillon, a Republican investment banker who had served as an Undersecretary of State under Eisenhower, was announced at the same time as the appointment of Heller. The Samuelson–Sproul differences were to become Heller–Dillon differences. They were not irreconcilable. Eventually the Administration's policies were a synthesis in which major elements of both approaches survived.

THE COUNCIL'S VIEW OF THE US ECONOMY IN 1961

In the perspective of recent experience the economy's overall performance in the eight Eisenhower years 1953–60 looks better than it did to the Council in 1961. Real gross national product grew at an average annual rate of 2.35 per cent, comparable to the 2.45 per cent average growth during 1973–86, even though the civilian labour force grew more rapidly in the second period: 2.2 per cent per year instead of 1.4 per cent. But the Council thought that the 1953–60 performance fell far short of the standards of the Employment Act.

Three recessions occurred during Eisenhower's two terms, in 1953–54 following the end of the Korean War, in 1957–58 and in 1960. The unemployment rate drifted up from 3 per cent in early 1953 to 5 per cent at the peak of the 1958–59 recovery. Kennedy's economic advisers, before and after election and inauguration, were disturbed by the record and by the fatalistic complacency with which it was generally viewed.

In our view, business cycles of such frequency and amplitude could be prevented, or at least significantly moderated, by federal fiscal and monetary policies. Instead, deliberate Federal Reserve monetary policies had contributed to all three recessions, especially the second and third. Moreover, official anxiety over a $13 billion budget deficit in the fiscal year 1959 had provoked contractionary fiscal measures that helped to bring on the 1960 recession. The anxiety was misplaced, because the deficit was largely a consequence of the depressed economic conditions of 1958.

In our view, the policies of the 1950s were cutting off recoveries before they were complete, at higher and higher rates of unemployment. We saw the recession conditions of early 1961 as stemming from inadequate aggregate demand, partly policy-induced and partly inadvertent. In either case, the appropriate short-run policy response was demand management: fiscal and monetary stimulus.

INTERPRETING THE RISE IN UNEMPLOYMENT

The Council's diagnosis of the rise in unemployment was not widely shared, even within the new Kennedy Administration. Most people, especially non-economists, viewed business cycles fatalistically and complacently, as immutable natural phenomena that policy neither caused nor could ameliorate. Likewise, they saw the upward drift of unemployment as the result of structural and technological trends in the economy. This was the well-publicized view of the Federal Reserve Chairman, William McChesney Martin, and it was shared by Representative Thomas Curtis of Missouri, the ranking Republican member of the Joint Economic Committee. The moral was that demand stimulus could not reduce unemployment but would ignite wage and price inflation.

This view appealed to conservatives, presumably because it could be used as an argument against policy activism. But similar interpretations of the rise of unemployment came from left-wing critics of capitalism. The views of Robert Theobald and other latter-day Luddites were fashionable among intellectuals: the economic system was obsolete because automation was destroying jobs and producing goods without disbursing the wages to buy them. Within the new Administration itself, leaders of the Labour Department emphasized policies tailor-made to the diverse problems of individual unemployed workers, and distrusted the Council's macroeconomic recipes for job creation.

To refute these interpretations of the rise in unemployment in the 1950s, the Council included in *The American Economy in 1961* a thorough statistical analysis finding that demographic and industrial breakdowns of unemployment showed no evidence that structural unemployment was increasing. What they showed was a general shortage of jobs of all kinds for workers of all kinds. Then and always, the Council recognized that much unemployment was structural, beyond the reach of macro remedies. We supported policies to help displaced workers and new job-seekers obtain the educations and skills required in the modern world, and to help them locate available jobs. We regarded macroeconomic and structural policies as complementary rather than competitive. We saw no reason that aggregate demand policies could not bring unemployment down to about 4 per cent, and even further as structural policies succeeded.

We economists looked at unemployment statistics not just as measures of the personal deprivations and hardships of the millions of unemployed, but also as barometers of the overall economic weather. Compared to the prosperity accompanying a 4 per cent unemployment rate, a 7 per cent rate signified bad news in many dimensions: among them production, incomes, profits, capital investment, capacity utilization and government budgets. This point was not widely appreciated. For example, Kennedy and his closest adviser on domestic policy, Ted Sorenson, wondered why raising the employment score from 93 to 96 per cent, 'A minus to A', deserved high political priority.

The Council undertook to document quantitatively the large changes in general economic conditions and well-being associated with small changes in employment and unemployment rates. Similar research had been done at the Joint Economic Committee by James Knowles. Much of the Council's work on the subject was done by Arthur Okun, before and after he joined the staff in Washington, DC. Thus was born 'Okun's Law', which proved to be one of the most reliable and useful empirical regularities of economics.

Okun estimated that three extra percentage points in unemployment meant a 10 per cent 'gap' between actual and potential GNP. Okun, like Knowles, estimated at 3.5 per cent per year the trend growth rate of potential GNP, that is, the real output associated with keeping unemployment constant at 4 per cent. Thus the mere avoidance of recession, conventionally defined as absolute decline in national output, meant the unemployment rate would be increasing by more than a point a year. That is why the Council stressed that the objective of policy should be to achieve and maintain full employment and potential output, not just to avoid recessions.

FISCAL POLICY

A gap between actual output and potential spelled also a shortfall in federal revenues and usually a budget deficit. But, as Keynesian fiscal analysis had long stressed, in these circumstances it is perverse policy to take austere measures to cut spending and raise taxes. This was a mistake made in the Great Depression and also in 1959, as previously remarked. The Council revived the full-employment budget concepts of the Truman Council and estimated them in the light of Okun's analysis.

In 1961 the continuing strength of the balanced-budget convention in political and financial circles foreclosed any major initiative of fiscal stimulus to promote recovery. The Council sought and exploited some small targets of opportunity – for example, starting sooner rather than later scheduled improvements in social security benefits, which were at the time 'off-budget' (as they now are once again), liberalization of unemployment insurance benefits, and early release to the states of allocations from the Interstate Highway Trust Fund.

The Berlin crisis at midyear occasioned a modest increase in defence spending. The instincts of the President and all his advisers except the Council were to ask for an equal increase in taxes. Kennedy, after all, had called on the nation to sacrifice for the cause of freedom, and a tax increase would demonstrate the nation's resolve. The Council argued that a tax increase was the last thing needed in an economy just beginning to recover, and Heller carried the day.

In 1962 Kennedy requested authority to initiate temporary income tax cuts when specified statistical evidence signalled incipient recession. This was the first of several similar proposals originating with the Council designed to facilitate timely countercyclical fiscal policy. Presidents Kennedy and Johnson regularly recommended them to Congress, which ignored all of them except a proposal for statistically triggered temporary increases in unemployment compensation.

In 1962 the Administration proposed a tax reform intended to be revenue-neutral. The principal item was the Investment Tax Credit, favoured by both Council and Treasury. As an incentive for business investment in equipment, it could enhance both short-run demand and long-run supply. At the same time the Treasury was liberalizing its tax rules on depreciation. The proposed revenue-increasing measures included both limits on deductibility of employees' expenses for meals, lodging and entertainment and withholding of taxes on interest and dividends. These got nowhere in Congress.

Heller eventually triumphed in his campaign to educate Kennedy, Dillon and Congress on the need for fiscal stimulus to ensure full recovery. The young recovery was faltering in 1962 and inflation was quiescent. The budget was not balanced despite the Administration's restraint. The business and financial communities were hostile to Kennedy in spite of his efforts to be fiscally 'sound'.

The President adopted the idea of an income tax cut in mid-1962 and proposed the legislation in January 1963. The Revenue Act of 1964 was passed and the cuts took effect only after his death. For the first time, fiscal stimulus was undertaken not to arrest a recession but to invigorate and prolong a recovery. Thus was accepted the Council's point that achieving and maintaining full employment, not just damping the business cycle, is the proper objective of policy under the Employment Act. Unfortunately, this triumph was not destined to be permanent.

At the time and since, the tax cut has drawn criticism from two sides. Some critics conceded the need for fiscal stimulus but preferred to obtain it by increasing federal non-military spending. The Council was sympathetic to this alternative, but it was not politically feasible at the time. (Indeed even the tax cut made it through Congress only on the wave of sentiment that followed Kennedy's assassination in November 1963.) The Council did not agree with Galbraith, who preferred no stimulus to a tax cut. His motto – never give away tax revenues because you may need them later – looked good in 1966–68 when President Johnson escalated Vietnam War spending without raising taxes, against the advice of his own Council.

Other critics preferred monetary to fiscal stimulus, encouraging investment relative to consumption in the interest of long-run growth. But international balance-of-payments problems ruled out a monetary policy significantly more expansionary than it was already. Heller was probably never as convinced of the efficacy and desirability of substituting monetary for fiscal stimulus as Samuelson, Solow and Tobin. The first priority of full employment was agreed by all.

ECONOMIC GROWTH

The Council wanted to expand demand enough to bring GNP back to its full-employment potential. But that was not all.

From the beginning, the Council supported policies that would eventually increase the rate of growth of potential output itself. This meant a focus on investment activities, broadly construed. As early as *The American Economy in 1961* we urged the importance of investment in physical, human and intellectual capital, and recommended policies to promote them. The 1962 Economic Report devoted one of its four chapters to making this case.

Two aspects of that chapter are worth emphasizing. First, its scope was very wide, ranging from natural resources (including timber and agricultural land) at one end of the spectrum, through plant and equipment, skill training and research and development, all the way to health and education at the other. Thus the Council asserted unambiguously that business investment in plant and equipment, while central to progress in a market economy, is by no means the sole vehicle of capital formation for future well-being. Of course, the Administration's Investment Tax Credit was a major incentive for business – not at first welcomed by its beneficiaries, though appetite grew with eating. Secondly, we pointed out the multiple purposes served by some forms of investment. Plant and equipment spending helps close employment and output gaps, while also lifting the trend of potential. Investments in human resources improve productivity and also help to equalize opportunity throughout society.

THE INTERNATIONAL BALANCE OF PAYMENTS

In the late 1950s a new element in the economic situation of the United States was our adverse balance in international payments. Foreign governments and central banks were accumulating dollars in liquid form, bank deposits and Treasury bills. Their holdings were potential claims on the US gold stock. As some were exercised, US gold reserves began to decline, after a long and massive buildup beginning in 1933. Financiers throughout the world were voicing suspicions that the United States might not always be able and willing to convert dollar claims into gold on demand. The influential head of the International Monetary Fund, Per Jacobsson, criticized the 1959 federal budget deficit from this standpoint.

As the Sproul Task Force urged, the balance of payments and confidence in the 'dollar' became constraints on US macroeconomic policies. Avoiding inflation, which would make US goods less competitive in world trade, took on heightened importance. Moreover, if monetary policy were to push US interest rates too low, funds would flow out to overseas markets where rates were higher. As a consequence, in 1960 the Federal Reserve held interest rates above their usual recession lows.

The Council's position can be summarized as follows:

1. The dollar problem was not a reason to abandon recovery and full employment as the major priorities of macroeconomic policies. The value of the dollar in gold and foreign currencies was not sacred writ. The Council was not proposing devaluation, even though the dollar appeared to be overvalued. But in our view devaluation would not be so cataclysmic that all other goals should be sacrificed to avert it. Eventually, it took a Republican President to devalue the dollar (as it did, for similar reasons, to make friends with Red China).
2. Greater emphasis would have to be placed on fiscal stimulus, and less on monetary stimulus, because of the dollar problem. The 'easy money, tight budget' policy mix desirable to raise future potential output would have to give way, to some extent, to a mix that would limit balance-of-payments deficits. Investment incentives that could not be given by low interest rates could, however, be given by tax legislation, the Investment Tax Credit and accelerated depreciation.
3. As economists committed to a liberal international trading system, we opposed protectionist measures, 'buy American' regulations such as tying foreign aid to purchases of US products, and other expedients for 'saving gold'.
4. National and international monetary measures could mitigate the imbalance in our external accounts and its consequences. We urged the Federal Reserve and the Treasury to shorten the maturities of outstanding federal securities, selling bills while purchasing bonds. Short interest rates seemed to be the more important for international flows of funds, while long rates were important for domestic investment, especially home-building. We wanted to twist the term structure, lowering long rates relative to shorts. Unfortunately the Federal Reserve, having committed itself to a 'bills only' policy in 1953, could not bring itself to intervene signifi-

cantly in long-term bond markets. The Treasury, while giving lip service to 'Operation Twist', was lengthening the debt by large-scale advance refundings of securities close to maturity. In the international arena, the Council favoured measures to take pressures off the dollar and gold by creation of alternative reserve assets through the International Monetary Fund. With gold scarce and the reserve status of the dollar questioned, the world faced a possible shortage of internationally accepted liquid assets.

INFLATION

President Kennedy and his Council were the first and last to specify a numerical target for full employment. Our 4 per cent unemployment target was cautiously chosen to be unlikely to set off excess-demand-pull inflation. For the Kennedy Administration, the silver lining of the two preceding Eisenhower–Martin recessions was that they had lowered the inflation rate from 4 per cent in 1957 to 1.5 per cent in 1961. Yet from the very beginning the Council was worried about the possibility of inflation's setting in before anything worth calling 'full employment' had been achieved. This fear was an after-effect of the 'creeping inflation' of the mid-1950s. The CPI had risen by a total of 6 per cent during two prosperous years 1955–57, and then by another 2.5 per cent in one year of recession between 1957 and 1958. Between 1960 and 1961 prices rose another 1 per cent; even that attracted attention in the press. Survivors of the 1970s may laugh, but the slightest inflation was unnerving then.

As a purely practical matter, the Council thought that there was so much slack in the economy that inflation was hardly a threat for the next few years. (That turned out to be right; when the unemployment rate finally fell to 4 per cent at the end of 1965, the price level was still rising less than 2 per cent per year with no serious acceleration.) We were worried, not because we thought that slow inflation was very damaging to the economy by itself, but because we could see that it could undermine the credibility of the expansionary policy that was the prime necessity.

Accordingly, *The American Economy in 1961* pointed out that most of the cumulative inflation of the past 15 years had occurred in two bursts of genuine excess demand: 1946–48, when wartime controls were lifted, and again at the time of the Korean War. If similar shocks were to happen again, one knew what to do. As a defence against 'premature inflation' we suggested active anti-trust enforcement (to preserve competition), accelerated productivity growth (to take advantage of nominal wage inertia), training and education programmes (to make for mobility of labour and to relieve localized skill shortages), and – even then – voluntary wage and price restraint.

By the time of the 1962 Economic Report this passage had grown into a whole chapter: 'Price Behavior in a Free and Growing Economy'. It talked a lot, rather didactically, about the need to combine flexibility of relative prices with stability of the general price level. This could only happen if some prices were free to fall. By that time we had learned that the Labour-Management Advisory Committee the President had established was going to be a disappointment to us, because it would not be the vehicle for changing either the ideology or the practice of collective bargaining. We were reduced to urging, rather unspecifically, that while it was perfectly acceptable for workers and employers to bargain unstintingly over the division of real revenue, it was not acceptable for them to join forces to pass their conflict on to the economy at large in the form of rising prices. The parties themselves seemed inclined to 'peace at any price level', and the fraternity of private and federal mediators and arbitrators acquiesced.

That chapter ended with the famous 'Guideposts for Noninflationary Wage and Price Behavior'. In form they were a description of the way wages and prices *would* behave in a well-functioning market economy free of market power and discretion in wage- and price-setting. The innocent hope was expressed that they would serve as a focus of public understanding and discussion, and thus help to bring about an atmosphere in which market power would be exercised 'responsibly'. Thanks largely to Kermit Gordon's foresight and initiative, the President and Secretary of Labour Arthur Goldberg began in 1961 to use their influence and good offices to preserve price stability, beginning with the bellwether steel industry. The Council tried to provide analytical underpinnings for this effort. We may even have guessed that the endemic problem of achieving full employment without inflation would prove intractable without organized 'incomes policy'. That still seems to be the case. We may not be able to do it with incomes policy; there is still little reason to believe that it can be done without incomes policy.

The intellectual framework that led the Council in this direction is clear in retrospect and was quite clear then. We believed we were trying to shift favourably the *level* of the Phillips curve, by talking it down in the first instance and by informal intervention if necessary. Phillips curves appeared on the backs of our envelopes. A.W. Phillips's original article had been published in 1958. The famous – some would say notorious – article by Samuelson and Solow, 'Analytical Foundations of Anti-Inflationary Policy', appeared in 1960. George Perry's PhD thesis was accepted in August 1961 and delayed in publication while he served on the Council staff.

Since then there has been much debate about the meaning and validity of a 'trade-off between unemployment and inflation'. The use made of this notion in the 1962 Economic Report has sometimes been characterized as naive. We do not think it was; but we may have banked too heavily on the stability of the Phillips curve indicated by post-war data through 1961.

The Council's estimate in 1961 was that 4 per cent unemployment was a reasonably safe 'interim target'. We meant to state our belief that expansion of aggregate demand could return the economy to an unemployment rate of 4 per cent – last achieved in 1957 – without much danger of wage-induced inflation. Since then, much research effort has gone into estimation of the 'natural rate of unemployment', a closely related but much more theory-laden concept. Some of that research suggests that 4 per cent was too low a target unemployment rate in 1961, and some suggests that it was close to being right. We observe that the unemployment rate did indeed get down to 4 per cent at the very end of 1965 without signs of labour market strain and with negligible acceleration of inflation. It took the clear wartime excess demand of 1966–68 to set off a wage–price–wage spiral.

CONCLUSION

No doubt we would write a somewhat different Economic Report were we to be transported back to the circumstances of 1961 with our 1987 mental furniture intact. It would be a sad comment on macroeconomics were that not so. Nevertheless we look back at *The American Economy in 1961* and the 1962 Economic Report with affection, respect and, indeed, defiant pride. We gladly reprint them now, not just because they may have historical interest but because we believe they contain much that is still valid and useful for macroeconomics and its relation to public policy.

NOTE

1. *January 1961 Economic Report of the President and the Economic Situation and Outlook.* Hearings before the Joint Economic Committee, 87th Congress, First Session, Washington, DC: US Government Printing Office, 1961, pp. 290–419, 563–614. The prepared statements reprinted in this book appear on pp. 310–92 and 564–74.

5. Okun's Law: how policy and research helped each other*

I want to relate to you an anecdote that illustrates the close two-way connection between economics as a scholarly, or perhaps in some sense a scientific, discipline and its applications to the problems, puzzles, issues and controversies of public policy. Economics used to be called 'political economy', after all, and its quantitative applications 'political arithmetic'. It developed from efforts to give practical advice, solicited or unsolicited, to rulers and legislators. Adam Smith, David Ricardo and John Maynard Keynes all made theoretical revolutions in the course of thinking through the big issues of political economy of their times.

The incident I will tell you about is much more recent and much less earthshaking in the history of ideas. But it is part of my own personal experience, and in its way makes the larger point.

I must begin by telling you who Arthur Okun was – he died, alas, in 1980 at the age of 51 – and what the Council of Economic Advisers (CEA) is and was.

Art Okun came to Yale as an instructor in economics in 1952. He was writing his PhD thesis at Columbia. He had received a bachelor's degree from Columbia College, with all sorts of academic honours. It was fortuitous that he came to Yale. As the fall term of 1952 was about to begin, we were short of teachers for introductory economics sections, and Professor Lloyd Reynolds put in some emergency calls to other graduate departments. When Art came to New Haven, I had been there for two years as an Associate Professor. We quickly found out that we were interested in the same subjects. We thought about them in very similar ways, and we stimulated each other.

Despite his brilliance, Art was shy and insecure. He was a perfectionist, and he never seemed satisfied enough with his thesis to submit it to Columbia. I became, among other things, his unofficial dissertation adviser and I finally got him to turn it in and accept his PhD in 1956. But the same characteristics kept him from publishing much, and his progress up the Yale ladder was slow. Yet I and a few others in the department who knew him well, plus cohorts of the best graduate students who still remember him as the

*Paper presented to The Club, New Haven Connecticut, April 1992.

principal source of their education, knew him to be a jewel in our crown, albeit a jewel not noticed very much elsewhere.

When the Cowles Commission for Research in Economics moved to Yale from Chicago in 1955, bringing very distinguished people with it (Tjalling Koopmans, Jacob Marschak, Gerard Debreu) along with some money, a library and a great tradition, I became its Director. One of the first things I did was to attach Okun to the Cowles Foundation (its name was changed by President Griswold) and get him into a research programme in macroeconomic forecasting for policy applications and into print.

I am about to tell you how the sequel was that Art went to Washington to work for the CEA to the President. He was in Washington for most of the rest of his life. He returned to Yale in 1963 and at last became a full Professor. He became a member of the CEA at the end of 1964 and its Chairman in 1968–69 until the change of Administration. For the last ten years of his life he was at the Brookings Institution in Washington, where he founded *Brookings Papers on Economic Activity*, which he made one of the most respected and best edited journals in our profession. Articles and books flowed from his pen. One I cherish is inscribed with his message: 'To Jim, who first taught me to be an economist and then led me into political economy'.

The CEA was established by the Employment Act of 1946, a bipartisan piece of legislation motivated by fear that the post-war economy might relapse into depression conditions like those of the 1930s. The Act dedicated the federal government to use its powers to promote 'maximum employment, production and purchasing power', an explicit commitment to use fiscal and monetary instruments for broad macroeconomic objectives rather than narrow financial goals. In a sense it ratified a political reality evident since the defeat of Herbert Hoover in 1932: that electorates would hold Presidents and Congresses, especially Presidents, accountable for the performance of the economy during their tenures.

The Act requires the President to report to Congress at least once a year on the state of the economy, the degree to which it is fulfilling the goals of the Act, and the President's proposals for achieving those goals. To help him fulfil those duties, the Act set up the CEA, composed of three members, one of whom the President designates as Chairman, all appointed by the President and confirmed by the Senate. It also set up a joint committee of the two houses of Congress now known as the Joint Economic Committee, which oversees the President's fulfilment of the purposes of the Act, and in particular receives and comments on the President's Economic Reports. They are submitted each year along with the Budget and the 'State of the Union' address.

The Council is a small agency, in the Executive Office of the President, with a staff of about 15 professional economists. It has no operating responsibilities. Consequently it has no power or influence, within the government or without, except to the degree that the President takes its advice seriously. That degree has varied considerably over the years, depending on the inclination of the President and the effectiveness of the Chairman and the other members in their relations with the White House. The annual Report is its *magnum opus*, but the CEA is busy all the time. Most CEA appointments have been drawn from the private sector, generally from academia. Effectiveness requires that the CEA and President be politically and personally simpatico. The Council cannot be an 'objective' Supreme Court of Economics. That was tried by the first Chairman, Edwin Nourse. After an indecisive session with Nourse, Harry Truman asked his Chief of Staff, Charlie Murphy, to find him a one-armed economist. Yale economics has had a good share of members – Henry Wallich, James Tobin, Arthur Okun (also Chairman), M.J. Peck, William Fellner, Paul MacAvoy, William Nordhaus.

President Kennedy in 1961 appointed a CEA of Walter Heller (Minnesota) Chairman, Kermit Gordon (Williams) and myself. We were quite dissatisfied by the performance of the economy during the Eisenhower years. There had been three recessions, in 1953–54, 1957–58 and, finally, in 1960, the election year – that recession probably gave J.F.K. victory over Nixon. The unemployment rate had been higher at each cyclical peak – 3 per cent in 1953, 4 per cent in 1957, 5 per cent in 1959 – and at the first two cyclical troughs. It was 7 per cent as we took office, and we wanted to do something about it. After all, J.F.K. had promised to 'get the country moving again'.

Moreover, we at the Council thought we knew how. We were Keynesians, though not literal adherents of the text of the Bible, *The General Theory of Employment, Interest and Money* published in 1936. We thought that a combination of monetary stimulus, lower interest rates and more abundant credit, engineered by the Federal Reserve, along with fiscal stimulus – yes, deficit spending (of modest amount by Reagan standards) resulting from either lower taxes or more expenditures – would do the job. We took the Employment Act seriously. We thought a goal of 4 per cent was an appropriate target for meeting the objectives of the Act, and our President was the first (and last) to be willing to announce a numerical target for 'maximum employment'. However, he was not initially willing to take the steps, or recommend to Congress the measures, to achieve this goal.

There were several reasons for his reluctance:

First, he had barely won the election. Congress, though Democratic, was run by conservatives, mostly Southern Democrats, who regarded him as a young whippersnapper.

Second, J.F.K. was afraid of Wall Street and the business community. He rightly thought they mistrusted a Democratic President and could do him great harm in the financial, foreign exchange and commodity markets. These were the days before a Republican President, Reagan, made deficit spending acceptable to those constituencies. In 1961 there was a strong taboo against deficit spending, and indeed a $12 billion deficit in the fiscal year 1959, the inadvertent result of the 1957–58 recession, was one reason for the Eisenhower Administration's belt-tightening, which helped bring about the 1960 recession.

Third, there was a strong belief among many politicians, policy-makers and pundits that the rise in unemployment in the 1950s was an inevitable and natural structural phenomenon, not remediable by government policy, not anyway remediable by monetary and fiscal policies to increase demand for goods and services and labour. These structural theories were popular on both the Left and the Right. Their common message was that we Keynesian macroeconomists were wrong, that we were misinterpreting what was some kind of change of life of the American economy.

There were several versions of the structural argument. One emphasized demographic changes: larger proportions of the labour force consisted of groups who were especially susceptible to unemployment, either because of their own choice or because of unemployability due to lack of needed skills or other attributes. This was, for example, the view of William McChesney Martin, the Chairman of the Federal Reserve – incidentally a loyal Yalie and a member of the Corporation. A more dramatic thesis was the view of Robert Theobald, a quasi-sociologist/economist guru whose widely read book contended that science and technology were making it possible to satisfy human desires without human work, resulting in mass unemployment in the midst of unimagined abundance and necessitating a wholly new system of generating the purchasing power by which the cornucopia would be distributed. Then there was our own Labour Department, which kept telling us that there was not one unemployment problem, as we macroeconomists thought, but as many as there were unemployed individuals. What we needed, they said, were programmes they would design and administer to deal with these millions of problems one by one.

These ideas reached the White House and, of course, Congress. We had to shoot them down. We did that with the help of a student of Bob Solow's at MIT. Solow himself we had enticed to come to Washington as our Senior Staff Economist. He became in reality a fourth Council member. Statistical research showed that the demographic and industrial structure of unemployment and employment were essentially the same as they had been since World War II. No structural changes of the alleged kinds could be detected.

The President's political concerns were more important. Sometimes we heard them from his own mouth, sometimes from his domestic policy Chief of Staff, Ted Sorenson. This was their argument: 'When I went to college, a 96 was an A and a 93 was an A minus. It seems to me that 7 per cent unemployment is a 93, an A minus. That's where we are now. Four per cent unemployment, that would be a 96, an A. That's where you want me to take the economy. I can't see why raising my economics grade from A minus to A, or really raising your grade from A minus to A, is worth spending my scarce political capital'. More than once, Ted Sorenson added that our professional reputations were not a major priority of the Administration. I should say that all of this was said in a friendly and jocular spirit, but it wasn't idle banter. It was a challenge we had to meet.

We knew that the differences between a 7 per cent unemployment economy and a 4 per cent unemployment economy were by no means so trivial. They were the differences between recession and prosperity, evident in many dimensions: personal incomes, profits and losses, bankruptcies, saving, investment, and state and local public finances. The unemployment rate was not, still is not, just a measure of unemployment *per se*. It was, it is, the prime business cycle barometer.

One overall measure naturally occurred to us as a concise and dramatic answer to Kennedy and Sorenson. This was to estimate the difference between GNP (always corrected for inflation, stated in dollars of constant purchasing power) at 7 per cent unemployment and at 4 per cent unemployment. I knew that this GNP gap would be a lot more than 3 per cent, but we needed as precise an estimate as we could get.

So I phoned Art Okun. I knew he could and would to the job. My colleagues in Washington had never heard of him, but they took my word for his competence. It was February 1961, and we were supposed to present the Administration's view of the economy to the Joint Economic Committee of the Congress early in March. (The 1961 Economic Report had already been submitted by the lame duck President and Council. Now the Committee wanted to know what the new team thought, and we wanted to tell them.)

Art enthusiastically undertook the assignment. Before long we had his answer. The evidence of the previous 15 years was that a three point difference in the unemployment rate was magnified into nearly a 10 per cent difference in GNP. We mutually decided to call the hypothetical GNP the economy was capable of producing at full employment, our 4 per cent target unemployment rate, potential GNP, and its percentage excess over actual GNP in any year or quarter-year the GNP gap or just the 'gap'. Okun's Law, as it came to be known, originated in this hurry-up research. Okun elaborated it in more academic and sophisticated journal articles subsequently published. The 'Law' was that a one percentage point increase in unemployment was associated with about a three point increase in the gap. The reverse would be true for decreases in unemployment and gap. A by-product of the exercise was an estimate of the rate of growth of Potential GNP, that is, of the productive capacity of the economy. At the time, Okun estimated it at 3.5 per

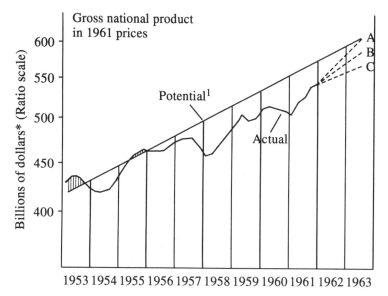

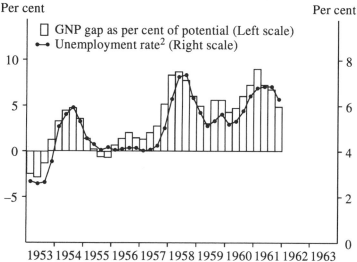

* Seasonally adjusted annual rates.
[1] 3$\frac{1}{2}$ per cent trend line through middle of 1955.

[2] Unemployment as per cent of civilian labour force; seasonally adjusted.

Note: A, B and C represent GNP in the middle of 1963 assuming unemployment rate of 4 per cent, 5 per cent and 6 per cent respectively.

Figure 5.1   Gross national product, actual and potential, and unemployment rate

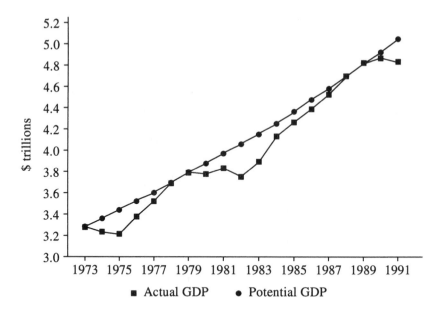

Figure 5.2   Actual and potential GDP, 1973–91

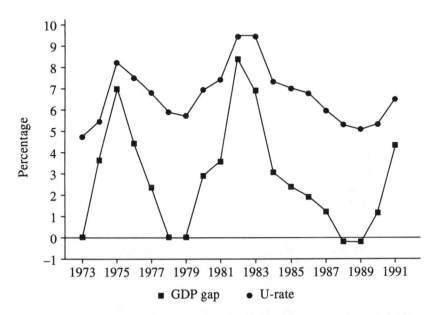

Figure 5.3   GDP gap and unemployment rate, 1973–91

cent per year, of which two points were due to growth in productivity and 1.5 to growth of the labour force. An implication of this finding plus the Okun's Law relation between unemployment and the gap was this: if actual GNP grows at 3.5 per cent the unemployment rate remains constant. If, however, actual GNP remains constant, the gap increases and unemployment grows at somewhat more than one point a year.

In Figures 5.1, 5.2 and 5.3 you can see the steady growth of Potential GNP. You can see also the actual GNP and the gap between the two. You can see that the gap is closely associated with the unemployment rate. Figure 5.1 is a copy of what was shown in our 1962 Economic Report. The other two are more recent history as I have graphed it. Notice how the paths of the gap and the unemployment rate fluctuate together, while the amplitude of the cycles in the gap is much the greater.

In comparison with 1962, the growth of Potential GNP has slowed down. Also, the consensus of economists is that the unemployment rate now regarded as 'full employment' has increased from 4 to 5.5 per cent, because of evidence in the 1970s that rates lower than that led to inflation. The Okun's Law coefficient appears to have declined from 3.2 to 2.5. But the essential point remains. Indeed Okun's Law – Art himself would never have used the term 'law' for any finding in economics – turned out to be one of the most durable empirical regularities of the US economy. It applies to other modern capitalist economies as well, though with different numerical parameters. The framework of the graphs is a very instructive way to decompose time series paths of GNP into long-run growth trends (represented by potential GNP) and cyclical fluctuations (shown by the paths of actual GNP and the gap). It is useful in teaching, too, from freshmen to graduate students.

One lesson is that the conventional definition of recession as negative changes in GNP and of recovery as positive changes is not very meaningful in a progressive economy. Par growth is not zero but the growth rate of potential, 3.5 per cent back in the 1950s and 1960s, 2.25 or 2.5 per cent now. For example, in this year (1992) we won't really have recovery unless GNP starts growing faster than that. Only growth faster than 2.5 per cent per year will lower unemployment.

Why is Okun's coefficient so high? *A priori* one might not expect a 3 per cent increase in labour input to be technologically capable of producing more than 3 per cent additional output. Indeed, one would probably expect less than 3 per cent, because other cooperating inputs – capital equipment and land – are not simultaneously increasing as much as employment. The answer to this puzzle is that the change in the unemployment rate is not a measure of the change of labour input. Kennedy and Sorenson had assumed it was – they thought that if the unemployment rate falls from 7 to 4 per cent then labour input must be rising from 93 to 96 per cent of a constant labour force. Okun pointed out that labour input rises much more. The same economic changes that diminish unemployment would concurrently have three other effects:

1. The labour force itself expands when unemployment falls and jobs become more available. People who had withdrawn from the labour force because they were discouraged by the unavailability of opportunities re-enter. House-spouses, students and retired persons are attracted when the right jobs come along. In the 1960s it sometimes seemed that two jobs had to be created to reduce unemployment by one person: one job for the unemployed person and one for someone else previously not in the labour force at all, not counted as unemployed.
2. Hours of work move pro-cyclically, increasing significantly as unemployment declines. Fewer workers are involuntarily confined to part-time jobs. More overtime work occurs. Thus employment in person-hours rises more than employment in persons.
3. The Census counts as employed anyone on a payroll. But workers can be on payrolls without being needed for current production. In business cycles many employers keep overhead workers and even production workers employed although they are temporarily redundant. Cyclical upswings in sales and production draw more labour input from already employed workers. This appears statistically as a surge in productivity, especially in the early phases of a recovery. Likewise, productivity per worker or worker-hour appears to decline in recessions.

In Table 5.1 the 1961 gap of $40 billion is allocated to the change in unemployment itself ($15 billion) and to the three complementary relationships: $4 billion to the labour force effect, $5 billion to the hours of work effect and $16 billion to the productivity effect.

Table 5.1   *Allocation of estimated $40 billion gap between potential and actual gross national product, 1961 (billions of dollars)*

Source	Associated increment of output
Total	40
Lower unemployment	15
Larger labour force in response to greater demand	4
Longer hours of work per man associated with higher utilization	5
Greater productivity per man-hour associated with higher utilization	16

Source: Council of Economic Advisers.

Okun's Law did help to persuade J.F.K. and Congress, perhaps even Chairman Martin, of the desirability of expansionary fiscal and monetary policy in the early 1960s. Thanks also to some good luck, recovery did achieve the 4 per cent unemployment target in 1965. J.F.K. gave a Commencement Speech at Yale in 1962 espousing the pragmatic and non-ideological approach to economic policy we had taught him. Art Okun joined the CEA staff part-time in the spring term 1961 and full-time thereafter. As I have already mentioned, he became Chairman of the Council later in the Johnson Administration.

A Yale alumnus who was an admirer of Okun has supported a series of lectures in his memory, and recently endowed an Okun Chair in economics.

6.   On Crotty's critique of q-theory*

NEOCLASSICAL AND OTHER INVESTMENT THEORIES

Tobin's first inclination was to turn the other cheek to Crotty's criticism elsewhere in this issue, but he didn't like being called a conflationist – ugh! Yes, q-theory works best if managers act in the interests of the stockholders. Yes, q-theory is in that sense a neoclassical theory of corporate investment. But ....

In the post-war discussion of the theory and econometrics of investment, 'neoclassical' meant emphasis on profitabilities, relative prices and cost-of-capital variables, in contrast to models that relied on output and sales and their 'acceleration' or on liquidity flows and stocks. Sometimes these latter models were called Keynesian, because some early English followers of Keynes downplayed interest rate effects. But Keynes himself presented a neoclassical theory of investment, namely that it is carried to the point at which the marginal efficiency of capital is equal to the interest rate. His theory was essentially the same as that of the great neoclassical theorist, Irving Fisher.

The heterodox element of Keynes's investment theory was his stress in Chapter 12 of the *General Theory* on the inevitable role of non-rational attitudes – optimism and confidence or their opposites – in forming estimates of the marginal efficiency. Even in insisting on the inapplicability of probability calculus to expectations of future investment returns, Keynes was not without mainstream precedents – his own *Treatise on Probability* and Frank Knight's distinction between risk and uncertainty.

So when Dale Jorgenson called his cost-of-capital investment equation 'neoclassical', he was rebelling against the accelerationists and other 'Keynesians' and not against Keynes. We proposed q-theory in the same spirit. We certainly did not thereby intend, any more than Keynes himself, to commit ourselves to a fully neoclassical macroeconomic theory.

*First published in *Journal of Post Keynesian Economics*/Summer 1990, **12** (4). (Written with William Brainard.)

MANAGERS AND STOCKHOLDERS

The first sentence of the Tobin–Brainard paragraph on which Crotty focuses criticism, a sentence omitted from the quotation on pp. 527–8, reads: 'The neoclassical theory of corporate investment is based on the assumption that the management seeks to maximize the present net worth of the company, the market value of the outstanding common shares'. The rest of the paragraph spells out the implications of this assumption.[1]

We are not asserting that the assumed identification of managers with stockholders' interests is an empirical fact. For this reason among others, we made clear that we regard q-theory as a testable hypothesis, not as an incontrovertible truth or a tautology. There surely are divergences of interest between managers and owners. At the same time, we observe that corporate Chief Executive Officers (CEOs) are very concerned (some would say obsessed) with the market value of their shares. Especially in these days of takeovers, they have to be. Consequently, one might expect financial markets to influence managerial decisions.

Our q-theory does *not* assume that stockholders and other market participants know better than managers what would increase the earnings and fundamental value of the firm in the long run. Speculators usually have short horizons and incomplete information.[2] Yet managers might make decisions they think the market will like and avoid those they fear the market will not like.

Nothing in our joint or individual writings on q-theory justifies Crotty's contention that 'Tobin's manager and his financial investor ... are equally knowledgeable and equally rational ...[and] virtually indistinguishable'. Nothing supports his statement that 'within Tobin's conflation it is the shareholders who are behaviorally active ... [and] management's only role is to execute decisions made for them in financial markets'. We imagined that managers propose projects and securities markets appraise them.

Nothing excuses the charge that 'Tobin places Keynes's stamp of approval on the rational expectations, efficient-markets general equilibrium models that are the modern extensions of the classical theory Keynes so vehemently opposed'. No one who has read a sample of what Tobin has written in macroeconomics over many years could attribute to him, as Crotty does, a Panglossian view of the stability and efficiency of market capitalism, especially when it is unassisted by government policy.

Crotty believes that management, far from being myopic or selfish, aims intelligently at 'the long-run reproduction, growth, and safety of the firm itself', resisting to the best of its ability the claims of uninformed and impatient stockholders as registered in financial markets or elsewhere. He associates Keynes with these characterizations, while criticizing Chapter 12 for assuming that managers supinely yield to these misguided pressures. Crotty exaggerates in both directions. Keynes says '... it is by no means always the case that speculation predominates over enterprise', and in section VII of the chapter he discusses the dependence of enterprise itself on 'animal spirits' and 'spontaneous optimism'.

In the 1977 paper at issue we offered numerous reasons, with examples, why we would not expect q, particularly as measured in practice, to explain investment all by itself. Since q is necessarily calculated as the average financial-market value per dollar of replacement cost of the existing reproducible capital of a firm or an economy, it may often fail to provide a measure of the marginal value of investments in quite different kinds of capital. Crotty's case, p. 536, of qualitatively new investments by American firms whose market shares and average q's were suffering from foreign competition could easily be interpreted as a marginal-average discrepancy, although Crotty cites it as a failure of q-theory and an example of managerial independence.

THE MACROECONOMIC SETTING OF q-THEORY

The intellectual motivations for 'q' were stated in the 1977 article. Since they will not be clear to a reader of Crotty, we will summarize them here. They mostly relate to the investment equations of short-run macro models.

First, following Abba Lerner (1940, p. 334), we thought that Keynes's investment function (Chapter 11, pp. 136–7) suffered from a stock-flow confusion. Keynes's condition that marginal efficiency of *capital* equal the rate of interest seemed not to determine a rate of net investment but a stock of capital. Indeed it is a condition for zero investment in a stationary economy. Investment should be modelled, we thought, as responding to the *difference* between the marginal efficiency and the interest rate. In this view we were in the tradition of Wicksell and of the Keynes of the *Treatise on Money* (who occasionally reappears in the *General Theory*, as in several sentences quoted by Crotty from Chapter 12). The q ratio is a convenient way of estimating that difference without requiring a separate measurement of the marginal efficiency of capital.

Second, we thought that rates of interest, nominal or real, on future obligations to pay money were not proper measures of the cost of capital for risky investment decisions. We need the discount rates 'for streams of return with the characteristics of business capital' (Tobin and Brainard, 1977, p. 245). These are implicit in stock market valuations, though not observable separately from expectations of future earnings. For example, many financial economists and pundits interpreted the low and even negative real-interest rates of the stagflationary periods of the 1970s as indicative of easy monetary and credit conditions. But the low q's of the same period signalled bad weather for investment. We think the central bank should keep its eye on q.

Third, it seemed to us common sense to find incentives for production of durable goods in the price of existing durable goods relative to the cost of reproducing them or their close substitutes. High prices for resale of houses or cars surely signal good opportunities for builders or automobile manufacturers. The q ratio applies that common sense idea to producers' capital formation. But used capital goods markets are not reliable sources of values because of the specificities, complementarities and irreversibilities of most producers' structures and equipment. The stock and bond markets provide valuations of whole businesses.

SHADOW PRICE q AND STOCK MARKET q

The literature contains 'q' models that are more strongly neoclassical than 'Tobin's q'. To understand the difference, consider the question: 'How can the capital stock ever be different from the optimal stock, given prevailing prices, interest rates and earnings expectations?'. If stock adjustment, no matter how large, costs neither time nor resources, actual and desired stocks will always be equal. Arbitrage via real investment would keep q continuously at 1. Irreversibility and durability make an exception: q will be less than 1 for redundant capital, in which gross investment is zero. Tax considerations may provide another reason why the par value of q is not 1. With these amendments, investment will be just the first time-derivative of the series for the desired capital stock, leaving no room for a separate theory of investment. In fact, Jorgenson got his 'investment' function only by postulating a distributed lag between demands for new capital goods and their delivery.

We cited the resource costs of adjustments to explain why capital stocks do not jump instantaneously in response to changes in marginal efficiencies and interest rates. Rapid exploitations of investment opportunities are expensive.[3] We did not introduce such costs into a firm's formal dynamic optimization problem. This has been done by other writers (Hayashi, 1982). The shadow price of investment at any time is a q-like variable, the value to the firm of the future returns to a dollar's purchase of capital goods that makes just worthwhile the current rate of investment. This value will not necessarily be equal to one or any other constant; it will be high when it is optimal for the firm to invest rapidly and incur high adjustment costs, low when it is optimal to invest little and economize on adjustment costs.

The logic here is similar to that of the neoclassical theory of the corporation as we stated it in the paragraph quoted by Crotty. But note that this formal q-theory does not require any stock market. This 'q' is not an observed or observable market price but an implicit shadow price. It is not an incentive for investment; rather it is determined jointly along with optimal investment. They are both functions of the data of the optimization problem, including the technologies of production and adjustment, expected prices, interest rates and taxes.

Empirically, it is quite obvious that stock market q's and formal implicit q's are not the same animals. Variations in marginal costs of adjusting capital stocks by investment would have to be implausibly large to be consistent with fluctuations in market valuations. Like Keynes, we believe that the stock market does not grind out values by mirroring the rational optimizations of informed managements but generates values of its own. These, we think, nevertheless provide incentives or disincentives for investment. We are so far from being thorough-going neoclassicals that we are quite comfortable in believing that corporate managers and other economic agents respond to market noise and are in any case sluggish in responding to the arbitrage opportunities of large deviations of 'q' from par.

CONCLUDING REMARKS

In the end Crotty does not disagree with us as much as he seems to think. The theme of his paper, according to its introduction, is that, contrary to most theories of macroeconomic instability, impediments to equilibrium may be rooted in either real or financial sectors, or in both. That is certainly our macroeconomics, and the only puzzle is why Crotty has created a fictional Tobin who thinks otherwise. In our macroeconomic models, both real and financial shocks affect q, indeed a shock to the marginal efficiency of capital cannot be classified as exclusively real or exclusively financial. It has both real and monetary consequences. Note that q itself is not a nominal or financial variable but a hybrid, the ratio of a financial market price to a commodity market price.

There are other points of agreement. Tobin has always emphasized the contrast between the liquidity of financial securities and the illiquidity of the underlying real assets. We agree with Crotty that neither managements nor stockholders dominate the other. We agree that q's are partly endogenous variables, that investments can influence q's as well as vice versa, and that the lags between exogenous changes in q and investment could be 'long and variable'.

Crotty, after describing scenarios in which investment fluctuations affect financial markets, says: 'On the other hand, a relatively autonomous rise in financial market optimism or decrease in investor risk aversion can lower the cost and improve the mood of management and thereby stimulate investment' (p. 537). So says q-theory.

NOTES

1. The paper is by Tobin and Brainard, but the latter is spared in Crotty's critique. The idea was first published in an earlier Brainard and Tobin paper (1968). Crotty does not refer to this paper or to any of the several others we have published jointly or individually on the subject. And why does he capitalize our symbol q?
2. Crotty says that Tobin substitutes 'well organized and efficient' markets for Keynes's irrational 'casino'. In the next sentence he refers to 'Tobin's stable and efficient financial markets'. This is a misunderstanding, indeed a misrepresentation. We did not use the word 'stable'. Our word 'efficient' referred only to technical market-clearing efficiency. We did not say or mean that stock markets come up continuously with fundamental valuations. In this 1977 article, which Crotty cites, and in others on 'q', we followed Keynes in believing that speculation makes market prices diverge from fundamental values. Again putting his own word in Tobin's mouth, Crotty says in his footnote 9 that in his 1984 article, 'Tobin appears to recant his belief in the valuation efficiency of financial markets'. The term 'valuation efficiency' does not appear in our 1977 article, and no other writing of ours, individual or joint, asserts such a belief. Tobin had nothing to recant.
3. This is an old idea, of course. Abba Lerner emphasized short-run increasing marginal costs in the capital goods industries. Eisner and Strotz (1964), pp. 60–337, stressed the firm-specific internal costs of absorbing changes in scale or technique.

REFERENCES

Brainard, William and James Tobin (1968), 'Pitfalls in Financial Model Building', *American Economic Review*, May, **56**, 99–122.

Crotty, James R. (1990), 'Owner–Manager Conflict and Financial Theories of Investment Instability: A Critical Assessment', *Journal of Post Keynesian Economics*, Summer, **12** (4), 519–42.

Eisner, Robert and Robert Strotz (1964), 'Determinants of Business Investment', *Impacts of Monetary Policy*, The Commission on Money and Credit, Englewood Cliffs, NJ: Prentice Hall.

Hayashi, Furnio (1982), 'Tobins' Marginal q and Average q: A Neoclassical Interpretation', *Econometrica*, January, **50** (1), 213–24.

Keynes, John Maynard (1971), *The Collected Writings of John Maynard Keynes*, 30 vols. London: Macmillan/St Martin's Press for the Royal Economic Society.

Lerner, Abba (1940), *The Economics of Control*, New York: Macmillan.

Tobin, James (1984), 'On the Efficiency of the Financial System', *Lloyds Bank Review*, July, 1–15.

Tobin, James and William Brainard (1977), 'Asset Markets and the Cost of Capital', in *Economic Progress, Private Values, and Public Policy: Essays in Honor of William Fellner*, Richard Nelson and Bela Balassa (eds), Amsterdam: North-Holland, pp. 235–62.

7. Review of 'Stabilizing an unstable economy'

By Hyman P. Minsky, Twentieth Century Fund Report Series, New Haven and London: Yale University Press, 1986.

Americans as individuals rely heavily on debt, but they distrust its role in the economy and the society. Borrowing enables consumers to own homes and cars and take vacation trips years before they could save up the money to pay for them. Borrowing enables businessmen to buy materials and hire labour before they reap the proceeds of selling the products the materials and labour make. Yet Americans admire Polonius's advice, regard debt as somewhat sinful, and suspect that it may be hazardous to the nation's health. They are an eager market for books and articles depicting coming disasters: financial crises and panics, defaults and bankruptcies, hyperinflations and great depressions.

The economics profession is also ambivalent. Irving Fisher's classic *Theory of Interest* shows how the loan market enables consumers to make mutually advantageous trades of consumption across time, and Arrow and Debreu apply the argument across contingent states of nature too. Irving Fisher also blamed debt, in combination with deflation, for the Great Depression of the 1930s.

Hyman Minsky is the most sophisticated, analytical and persuasive of those contemporary economists who believe that leverage is the Achilles heel of capitalism. This book is a full and mature statement of a thesis he has been advancing for three decades: capitalist economies are unstable because of capitalist financial markets and institutions.

Do not confuse Minksy with the many economists who have lately discovered the perils of excessive debt. They complain of US federal deficits and overseas borrowing in the 1980s. Most of them think the resulting difficulties could have been avoided, and can even now be resolved, by sensible macroeconomic policies. Minsky does not think the problems are so new, so easy to solve, or so exclusive to public borrowing.

*First published in *Journal of Economic Literature*, **xxvii**, March 1989.

The reliance of enterprise on debt finance, Minsky argues, makes capitalism intrinsically unstable. Periods of steady expansion are not the stable equilibrium paths beloved of neoclassical theorists. These 'tranquil' periods sow the seeds of their own destruction. They lull borrowers and lenders alike into complacent underestimation of normal business risks. Ever greater leverage is sought, and obtained. Investment and business activity are stimulated. Prices rise, but have to rise still further to validate the debts that finance the investments. Increasing numbers of businesses and banks suffer troubled balance sheets and straitened cash flows. As these difficulties spread, they deal deflationary (or disinflationary) shocks to the whole economy, threatening a Fisherian debt-cum-deflation depression.

This scenario, it seems, is intended as an endogenous systematic business cycle, for which no external stochastic fuel is required beyond normal microeconomic business risks. Minksy does not provide a rigorous formal model, and without one readers cannot judge whether an undamped endogenous cycle follows from the assumptions or not. Rational expectations adherents will doubtless object that the alleged cycle would vanish as soon as borrowers and lenders understood it. I guess Minsky would give an empirical answer: the participants in every new era of prosperity extrapolate it, finding many reasons not to temper their optimism by the lessons of history.

The only formal theorizing in the book, the only algebra except for Appendix A elaborating Minsky's taxonomy of finance, occurs in Chapters 7 and 8 and Appendix B, all on prices, profits and investment. 'Profits equal investment', Minsky says, 'is a profound insight into how a capitalist economy works' (p. 151). Since this implication of the 'IS' equation depends on the assumption that workers do not save and capitalists do not consume, it does not seem relevant to actual modern capitalist economies. Anyway, Minsky's algebra amends the model and the aphorism to allow government purchases, taxes and transfers, and also exports and imports. The main problem is that this 'post-Keynesian' theory is not convincingly linked to the central message of the book, the financial theory of business cycles. Minsky's excellent account of asset pricing and investment decisions is separable from his theory of prices, wages and profits. It sounds like 'q' theory to me.

Minsky cites the travails of the US economy since 1965 in support of his central thesis. Certainly many more crises of both non-financial enterprises and financial institutions have made headlines in the 1970s and 1980s than in the three prior decades: Real Estate Investment Trusts, Franklin National, Chrysler, New York City, Penn Square, Continental Illinois, Pan Am, International Harvester, Seafirst, Bank of America and lots more. However, the macroeconomic disappointments of the period are easily attributable to other sources: to an unprecedented series of severe macro shocks, notably the

Vietnam War and its financing, two oil supply and price shocks, and the collapse of the Bretton Woods world monetary system.

To many observers, the structural feature of the economy that rendered it vulnerable to those shocks was not the financial system but the evident conflict in labour and product markets between full employment and stability of nominal wages and prices. All the recessions during this period, and most previous post-war recessions as well, were the result of deliberate counter-inflationary Federal Reserve policy. The Fed had not lost control of the financial system, far from it.

As Minsky emphasizes, the Fed is the lender of last resort, not just for depository institutions but for the whole financial system. The tension in its role is clear. Banks and other financial enterprises can abuse the safety nets the government has established to protect the public, relying on the Fed to bail them out lest their troubles engulf the whole economy. Yet contrary to Minsky's thesis, the Fed has managed to reconcile its lender-of-last-resort and macroeconomic responsibilities. The Fed has lent generously to troubled institutions without being drawn into an overall easier monetary stance on that account, as the Continental Illinois episode clearly illustrates. Likewise, the Fed has prevented the defaults and failures that have occurred from throwing the whole economy into tailspin. Indeed in October 1987 we did at last have a 1929-class stock market crash, and the Fed was able to keep the economy on an even keel.

Nightmares of 1930s-style financial panics and epidemic bank failures haunt current discussions, even Minsky's, to an unreasonable degree. The problem then was a massive shift from bank deposits in general to currency. That has not been a problem since 1932 and is not today. But if a generalized bank run, as opposed to a run from one institution to others, were to occur, today's Fed, unlike its 1930–32 predecessor, could and would supply all the currency demanded. There would be no liquidity crunch.

Even though macroeconomic policies have so far not been crippled, Minsky is right that reforms are urgent to forestall abuses of the safety nets at taxpayers' expense and at possible future hazard to Federal Reserve control. The Fed and other regulatory authorities have been too anxious to prevent failures of large institutions. Thoughtless deregulation has opened the door to reckless interest rate competition, led by institutions, mostly savings and loan associations, desperate for funds to cover illiquid and non-performing assets. Since the government stands behind the deposits, inclusive of whatever interest they 'earn', depositors send money where proffered yields are highest.

Minsky is an informed, perceptive and stimulating analyst of the financial system. He is right to stress that 'inside' monetary and financial institutions and market make a big difference, and to reject 'Modigliani–Miller' theorems that assets and debts which wash out in accounting aggregations wash out in economic effects as well.

Minsky's classifications of debt finance – 'hedge', 'speculative' and 'Ponzi' – are suggestive and helpful. Hedge and speculative project-debt packages have positive present values with high probability. But while hedge packages promise with high probability excesses of cash flow over debt service commitments in all periods, speculative packages do not. They involve refinancings and are therefore vulnerable to interest rate changes. Ponzi packages have, with high probability, negative net present value and depend on continued sale of new debt to meet debt service commitments. Capitalism depends on speculative finance, the function of commercial banking and other financial institutions and markets. But speculative finance tends to slip into Ponzi finance.

I turn now to a prominent feature of the book on which I am scarcely disinterested, the gratuitously combative attacks on mainstream economic thought. Minsky indiscriminately lumps together everybody he discerns to his 'right', not only 'new classicals', monetarists, and 'supply-siders' but also many of us who regard ourselves as eclectic Keynesians.

Minsky's sharpest thrusts are directed at the architects and adherents of the 'neoclassical synthesis' of Keynesian macroeconomics and standard micro-economics – Samuelson, Hicks, Modigliani, Solow, Tobin *et al*. Minsky grossly misrepresents their views, identifying them with those of Don Patinkin (1965) and stating that: 'This neoclassical synthesis is also the underpinning of Milton Friedman' (p. 5, fn. 4). He accuses the misguided Keynesians of embracing the Pigou–Patinkin real balance effect as a proof that flexibility of wages and prices ensures full employment so that governmental macro-economic interventions are not needed. This is just not true. I, for example, say the opposite in publications that Minsky knows and actually cites. Readers who are interested in an accurate and dispassionate exposition of the 'neoclassical synthesis' can consult Olivier Blanchard's article in *The New Palgrave*.

In the same spirit Minsky criticizes both sides of the debate between monetarists and Keynesians for assuming that the effects of a given injection of money are independent of the transactions by which the money is created. In fact, this was one of the major points of contention (see Gordon (1974).

These days there are plenty of influential economists beguiling the profession and the public with Panglossian views of market capitalism. Better the author should fire at them, not at his own allies.

The book betrays the long period of preparation of which its sponsor, the Twentieth Century Fund, politely complains in the foreword. Initial statements of the thesis in the early chapters are illustrated by tales and tables of the 1970s, with brief 1980s addenda as afterthoughts. The book has not caught up with some institutional changes of moment: for example the payment of market-determined interest rates on deposits.

Lapses of memory and failure of editing have left in the book repetitions of identical points, references and language (see, for example, pp. 100 and 288). There are also anomalies of order and organizations. For example, the important taxonomy of types of finance first appears in a footnote on page 202 and is used in the text before it is introduced and fully explained beginning on page 206. The index is incomplete.

The book ends with a long catalogue of recommended economic reforms and policies, inspired by the issues and problems of the 1980s. They cover many more aspects of the economy than the preceding chapters discuss. Even the financial reforms suggested are only loosely related to the diagnoses earlier in the book. Maybe these recommendations would 'stabilize an unstable economy', but Minsky does not really tell how. Nevertheless, the recommendations are undoctrinaire, sensible and pragmatic. Minsky is a fine political economist. He should write another book arguing specifically and fully for the programme he outlines in his 'Agenda for Reform'.

REFERENCES

Eatwell, John, Murray Milgate and Peter Newman (eds) (1987), *The New Palgrave Dictionary of Political Economy*, vol. 3, London: Macmillan, 634–6.

Fisher, Irving (1930), *Theory of Interest*, New York: Macmillan.

Gordon, Robert J. (ed.) (1974), *Milton Friedman's Monetary Framework: A Debate with his Critics*, Chicago: University of Chicago Press.

Patinkin, Don (1965), *Money, Interest, and Prices*, 2nd ed., New York: Harper and Row.

PART II

Monetary Policy

Part II   Monetary policy

To overcome the burst of inflation following the Iranian revolution and the second oil shock of 1979, the US Federal Reserve pursued a strict monetarist policy for three years. A deep recession drove unemployment up to 10.7 per cent and succeeded in cutting the inflation rate in half, to about 5 per cent. In the autumn of 1982 the Fed, under its Chairman Paul Volcker, reversed course, abandoned its monetarist targets, and promoted a six-year recovery which reduced unemployment to less than 6 per cent while inflation continued to subside.

In 1987–89 the Fed tightened in fear of overheating, and another slowdown and recession, relatively mild but prolonged, followed. The Fed eased slowly but eventually sufficiently to bring about a recovery, with fairly brisk growth in 1993, continuing and quickening in 1994 even as the Fed tightened once more. Unemployment fell below 6 per cent again, and inflation continued to subside.

The opening chapter of this Part is a primer on monetary policy written for an encyclopaedia of finance. Chapter 9 argues for caution in deregulating banks and other depositories, and advocates reforms to eliminate taxpayers' residual liabilities for deposit insurance when these institutions fail. These are followed by four commentaries on these developments, in retrospect (Chapter 10) and as they were happening (Chapters 11, 12 and 13). Chapter 13 argues in particular that the central bank should gear policy to domestic considerations and not to the foreign exchange rate, a position that is now Federal Reserve and Administration doctrine, despite criticism from private financiers and foreign financial officials. In Chapters 14 and 15 I argue against mandating the Fed to aim at an inflation target of zero or at any inflation target to the exclusion of other measures of macroeconomic performance, notably unemployment and real growth. I also advocate measures to confine decision-making officers of the Federal Reserve System to persons appointed by the President and confirmed by the Senate. While the central bank needs to be shielded from short-term political interference, its legitimacy depends on its accountability to elected officials who themselves are held accountable by the electorate for the performance of the economy.

8.   Monetary policy*

Paul Volcker, while Chairman of the Board of Governors of the Federal Reserve System (1979–87), was often called the second most powerful person in the United States. Volcker and company triggered the 'double-dip' recessions of 1979–80 and 1981–82, vanquishing the double-digit inflation of 1979–80 and bringing the unemployment rate into double digits for the first time since 1940. Volcker then declared victory over inflation and piloted the economy through its long 1980s recovery, bringing unemployment below 5.5 per cent, half a point lower than in the 1978–79 boom.

Volcker was powerful because he was making monetary policy. His predecessors were powerful too. At least four of the previous seven post-war recessions can be attributed to their anti-inflationary policies. Likewise, Alan Greenspan's Federal Reserve bears the main responsibility for the 1990–91 recession and the subsequent recovery.

Central banks are powerful everywhere, although few are as independent of their governments as the Fed is of Congress and the White House. Central bank actions are the most important government policies affecting economic activity from quarter to quarter or year to year.

Monetary policy is the subject of a lively controversy between two schools of economics: monetarist and Keynesian. Although they agree on goals, they disagree sharply on priorities, strategies, targets and tactics. As I explain how monetary policy works, I shall discuss these disagreements. At the outset I disclose that I am a Keynesian.

COMMON GOALS

Few monetarists or Keynesians would disagree with this dream scenario:

- First, no business cycles. Instead, production – as measured by real (inflation-corrected) gross national product – would grow steadily, in step with the capacity of the economy and its labour force.
- Second, a stable and low rate of price inflation, preferably zero.

*First published in D.R. Henderson (ed.), *Fortune Encyclopaedia of Economics*, Time Warner, 1993.

- Third, the highest rates of capacity utilization and employment that are consistent with a stable trend of prices.
- Fourth, high trend growth of productivity and real GNP per worker.

Monetary policies are demand-side macroeconomic policies. They work by stimulating or discouraging spending on goods and services. Economy-wide recessions and booms reflect fluctuations in aggregate demand rather than in the economy's productive capacity. Monetary policy tries to damp, perhaps even eliminate, those fluctuations. It is not a supply-side instrument. Central banks have no handle on productivity and real economic growth.

PRIORITIES

The second and third goals frequently conflict. Should policy-makers give priority to price stability or to full employment? American and European monetary policies differed dramatically after the deep 1981–82 recession. The Fed 'fine-tuned' a six-year recovery and recouped the employment and production lost in the 1979–82 downturns. Keeping a watchful eye on employment and output, and on wages and prices, the Fed stepped on the gas when the economic engine faltered and on the brakes when it threatened to overheat. During this catch-up recovery the economy grew at a faster rate than it could sustain thereafter. The Fed sought to slow its growth to a sustainable pace as full employment was restored.

European central banks, led by the German Bundesbank, were more conservative. They did little to help their economies catch up. They regarded active monetary stimulus as dangerously inflationary, even when their economies were barely emerging from recession. They were determined never to finance more than sustainable non-inflationary growth, even temporarily. Europe recovered much more slowly than America, and its unemployment rates have ratcheted up from the 1970s.

Priorities reflect national dreams and nightmares. German horror of inflation, for example, dates from the 1923 hyperinflation and from a second bout of inflation after World War II. Priorities also reflect divergent views of how economies work. European monetary authorities were acting like monetarists, Americans like Keynesians, although both would disavow the labels.

Here is the crucial issue: expansionary monetary policy, all agree, increases aggregate spending on goods and services – by consumers, businesses, governments and foreigners. Will these new demands raise output and employment? Or will they just raise prices and speed up inflation?

Keynesians say the answers depend on circumstances. Full employment means that everyone (allowing for persons between jobs) who is productive enough to be worth the prevailing real wage and wants a job at that wage is employed. In these circumstances more spending just brings inflation. Frequently, however, qualified willing workers are involuntarily unemployed; there is no demand for the products they would produce. More spending will put them to work. Competition from firms with excess capacity and from idle workers will keep extra spending from igniting inflation.

Monetarists answer that nature's remedy for excess supply in any market is price reduction. If wages do not adjust to unemployment, either government and union regulations are keeping them artificially high or the jobless prefer leisure and/or unemployment compensation to work at prevailing wages. Either way, the problem is not remediable by monetary policy. Injections of new spending would be futile and inflationary.

Experience, certainly in the Great Depression and also in subsequent recessions, indicates that downward adjustments of wages and prices cannot avoid damage to output and employment. Moreover, wage and price cuts may actually reduce demand by generating expectations of further disinflation or deflation.

A.W. Phillip's famous curve showed wage inflation varying inversely with unemployment. Keynesians were tempted to interpret it as a policy trade-off: less unemployment at the cost of a finite boost in inflation. Milton Friedman convinced the economics profession in 1968 that if monetary policy persistently attempts to bring unemployment below 'the natural rate of unemployment' (the rate corresponding to Keynes's 'full employment'), it will only boost the inflation rate explosively. Friedman's further conclusion that monetary policy should never concern itself with unemployment, production or other real variables has been very influential. But in situations of Keynesian slack, as recent American experience again confirms, demand expansion can improve real macroeconomic performance without accelerating prices.

STRATEGIES

Here too the monetarist–Keynesian controversy is exemplified by Federal Reserve and Bundesbank policies in the 1980s. The issue is this: how actively and frequently should policy-makers respond to observed and expected departures from their targets? Friedman wants them to follow the same routine regardless of the economic weather, increasing the money supply at a constant rate. In his view trying to outguess the economy usually exacerbates fluctuations.

While not all monetarists endorse Friedman's rule, they do stress the importance of announced rules enabling the public to predict the central bank's behaviour. In principle, announced rules need not blind policy-makers to changing circumstances; they could specify in advance their responses to feedback information. But it is impossible to anticipate all contingencies. No central bank could have foreseen the OPEC shocks of the 1970s and decided its responses in advance. Any practicable rule is bound to be simple. Any reactive policy, like the Fed's fine-tuning after 1982, is bound to allow discretion.

RELATION TO FISCAL POLICY

In monetarists' view government budgets have important supply-side effects for good or ill but have no demand-side role unless they trigger changes in monetary policy. In Keynesian theory fiscal policy is a distinct demand-side instrument. The government affects aggregate demand directly by its own expenditures and indirectly by its taxes.

Prior to 1981, Presidents and Congresses in making annual budgets considered their macroeconomic effects. In the 1980s budget-making became slow and cumbersome, and the explosion of deficits and debt made counter-cyclical fiscal policy very difficult. In the 1990s the burden of stabilization policy falls almost entirely on monetary policy.

Monetary and fiscal policies are distinct only in financially developed countries where the government does not have to cover budget deficits by printing money but can sell obligations to pay money in future, like US Treasury bills, notes and bonds. In the United States, Congress and the President decide on expenditure programmes and tax codes and thus – subject to the vagaries of the economy – on the budget deficit (or surplus). This deficit (or surplus) adds to (or subtracts from) the federal debt accumulated from past budgets. The Federal Reserve decides how much, if any, of the debt is 'monetized', that is, takes the form of currency or its equivalent. The rest consists of interest-bearing Treasury securities. Those central bank decisions are the essence of monetary policy.

MECHANICS OF MONETARY POLICY

A central bank is a 'bankers' bank'. The customers of the 12 Federal Reserve banks are not ordinary citizens but 'banks' in the inclusive sense of all depository institutions – commercial banks, savings banks, savings and loan associations, and credit unions. They are eligible to hold deposits in, and borrow from, Federal Reserve banks and are subject to the Fed's reserve requirements and other regulations.

At year-end 1990, federal debt outstanding was $2,569 billion, of which only 12 per cent, or $314 billion, was monetized. That is, the Federal Reserve banks owned $314 billion of claims on the Treasury, against which they had incurred liabilities in currency (Federal Reserve notes) or in deposits convertible into currency on demand. Total currency in public circulation outside banks was $255 billion at year-end 1990. Banks' reserves – the currency in their vaults plus their deposits in the Fed – were $59 billion. The two together constitute the monetary base (M0): $314 billion at year-end 1990.

Banks are required to hold reserves at least equal to prescribed percentages of their checkable deposits. Compliance with the requirements is regularly tested every two weeks for banks accounting for the bulk of deposits. Reserve tests are the fulcrum of monetary policy. Banks need 'federal funds' (currency or deposits at Federal Reserve banks) to pass the reserve tests, and the Fed controls the supply. When the Fed buys securities from banks or their depositors with base money, banks acquire reserve balances. Likewise the Fed extinguishes reserve balances by selling Treasury securities. These are open-market operations, the primary *modus operandi* of monetary policy. These transactions are supervised by the Federal Open Market Committee (FOMC), the Fed's principal policy-making organ.

A bank in need of reserves can borrow reserve balances on deposit in the Fed from other banks. Loans are made for one day at a time in the 'federal funds' market. Interest rates on these loans are quoted continuously. Central bank open-market operations are interventions in this market. Banks can also borrow from the Federal Reserve banks themselves, at their announced discount rates, in practice the same at all 12 banks. The setting of the discount rate is another instrument of central bank policy. Nowadays it is secondary to open-market operations, and the Fed generally keeps the discount rate close to the federal funds market rate. However, announcing a new discount rate is often a convenient way to send a message to the money markets. In addition to its responsibilities for macroeconomic stabilization, the central bank has a traditional safety-net role in temporarily assisting individual banks and in preventing or stemming systemic panics as 'lender of last resort'.

TACTICS: OPERATING PROCEDURES

Through open-market operations, the FOMC can set a target federal funds rate and instruct its trading desk at the Federal Reserve Bank of New York to enter the market as necessary to keep the funds rate on target. The target itself is temporary; the FOMC reconsiders it every six weeks or so at its regular meetings, or sooner if financial and economic surprises occur.

An alternative operating procedure is to target a funds quantity, letting the market move the funds interest rate to whatever level equates banks' demands to that quantity. This was the Fed's practice in 1979–82, adopted in response to monetarist complaints that the Fed had been too slow to raise interest rates in booms to check money growth and inflation. The volatility of interest rates was much greater in this régime than in the interest-rate-target régime.

How is the Fed's control of money markets transmitted to other financial markets and to the economy? How does it influence spending on goods and services? To banks, money market rates are costs of funds they could lend to their customers or invest in securities. When these costs are raised, banks raise their lending rates and become more selective in advancing credit. Their customers borrow and spend less. The effects are widespread, affecting businesses dependent on commercial loans to finance inventories; developers seeking credit for shopping centres, office buildings and housing complexes; home-buyers needing mortgages; consumers purchasing automobiles and appliances; credit card holders; and municipalities constructing schools and sewers.

Banks compete with each other for both loans and deposits. Before 1980 legal ceilings on deposit interest restricted competition for deposits, but now interest rates on certificates of deposit, savings accounts and even checkable deposits are unregulated. Because banks' profit margins depend on the difference between the interest they earn on their loans and other assets and what they pay for deposits, the two move together.

Banks compete with other financial institutions and with open financial markets. Corporations borrow not only from banks but also from other financial intermediaries: insurance companies, pension funds and investment companies. They sell bonds, stocks and commercial paper in open markets, where the buyers include individuals, non-profit institutions and mutual funds, as well as banks. Households and businesses compare the returns and advantages of bank deposits with those of money market funds, other mutual funds, open-market securities and other assets.

Thanks to its control of money markets and banks, the Fed influences interest rates, asset prices and credit flows throughout the financial system. Arbitrage and competition spread increases or decreases in interest rates under the Fed's direct control to other markets. Even stock prices are sensitive, falling when yields on bonds go up, and rising when they fall.

The Fed has less control over bond yields and other long-term rates than over money market and short-term rates. Long rates depend heavily on expectations of future short rates, and thus on expectations of future Fed policies. For example, heightened expectations of future inflation or of higher federal budget deficits will raise long rates relative to short rates, because the Fed has created expectations that it will tighten monetary policy in those circumstances.

Another mechanism for transmitting monetary policy to the demand for goods and services has become increasingly important in the last two decades. Since 1973 foreign exchange rates have been allowed to float, and obstacles to international movements of funds have steadily disappeared. An increase in US interest rates relative to those in Tokyo, London and Frankfurt draws funds into dollar assets and raises the value of the dollar in terms of yen, pounds sterling and Deutsche marks. American goods become more expensive relative to foreign goods, for buyers both at home and abroad. Declines in exports and increases in imports reduce aggregate demand for domestic production. High interest rates and exchange appreciation created a large and stubborn US trade deficit in 1981–85. Since 1985, as the interest advantage of dollar assets was reduced or reversed, the dollar depreciated and the US trade deficit slowly fell, relative to the size of the economy.

TARGETS: MONETARY AGGREGATES OR MACROECONOMIC PERFORMANCE?

People hold dollar currency because it is the means of payment in many transactions. But checkable deposits are usually more convenient. They are not confined to particular denominations, cannot be lost or stolen, pay interest and generate records most of us find useful.

The use of deposits in place of currency greatly economizes on base money. The $59 billion of bank reserves at year-end 1990 supported about $580 billion in checkable deposits. (The $521 billion of other assets behind those deposits were banks' loans and investments. In this sense banks 'monetize' debts of all kinds.) These deposits plus the $255 billion in circulating currency provided a stock of transactions money (M1) of $835 billion. But time deposits and deposit certificates, though not checkable, are close substitutes for transactions deposits in many respects. So are money market funds and other assets outside banks altogether. Consequently the Fed keeps track of a spectrum of monetary aggregates, M1, M2, M3, each more inclusive than the preceding, capped by measures of liquid wealth (L) and debt.

The same open-market operations that move M0 up and down and interest rates down and up change the quantities of M1 and other monetary aggregates. Operations that reduce federal funds rates and related short-term interest rates add to bank reserves, and thus also to bank loans and deposits. In 1990 reserve requirements averaged about 10 per cent of checkable deposits. (In 1992 the Fed reduced the required reserve ratio by two percentage points.) Thus in 1990 a $1 increase in the bank reserves component of M0 meant roughly a $10 increase in the deposit component of M1. In contrast, a $1 increase in the currency component of M0 is always just a $1 increase in M1.

If the public consistently held deposits and currency in the same proportion, 580/255 in the year-end 1990 example, a $1.00 increase in M0 would mean a $2.70 increase in M1. This is the 'money multiplier'. It does not stay constant, for several reasons. The Fed occasionally changes the required reserve ratio. Banks sometimes hold excess reserves and sometimes borrow reserves from the Fed. The public's demand for currency relative to deposits varies seasonally, cyclically and randomly. Thus the Fed's control of M1 is imprecise, and its control of broader aggregates is still looser.

Monetarists urge the Fed to gear its operations to steady growth of a monetary aggregate, M1 or M2. Under congressional mandate the Fed twice a year announces target ranges for growth of monetary aggregates several quarters ahead. In the 1970s the FOMC tried to stay within these ranges but often missed. Monetarist criticism became especially insistent when money growth exceeded Fed targets during the oil shocks. In October 1979 Chairman Volcker warned the public that the Fed would stick to its restrictive targets for monetary aggregates until inflation was conquered. Three years later, however, the Fed stopped taking the monetary aggregates seriously.

Monetary aggregates are not important in themselves. What matters is macroeconomic performance as indicated by GNP, employment and prices. Monetarist policies are premised on a tight linkage between the stock of money in dollars, say M1, and the flow of spending, GNP in dollars per year. The connection between them is the velocity of money, the number of times per year an average dollar travels around the circuit and is spent on GNP. By definition of velocity, GNP equals the stock of money times its velocity. The velocity of M1 was 6.6 in 1990. If it were predictable, control of M1 would control dollar GNP too. But M1 velocity is quite volatile. For the 1961–90 period its average annual growth was 2.1 per cent, with standard deviation of 3.0 per cent. That is, the chance is about one in three in any year that velocity will either rise by more than 5.1 per cent or decline by more than 0.9 per cent. For the 1981–90 period the mean was –0.15, with a standard deviation of 4.0. (M2 velocity is less volatile, but M2 itself is less controllable.)

Velocity depends on the money management practices of households and businesses throughout the economy. As transactions technologies and financial institutions have evolved and an increasing array of money substitutes has arisen, velocity has become less stable and monetary aggregates have become less reliable proxies for aggregate spending and economic activity. The 1981–82 recession was deeper than the Fed intended because the FOMC stuck stubbornly to its monetary aggregates targets while velocity was precipitously falling.

Accounting for aggregate demand as the product of a money stock and its velocity is inadequate shorthand for the complex processes by which monetary policies are transmitted – via interest rates, banks and asset markets – to spending on GNP by households, businesses and foreigners. The Fed does better by aiming directly at desired macroeconomic performance than by binding itself to intermediate targets.

9. The case for preserving regulatory distinctions*

The structure of the monetary, banking and financial institutions of the United States is currently a topic of unusual excitement and controversy. Divers reforms have been proposed, some in legislative form. No consensus has been reached, and at present there appears to be a political stalemate. Meanwhile, the structure is changing in a piecemeal and anarchic fashion, as a result of technological and institutional innovations, private initiatives, accidental quirks of ancient laws, administrative and judicial decisions, and actions by various states. As recent events attest again, Congress cannot agree on basic solutions and tries half-heartedly to arrest the disorderly drift.

Two sets of issues are before the Congress, the Executive, the courts and the country. One concerns the range of activities permitted to various types of financial and non-financial enterprises and their affiliates or subsidiaries. Should banks and other depositories, or their holding companies, be allowed to engage in various businesses from which they are now excluded – underwriting and other investment banking activities, insurance, real estate and other non-monetary and even non-financial transactions? Should other private enterprises, financial and non-financial, be allowed to engage in commercial banking and/or to accept insured deposits, either directly or through affiliates or subsidiaries? Issues of this type touch conflicting private interests and privileges, the principal stuff of politics. Consequently, they are the focus of attention in the affected industries, in the media and in legislative debate.

Nevertheless, I think a second set of issues is more crucial and deserves priority. I refer to the structure of the monetary, banking and depository system itself. We need to protect the system of monetary payments, ensure the availability of safe and convenient media of exchange and other assets to the general public, preserve effective macroeconomic monetary control by the Federal Reserve System, and maintain the sovereign power and responsibility of the federal government, under the Constitution, to 'coin money and regulate the value thereof'.

*First published in *Restructuring the Financial System*, Federal Reserve Bank of Kansas City, 1987.

The deposit insurance systems, on which we have relied heavily for a half century, no longer appear adequate to achieve these basic objectives. There is a danger that these problems will be neglected or subordinated to the politically charged issues of the first set. To me, it makes more sense to settle on a viable monetary and depository system for the future *prior* to deciding what activities members of that system should be allowed to engage in and what monetary and depository activities other private institutions should be permitted.

For these reasons, I shall take up the second set of issues first.

FEDERAL SAFETY NETS AND MORAL HAZARD

Can Large Financial Enterprises be Allowed to Fail?

Depository institutions, banks and thrifts, have been failing in numbers alarming to a public accustomed to thinking that failures were a depression problem solved by New Deal legislation in ancient times. By the same token, the spectres of bank runs, financial collapse and depression itself haunt regulators, legislators and other policy-makers. They have used powers and instruments unavailable to their predecessors in the 1920s and early 1930s to control and contain the damage, quite successfully to date.

Large banks and their depositors have been virtually guaranteed rescue, by giant loans 'of last resort' and by *de facto* extension of deposit insurance to 100 per cent coverage. This was the precedent set by the Continental Illinois case. Although management and stockholders did not escape unscathed, the ability to shift risk to the federal government is bound to tempt depositors and managers to take more risk.

The memory of the Great Depression was a big reason for the policy of rescue, but in my opinion not a good reason. The analogy is misplaced. Bank runs in the Depression were an economy-wide catastrophe because they became a general run of depositors to currency. The banking system was drained of reserves, and the Federal Reserve was unable or unwilling – it is not necessary here to enter the debate which – to expand the supply of base money enough to offset the drain. Shift from bank money requiring only fractional reserves to 100 per cent currency money cut down the total money supply – that is the monetarist way to look at it – and reduced the supply of loanable funds from banks – that is the eclectic way to put it.

In the 1980s runs to currency are not the problem. The deposit shifts we have seen have been from threatened institutions or particular types of institutions in particular jurisdictions to similar deposits elsewhere. Such shifts do not destroy bank reserves in aggregate. Indeed, central bank lending to the reserve-losers – recall that Federal Reserve loans to Continental Illinois were $6 to $7 billion, compared with normal aggregate borrowing at the discount window of $1 billion or less – actually increased total reserves. To maintain a stable overall monetary stance, the Federal Reserve had to remove a roughly equal amount by open-market sales.

Should there be a run to currency, rather than from one bank to another, today's Federal Reserve would not be deterred by the obstacles that prevented the Federal Reserve of the early 1930s from supplying the currency. Federal Reserve banks are no longer required to hold gold or other specified assets as backing. They can lend to depositories and buy paper in the open market without limit. Unlike their predecessors, they would presumably be free of doctrinal, political and psychological inhibitions against such actions.

In the early 1930s, we were still on the gold standard, and a run to foreign currency or gold panicked US authorities. Thanks to floating exchange rates, their successors are spared this anxiety. They may not, of course, welcome a decline in the market value of the dollar, but the trauma is of a lower order of magnitude.

For these reasons, I see no convincing macroeconomic reason for the US government to guarantee that a large depository will not be allowed to fail. Without doubt, there would be turmoil in financial markets for a few days on news of such a failure, but such frenzies have few consequences for the vast economy and population engaged in producing goods and services. I observe that the financial markets have taken in stride large banks' recognition of losses on their foreign loans.

Of course, the prospective failure of any large company, non-financial or financial, generates strong economic and political pressures for government rescue. Even some economists and policy-makers who are generally suspicious of the arguments used in such cases find special reasons for bailing out large financial enterprises. Given the proclivity of the monetary and financial regulators for averting failures of large depositories, proposals to restructure the financial system should guard against changes that make rescues even more compelling.

The system of depositories is drifting towards oligopoly of giant nation–wide banks and bank holding companies, and to conglomerates engaged in a host of financial and non-financial businesses. An unfortunate by-product of this drift would be that the government would be so fearful of the consequences of a failure of these giants that their survival would be guaranteed – whatever the nature of their difficulties, whether they presented any threat to the payments system or not, indeed whether they were connected to financial or non-financial activities.

The Abuse of Deposit Insurance

The truly urgent problem, I think, is the abuse of deposit insurance. Ironically, it was the innovation of deposit insurance in 1935 that has been credited for the avoidance of epidemic runs from banks ever since.

Deposit insurance is a delegation to private enterprises of the government's sovereign right to coin money. The government promises to coin money to meet the depository's promises to its creditors in case it is unable to redeem them itself.

For the contagious runs to currency 55 or 60 years ago, deposit insurance, financed by uniform premiums, made sense. Confidence in the system was a public good to which all institutions, whatever their individual balance sheets, could be expected to contribute. Of course, some institutions were insolvent because of bad loans and investments, but it was possible to argue that these were largely macroeconomic and stochastic in origin.

Today, however, there appears to be a much greater component of imprudence and adventurism, even self-dealing, in the incidence of failure. Moral hazard is rampant. The sounder and luckier – it is not easy to distinguish – members of federal insurance corporations understandably balk at paying higher premiums to salvage the depositors of failed members. The taxpayer can be left holding the bag. Congress affirmed the government's ultimate guarantee just the other day.

As has long been recognized, deposit insurance dulls the incentives of depositors to scrutinize the soundness of the depository's assets and the incentives of the institution itself to maintain liquidity and asset quality sufficient to limit to low probability the contingency that it will be unable to meet withdrawals.

These dilutions, it seems, began to be a serious problem when interest on insured deposits was deregulated, even to the extent that deposits effectively payable or transferable on demand became interest-bearing. The history is revealing. Interest prohibitions and ceilings were legislated in the 1930s, mainly because of the perception that previously deposit interest competition had contributed to bank failures. The argument was that banks had to reach out for high-return but unsafe loans and investments in order to pay competitive deposit interest rates. In the post-war debate about the regulation of deposit interest, that argument was discredited on both theoretical and empirical grounds. Anyway, it was alleged, deposit insurance by itself had solved the problem that motivated the 1930s legislation, so that interest regulation was redundant.

However, the combination of unregulated deposit interest and deposit insurance does enable depositories to attract deposits to finance adventurous and even corrupt asset management, as the recent examples of Texas thrift institutions dramatically illustrate. Depositors who enjoyed high certificate of deposit (CD) rates are kept whole at the expense of those of other institutions whose deposit insurance premiums pay them off or of general taxpayers.

A minor reform would mitigate the attraction of above-market interest rates to finance unsound loans and investments. This would be to subtract from the amount of a depositor's balance, in reckoning the amount insured, all interest credited or paid in excess of some standard rate, the Treasury bill rate or the Federal Reserve discount rate.

A remedial proposal that comes naturally to economists is to scale premiums to risk, just as auto insurance premiums vary with the risk categories of drivers. However, it does not seem possible to gauge the riskiness of asset portfolios in advance, and basing them on 'accident' experience is too late. For similar reasons, surveillance by examiners is not wholly effective.

'Deposited Currency'

I believe, therefore, that the monetary and depository system should be restructured to reduce the reliance now placed on deposit insurance to protect the monetary payments system. I have two proposals. One is to provide a kind of deposit money, so safe that it does not have to be insured. The second is to make in advance a sharp distinction between insured and uninsured liabilities, and to stick to it. This involves separating 'commercial banks', which accept insured deposits, from 'investment banks', which do not.

To diminish the reliance of the payments system on deposit insurance, I have proposed making available to the public what I call 'deposited currency'. Currency – today virtually exclusively Federal Reserve notes – and coin are the basic money and legal tender of the United States. They are generally acceptable in transactions without question. But they have obvious inconveniences – insecurity against loss or theft, indivisibilities of denomination – that limit their use except in small transactions (or in illegal or tax-evading transactions). These disadvantages, along with zero nominal interest, lead to the substitution of bank deposits for currency. But deposits suffer from their own insecurity, unless guaranteed by the government; and the guarantes of deposit insurance are subject to the abuses discussed above.

I think the government should make available to the public a medium with the convenience of deposits and the safety of currency, essentially currency on deposit, transferable in any amount by cheque or other order. This could be done in one or more or the following ways:

1. The Federal Reserve banks themselves could offer such deposits, a species of 'Federal Funds'. Presumably they would establish conveniently located agencies in private banks or post offices. The Federal Reserve banks would pay for the services of the agents. Potential agents could

bid for the contracts. Transactions between holders of deposited currency accounts, or between them and, directly or indirectly, other Federal Funds accounts would be cleared through the Federal Reserve. Wire transfers, as well as cheques, would be possible. Giro-type payment orders to other accounts in the system could be made. Overdrafts would not be allowed. Computer capabilities should soon make it possible to withdraw conventional currency at any office or agency, and even to order payments to third parties by card or telephone. Interest at a rate sufficiently below the rates on Treasury securities to cover costs could be paid, and some costs could be charged to account-holders.

2. Banks and other depository institutions could offer the same type of account, or indeed be required to do so. The deposited funds would be segregated from the other liabilities of the institution, and invested entirely in eligible assets dedicated solely to those liabilities. These would be Federal Funds or Treasury obligations of no more than three months' maturity. As in case (1), interest might be paid on Federal Funds in such segregated portfolios.

In either case, deposited currency accounts would not have to be insured against illiquidity or insolvency, only against malfeasance by the agent or depository, a much smaller risk. Thus a part of the payments system would be secure without the help of deposit insurance. Members of the public who value the security of currency at sacrifice of interest, largely the poorer and less sophisticated population, would be accommodated. Moreover, assuming statutory limits on insurance of other deposits are made effective, depositors who wish safety and liquidity on larger sums would be served.

I should like to make clear that, unlike my good friend and former student Robert Litan (1987), I do not propose the offering of accounts of this kind by banks as an option for which the bait is permission to engage in financial and non-financial activities now proscribed. I separate the issues and advocate these accounts for their own sake.

'Commercial Banks' Redefined

I would carry further departmentalization and asset segregation in banks and other depositories. A 'commercial bank', generally an affiliate of a bank holding company, would be confined to liabilities eligible for deposit insurance, although only up to specified limits per depositor (not per account). Deposits in other affiliates or other financial institutions would not be federally insured.

'Commercial bank' asset portfolios would be subject to regulations, and generous capital-account reserves against losses on these portfolios would be required. Fixed-nominal-interest bonds and mortgages of long maturity are not suitable assets for insured depositories, especially in an era of volatility of actual and expected interest rates and inflation. Asset portfolios heavily concentrated in consumer paper and credit card debts are clearly unsuitable. Commercial banks, with insured deposits, should hold diversified portfolios of relatively short-term paper, including Treasury bills as secondary reserves, marketable commercial paper, non-marketable commercial loans, consumer debts, and longer-term variable-rate bonds and mortgages. They should not be using depositors' money to play zero-sum games in foreign exchange, interest rates and securities prices.

As for the capital-account requirement, this could take the form of the most senior securities, preferred stock or debt, of the holding company of which the bank is a subsidiary, equal at least to a federally set fraction of the bank's assets, surely not lower than 5 per cent. The capital requirement would be larger if, as is suggested as a possibility below, the bank holding company also has an underwriting affiliate.

Note that the defining characteristics of commercial banking would be the incurring of insured deposit liabilities as well as the making of commercial loans. The absurdity of non-bank banks would be ended, with some transitional grace period for the existing ones to convert.

The linking of deposit money and commercial banking is an accident of history, rationalizable by 'real bills' doctrine because of the short-term nature of the assets and their financing of inventories and work in progress. Commercial lending is an important economic function. A banker formerly was expected to be an expert in appraising the risks of particular loans, and his continuing relationship to borrower-customers served both them and the economy at large. Although the proposed 'deposited currency' partially breaks the link of deposit money to commercial lending, that historic link is continued and even reinforced by the proposed redefinition of commercial banking.

One corollary of the redefinition is abolition of the distinction between banks and thrift institutions. The distinction has been crumbling anyway, as savings and loan associations turn themselves into banks, functionally and legally. Under the proposal, those associations could place most of their mortgages into an investment affiliate without insured deposits and their insured deposits into a commercial banking affiliate.

Likewise, the two federal insurance systems, the Federal Deposit Insurance Corporation and the Federal Savings and Loan Insurance Corporation, would be consolidated.

Of course, many depositors will prefer the chequing accounts, savings and time deposits, and CDs of these commercial banking departments to deposited currency because they will generally pay higher interest rates. It is this affiliate that would be subject to fractional reserve requirements and have the privilege of borrowing from the Federal Reserve. As now, these banks would be the major fulcrum of monetary policy.

Digression on Reserve Discipline

The basic requisite of monetary control is that the central bank control the supply of something the private sector demands. In the United States, this something is base money, and the marginally active demand is that of the depositories for reserves to satisfy legal requirements and to meet clearing debits to other depositories. Reserve discipline can be maintained whatever the legal fractional reserve requirement. Franklin Edwards suggests (1987, Chapter 1) that no reserves need be required. He is correct if he means, as I assume, that depositories must meet a zero requirement in the same way they have to meet a positive one now, that is, by having reserve balances, averaged over the computation period, not less than those required. If the fraction were zero, a depository must not be 'overdrawn'. If depositories can borrow or overdraw without limit, then, of course, there can be no reserve discipline. If they cannot, the central bank could retain control even if the required fraction were negative, permitting overdrafts up to a prescribed line of credit.

While it is possible to operate the system with zero reserve ratios, that does not mean it is a good idea. For one thing, distributional equities are at stake. The taxpayers would lose the cheap placement of part of the national debt in required interest-free holdings. Moreover, a zero required reserve would mean that demands for Federal Funds would depend entirely on individual depositories' precautionary decisions to hold excess reserves and to borrow at the discount window. These depend on uncertainties that the central bank would find difficult to forecast in aggregate. The more predictable demands for required reserves would be non-existent.

The United States bases reserve requirements on deposit liabilities, but this convention is not essential. They could be based on asset volume, exempting an amount equal to capital. Computerization is likely to lead to increasing extension of overdraft credit lines by commercial banks to their depositors. If so, deposits will be an ambiguous and unsuitable base for reserve requirements. Assets, including overdrafts in use, will be more meaningful.

Daylight overdrafts create a short-run problem of reserve discipline, distinguishable from the regular reserve tests based on comparison of averages of end-of-day deposits and reserve holdings. It is difficult for a layman to understand why a depository using Fedwire cannot be held to a continuous requirement that its balance be not less than zero or some other prearranged amount. Leaving aside computer capabilities, which I presume can eventually be upgraded, I guess that the problem is that the depository cannot know all the debit charges to its Federal Reserve account. If this is because it has delegated the initiation of wire charges on its account to its clients, that practice should not be allowed. If it is because various employees are authorized to make such transactions, then the bank should hold enough excess reserve balances to make sure it is not overdrawn within a period when some responsible officer of the bank can learn what his agents are doing and take the necessary steps. If it is because cheque clearings deplete the account in amounts and at times the bank does not control or know, then excess overdrafts restricted to this quantity could be allowed until the end of the day, as was the practice before the dominance of wire transfers.

The Federal Reserve's nightmare appears to be that a run on a bank on a given day could lead to large overdrafts that could not be settled at the end of the day without generous Federal Reserve credit. The Federal Reserve would have no choice but to grant it, because otherwise a whole chain of payees would not hold the credits to their accounts they expected. The Federal Reserve's credit might have to continue day after day if the initial run were not reversed. It seems to be in the Federal Reserve's power to impose enough continuous discipline to avert this nightmare.

Tighter control by the Federal Reserve would presumably lead to tighter control by banks over customer overdrafts. A movement to a 'debit card' or giro system, eliminating float, is greatly to be desired. For maintaining control, the giro sequence of payments orders and information – payor to payor's bank to central clearing to payee's bank to payee – is preferable to the cheque sequence – payor to payee to payee's bank to central clearing to payor's bank. Incidentally, the giro system would eliminate the considerable volume of transactions undertaken to earn double interest during float. Even under the cheque system, these transactions could be made unprofitable by prohibiting banks from paying interest on funds deposited before they are actually collected.

Investment Affiliates

I would allow a bank holding company to have one or more investment bank affiliates, whose liabilities would be entirely uninsured, and whose assets would be free from commercial banking restrictions. Such an affiliate, I should think, would be subject to disclosure requirements like those of the Securities and Exchange Commission and to balance sheet restrictions like those of the Investment Company Act of 1940. An investment banking affiliate would not be allowed to trade with, or borrow from, the commercial banking affiliate.

Owners of claims on the investment bank could be offered facilities for redeeming their claims and simultaneously transferring the proceeds to third parties, as owners of mutual funds have now, but not for transferring the claims themselves. To provide these facilities, the investment affiliate would presumably hold a checkable deposit in its commercial banking sister.

The commercial bank would be, as now, limited in the proportion of its assets representing liabilities of any one borrower, and a similar rule would apply to the total claims of the commercial and investment banks combined against any one (non-federal) entity. These restrictions should prevent abuse while allowing the two banks together to develop an efficient broad-spectrum financing relationship with a customer.

For a current commercial bank or equivalent insured depository, an investment affiliate would be established by the transfer of uninsured liabilities and equivalent value of assets from the commercial bank. These transfers would move the commercial bank towards compliance with the new and stricter regulations about asset portfolio composition. Of course, the transition will have to allow ample time for orderly compliance.

WHO SHOULD BE ALLOWED TO DO WHAT?

I turn now to the first set of issues. However, I cannot share the frenzy of excitement about them, unless the monetary and depository system is reformed along the lines I have outlined.

Deregulation in Perspective

I suggest scepticism of blanket deregulation justified simply as an application of general propositions on the optimality of the outcomes of free competitive markets. There is nothing in Adam Smith, or in Arrow and Debreu, that justifies the naive confidence of the deregulation ideology that unfettered growth and unrestrained combinations of firms – vertical, horizontal, conglomerate – will yield the socially best allocations of resources to activities. Oligopolies, monopolistic competition, non-price competition and non-market third-party effects (externalities) are excluded by assumption in any careful statement of 'invisible hand' propositions.

Combinations supplant market transactions with internal administrative procedures. Adam Smith and his disciples to this day have viewed competitive markets as the mechanisms of social coordination and cooperation, of specialization and the division of labour. It is ironic that free market enthusiasts are so ready to promote combinations, which remove resource allocations from market discipline.

The case for bigness depends on economies of scale and scope. The case against is that bureaucracies are inflexible and inefficient – the same case that free market exponents make against government. So far as I know, there is no convincing theoretical or empirical demonstration that the markets for businesses, so active nowadays, resolve the conflict rationally and optimally. That combinations will be made, if allowed, if and only if they are in society's interest, is simply an ideological article of faith.

Synergies in production technology and management seem very often to be less crucial considerations than empire-building. Managerial remuneration and prestige depend on size and on the height of the hierarchical pyramid. The market in businesses has not been very successful even in improving profits, let alone adding to national economic welfare. Financial pages report regularly the divestments of divisions or affiliates acquired only a few years earlier amid fanfare about synergistic fit.

Even when combinations increase profits, they may not be economic in a more comprehensive sense. Private gains may come, thanks to quirks of tax law, at the expense of taxpayers. Or as in the financial industries of concern to us here, they may arise from taking aggressive advantage of federal safety nets, deposit insurance and last-resort lending.

Although financial markets come closer than non-financial markets to the perfect markets of economic theory, non-price competition is rampant in financial services. It is easy to proliferate 'products', and competing financial firms devote considerable resources to differentiating and advertising products. As the competition for Individual Retirement Account money exemplifies, the alleged differences are generally trivial and superficial. Arrow–Debreu theorems do not apply when the list of products is endogenous. Chamberlinian 'wastes of monopolistic competition', or of oligopolistic competition, are a real possibility.

To an extent not shared by most other industries, monetary and financial institutions involve some externalities, public goods and bads, and their functioning in the public interest requires wide availability of accurate information. The payments system and the integrity of the medium of exchange are public goods. The sovereign monetary fiat, partially delegated to private agents, must be protected. Consequently regulations are essential, although not necessarily those that now exist. In addition, there is a general conservative principle. Just as 'old taxes are good taxes', old regulations may be good regulations in the sense that it is better not to repeal them even if they would not be adopted *de novo*.

Are there Significant Synergies?

Economies of scale in banking do not appear to justify 'megabanks'. The evidence is that these economies are exploited by medium-size banks, which do better than both very small and very large firms. No doubt there are some efficiencies to be realized by branching and interstate banking, but we do not need an oligopoly of a few coast-to-coast giant banks.

Economies of scope are the major rationale invoked for allowing conglomeration of various financial activities under common ownership and management, even in combination with non-financial businesses. Evidence of their importance, especially for the economy at large, remains scanty. I doubt there could be detectable increment in GNP. Indeed, I suspect that involving even more bright people in frenzied financial activities could be counter-productive.

'One-stop' banking and financial servicing is a popular slogan, but it tends to fall apart under close scrutiny. Collecting various services under one roof will not make your visit 'one-stop' except for parking your car. Inside the supermarket you will have to visit, and wait for, the various specialists – teller, broker, insurance agent, mortgage officer, auto loan manager, and so forth.

'One-statement' finance is probably another mirage. At least in my experience, combined statements do not diminish paper overload and are confusing and prone to error. Moreover, it is predictable that the multiproduct financial firm is going to proliferate extravagantly promoted tie-in deals, just about as advantageous to the customers as the life insurance the lender's agent assumes you want when you take out a mortgage or an auto loan.

Common location does not necessitate common ownership. Distinct specialized firms can have offices in the same building or shopping centre, or even within a bank's premises.

Anyway, is not 'no-stop' finance the wave of the future? Will not telephone lines and computer networks replace automobile trips? You may pay for your groceries at the checkout by inserting a card, and pay your bills likewise at more versatile ATM stations conveniently located, even at your own phone. You may manage your investment portfolio the same way. The current examples of ATMs and credit cards indicate that these facilities can be provided without combination and conglomeration.

That is true also of transactions other than those of consumers. While a large bank can mobilize the excess deposits of some branches to finance the excess loans of others, the same function is performed by secondary markets in mortgages, loans, securities, Federal Funds and interbank deposits. As noted above, the question is whether internal administration can do these things better than the markets.

Robert Litan (1987, Chapter 3) finds the major case for activity diversification not in technological and managerial synergies but in risk reduction. Possibly the variance of earnings on assets and on net worth can be diminished, without sacrifice of expected return, by conglomeration, especially if returns on new activities are negatively correlated with those on traditional banking operations. On the other hand, the new activities may be instrinsically more risky.

I am afraid I do not find this case very convincing. I have argued that the moral hazards of federal safety nets have to be attacked head on. Companies owning banks must be prevented from placing the risks of their various activities on those safety nets. Once that is assured, conglomeration may not be so attractive. And in one sense it seems redundant. It might be that the profitability of chewing-gum turned out empirically to be strongly negatively correlated with earnings in banking. Does it therefore make sense for chewing-gum companies to operate banks or vice versa? Individual savers do not need conglomerate firms in order to diversify. They can do so, possibly with the help of mutual funds, in their own portfolios, and could do so even in a world of firms with specialized product lines.

Should non-financial activities and commercial banks, as redefined above, be combined under common ownership and top management? My judgement, like that of Paul Volcker and Gerald Corrigan (1987), is not to allow such marriages. The danger that the bank would be used to assist the non-financial activities, increasing the risks to depositors and to the federal government, is too great, whatever regulations are written to forestall such abuse. The countervailing social advantages do not seem important. Anyway, in the structure I have sketched above, nothing would stop conglomeration of non-financial business and non-banking financial activities.

Should bank holding companies, which by definition would have a commercial banking affiliate, be allowed to underwrite securities? This is a difficult judgement call, and I do not feel at all expert. I see the advantages to the bank holding company and to its customer of a relationship that covers short-term finance (the commercial bank affiliate), long-term finance (the investment bank affiliate) and underwriting services (still another affiliate). This seems a more likely synergy than those alleged for consumer banking and finance. Underwriting is a risky activity, however, and depends on a range of skills different from banking, in particular those involved in the 'due diligence' investigations required by the Securities and Exchange Commission.

I would require an underwriting affiliate to be heavily capitalized, and I would raise the senior capital protection requirement of the commercial bank affiliate of any holding company doing underwriting. Limits on the commercial and investment bank holdings of any one company would prevent the underwriting affiliate from regarding its sisters as fallback customers. Likewise, the underwriters would not be allowed to borrow from their sisters.

Prohibiting the use of deposits, especially insured deposits, from financing underwriting would make banks less threatening to that industry than usually touted, but even so, thanks to the general financial expertise of banks, their competition could reduce the toll booth profits now protected by Glass–Steagall.

CONCLUSION

In summary, the strategy I favour is, first, to restructure the systems of depository institutions so as to reduce significantly the moral hazard of federal safety nets, particularly deposit insurance. I would not turn banks loose to enter new fields, or throw the gates of banking open to non-bank firms, as long as it remains possible for additional risks to be passed to depositors, taxpayers and prudent members of deposit insurance systems. Once a restructured system of depositories was relatively immune to this danger, I would let commercial banks have investment banking and, possibly, underwriting affiliates. But I would draw the line at letting non-financial firms have banks, anyway the kinds of banks that would do them any good.

REFERENCES

Corrigan, E. Gerald (1987), *Financial Market Structure: A Longer View*, New York: Federal Reserve Bank of New York.

Edwards, Franklin (1987), *Restructuring the Financial System*, Federal Reserve Bank of Kansas City, Chapter 1.

Litan, Robert E. (1987), *What Should Banks Do?*, Washington: Brookings Institution.

10.   Monetary policies in the 1980s*

Speaking about Paul Volcker right after Paul Volcker, I am not in an enviable position. Imagine an academic critic following Douglas MacArthur in a retrospective discussion of the general's campaigns.

I shall discuss only briefly the three years from October 1979, the period of serious quantitative medium-run targets for monetary aggregates and of short-run operating targets for quantities of reserves. History will confirm the praise that Paul Volcker earned from his contemporaries for his resolute generalship of the war against the inflation of the late 1970s. The recessions did not reduce inflation to zero, but they did lower it to a comfortable rate, 4–5 per cent, which proved to be stable during the subsequent cyclical expansion.

In 1979–80, many economists contended that the way monetary policy-makers could bring about a relatively rapid and painless disinflation would be to announce strict monetarist targets and operating procedures and to commit themselves to stick with them regardless of what happened to business activity and employment. Thus business managers and workers would be put on notice that their livelihoods and jobs depend on their own price and wage decisions – they must disinflate. This popular academic view may have influenced the climate of opinion in the Federal Reserve System and the financial markets. I gather that it was not as important in Volcker's own thinking as the need to obtain and display consensus in the System for a policy move appropriate to prevailing economic conditions.

If a 'credible threat' was intended in the October 1979 revolution, it was attenuated by the policy roller coaster in 1980, severely criticized by Michael Mussa in his background paper and unapologetically reviewed by Paul in his remarks. Why Carter's credit controls were so powerful a restraint on aggregate demand and on money supplies remains a mystery. Evidently, their effects both on imposition and on removal greatly confused the Fed. Anyway, beginning in September 1980, a determined monetarist policy was followed for nearly two years. Did the policy make the disinflation faster and less painful than it would have been otherwise? The economic literature renders a

*First published in M. Feldstein (ed.), *American Economic Policy in the 1980's*, National Bureau of Economic Research, 1994. References to Mussa's paper are to his Chapter 2 of that volume. The paper was presented at a conference in Williamsburg, Virginia, 18–20 October 1990.

mixed verdict. Certainly, it took substantial pain and suffering, not just threat, to get wage and price inflation rates down.

Was there any way to limit the cost? Some economists, myself included, had suggested combining the announcement of a firm disinflationary monetary policy with some variant of incomes policy, at least guideposts. There had been a stab at incomes policy in the Carter Administration in 1979, but it was abandoned just at the crucial time. Rumour was that this decision was related to the contest for the Democratic Presidential nomination, specifically to the position of organized labour. No incomes policy was conceivable in the new Administration, although President Reagan's tough stand against the air traffic controllers in 1981 taught an exemplary lesson. One could say that the Fed itself was carrying out an incomes policy, albeit one that worked via actual pain and cost rather than by conjectural fears.

I hope that history will give Paul and his colleagues the praise that they deserve not only for fighting the war against inflation but also for knowing when to stop, when to declare victory. They reversed course in the summer of 1982, probably averting an accelerating contraction of economic activity in the United States and financial disasters world-wide. Many observers, knowing that the Fed takes seriously its responsibilities for financial stability, have assumed that the Mexican debt crisis and other financial threats were the main considerations in the Fed's decisions in 1982. According to Volcker, however, domestic non-financial business conditions were the main concern of the Federal Open Market Committee (FOMC).

I know that there are some hawks who thought then and think now that the anti-inflation crusade should have been pursued to the bitter end and that there are some who would resume now the push to zero inflation. I think that it was an act of genius, worth trillions of dollars of GNP – yes, real GNP – to have led the country to regard 5 per cent inflation as zero, and I think that it is mischievous to rock the boat now.

The monetary management of the expansion of the last eight years – perhaps this record expansion has ended or is about to end – is my main topic. For the management of aggregate demand, monetary policy has been the only game in town since 1981. The Reagan Administration disabled fiscal policy as a tool of macroeconomic stabilization and dedicated it wholly to other goals, as discussed in other sessions of this conference. Structural budget deficits far beyond previous peacetime experience clouded the environment to which the Fed had to adapt. No doubt the economic and political implications of the federal budget complicated the Fed's decision problems. There were other new complexities and uncertainties: dramatically increasing international capital mobility; Latin American and other Third World debts; structural and regulatory changes in American banking and finance; and insolvencies, threatened and actual, among American financial institutions.

Despite these handicaps, the Fed has been quite successful. Volcker and company, and then Greenspan and company, restored the reputation of fine-tuning and made it into a fine art. The proof is in the pudding. The economy grew steadily, if sometimes slowly, and eventually recovered the ground lost in the recessions. In 1988–89, unemployment was lowered well below what economists considered the lowest inflation-safe rates ten years earlier. Finally, after managing a 'soft landing' at this new and lower non-accelerating-inflation rate of unemployment (NAIRU), for the last two years the Fed has managed to steer the economy between the Scylla of price acceleration and the Charybdis of recession. I don't know how long that will be true, but it is true so far.

Demand management cannot take major credit for the improvement in the NAIRU, except that the previous deep recession may have helped discipline subsequent wage- and price-setting practices. Sharper foreign competition helped, a thin silver lining to the dark cloud of dollar appreciation. The decline in oil prices prior to August 1990 was a welcome contrast to the 1970s. Whatever cleared the path for expansion, the Fed does get credit for following the path into new territory, cautiously keeping the recovery going as long as inflation remained well behaved.

For the improved price performance of the 1980s, Mussa gives important weight to the new macroeconomic policy mix, loose fiscal policy and tight money. He echoes previous rationales for this combination. The argument is that the 1982–86 currency appreciation lowered the inflation rate associated with a given outcome in real output and employment. I am still sceptical. For the United States, the impact of appreciation on overall price indexes is small. Besides, it is temporary, essentially a loan from other countries that must be paid back. Later, the currency has to be depreciated, and the borrowed price reduction has to be reversed. Even in the short run, the gain from an appreciation is one shot; it lowers not the rate of inflation but the level of price indexes. The policy mix in question has serious costs in long-run growth and foreign indebtedness, costs that dwarf any small short-run macro-economic advantages.

I have no inside information about how the Fed has done its fine-tuning. The interpretation that follows is simply inference from an outsider's observations. The new Fed monetary regime, beginning in the fall of 1982, changed both medium-run targets of policy and operating procedures. Although target ranges for intermediate monetary aggregates are still voted on and announced as required by law, they have lost importance, as the markets know very well (see Mussa's figures 2.8 and 2.9).

The Federal Reserve recognized that intermediate monetary aggregates had lost whatever meaning they had because of regulatory and technological changes in the financial industries. Downgrading the monetary targets finessed at least one source of error in monetary policy, unexpected (or even systematic) changes in velocity. Mussa's Figure 2.10 shows what happened to M1 and M2 velocities. Liberated from the Ms, the Fed is enabled to respond to shocks that change velocity but not the aggregates and is excused from responding to M changes that simply reflect velocity shocks. Tactically, in 1982, the changing and uncertain meanings of the Ms gave the Fed some cover for making changes in policy substance and operating procedure that Paul and his colleagues wanted to make anyway.

The Fed has aimed directly at observed and projected macroeconomic performance, as measured not by monetary aggregates but by variables that matter: real GNP growth; unemployment, excess capacity and other indicators of slack; wage and price inflation. The weights on different measures of performance are not explicit; indeed, they doubtless differ among members of the Open Market Committee. The bottom line is likely to be some agreed on or compromise range for real GNP growth, higher or lower depending on the weights the Committee is putting on the other variables.

Short-run operating instruments are no longer reserve quantities but, as in pre-1979 days, Federal Funds rates. The differential between the funds rate and the discount rate reflects the pressure on the banks' reserve positions. Like most controllers, the Fed is a feedback mechanism, changing its instrument settings in response to discrepancies significant in size and duration between actual readings and projections of its target variables, on the one hand, and desired target paths, on the other.

Not surprisingly, Federal Funds rates, and other interest rates as well, have been less volatile since 1982 than in the preceding monetarist régime. Paul admits that he was astounded by their volatility in 1980–82. Most of their recent volatility has been deliberate policy. When the Fed saw aggregate demand growing too slowly, the FOMC lowered the funds rate substantially (down 564 basis points in six months from July 1982). When demand was perceived to be growing too fast, the FOMC raised the rate (up 205 basis points in six months from February 1984). Likewise, the funds rate was lowered 163 points in the seven months from February 1986 and raised 210 points in the eight months from July 1988. Other interest rates moved in the same directions, longer rates of course by fewer points (see Mussa's Figure 2.4).

In retrospect, the tightening in 1984 looks excessive to me and too long maintained. The recovery was little more than a year old, and there was plenty of slack left in the economy. At the time of the February 1984 'Monetary Policy Report', the Board believed that real GNP had grown 6 per cent from 1982:4, then thought to have been the recession bottom, to 1983:4 and that growth had slowed to 4.5 per cent in 1983:4. The Fed reported that 1983 growth was in considerable measure due to rebuilding of inventories. The unemployment rate was said to be down 2.5 points, but it was still about 8 per cent. Wage and price inflation was still abating. Yet the Fed was aiming for only 4.5 per cent growth in 1984, fourth quarter to fourth quarter – they got it, now revised to 5 per cent. (This is the only time that I found so explicit a target in a 'Monetary Policy Report to Congress'. Generally, the growth target is unstated or is implicit in the FOMC members' projections. In his remarks, Paul warned us against reading any policy intentions into those projections.)

In most post-war recoveries, growth was 6 per cent or better in the first year. I have never found convincing the 'speed limit' theory, which argues that high growth rates are dangerously inflationary even in very slack economies. Demand management, I think, should aim for high growth at the beginnings of recovery and gradually reduce stimulus as the margin of economic slack declines. The Fed's foot was a bit heavy on the brake.

I mention this episode because it did unintended and unexpected long-lasting damage. The return of double-digit short interest rates in mid 1984, raising long-term bond rates above 13 per cent again, ratcheted the dollar up another big notch (20 per cent nominal, 19 per cent real, in the multilateral trade-weighted index). I realize that, as Paul Krugman convincingly argued, there must have been significant speculative content in the appreciation of the dollar. But US interest rates had a lot to do with it. The merchandise trade deficit grew from $21.7 billion in 1983:4 to $29.3 four quarters later, the current account deficit from $18.3 to $30.0. Reversal of the deterioration proved to be a slow and difficult process, even after the dollar's exchange value fell.

By 1980, economists inside and outside the Federal Reserve and the Treasury understood the qualitative role of exchange rates, capital movements and trade imbalances in the transmission of monetary measures – and fiscal measures, too – to the economy in a world of floating exchange rates and mobile financial funds. Qualitatively, things happened the way our theory said they would. But I guess that no one, even in the Fed's international shop, foresaw how large these effects could be, how long they could persist and how difficult they might be to reverse.

The drag of the import surplus was one reason that the recovery of real GNP proceeded even more slowly in the two years after 1984, 3.6 per cent in 1985 and 1.9 per cent in 1986, while unemployment hovered around 7.0 per cent. Only in 1987–88, after the cautious easing of 1986 finally took effect, was the recovery completed, five and a half years after it had begun.

Real interest rates averaged 400 or 500 basis points higher in the 1980s recovery than in previous post-war expansions. This is the proximate cause of several well-known adverse developments in the US economy and the symptom of others. Like most people in this room, I place most of the blame on federal fiscal policy. But the Fed could have lowered rates sooner and further in the period 1984–87.

I tell monetary policy sceptics like my friend Bob Eisner that we could have had – indeed, we would have had – the same recovery in the 1980s without the extraordinary fiscal stimulus, the same performance in GNP and employment without the negative by-products. I have based this claim on the generous interpretation of Fed policy that I have given above. Assuming that the Fed's targets for macroeconomic performance would have been the same had fiscal policy been pre-Reagan normal, I say that the Fed had plenty of room to lower interest rates in pursuit of those targets and would have used it. Maybe, in fact, sound fiscal policy would have made the Fed more expansionary. Maybe our central bankers held back at times in the hope of sending a message about fiscal policy to the President and Congress.

I am still saying these things, now to people who worry whether budget correction will cause recession. I hope I am right. The Fed might have to act faster, in larger steps, than it did in 1984–86. Twenty-five basis points every FOMC meeting would not be enough.

Sometimes, I am afraid, defence of the dollar has been given more weight than it deserves. I am not referring to the fall of 1979, when Paul tells us that the dollar's weakness and the complaints of major foreign central bankers simply reinforced the sufficient domestic reasons for a contractionary move. But supporting the dollar was a consideration in 1984 and again after the Group of Five agreed at the Louvre in early 1987 that the 1985–86 depreciation had gone far enough. (According to Paul, this was Treasury policy, not his preference. The idea that exchange rate policy is the province of the Treasury and that monetary policy is the province of the Federal Reserve seems dangerously anomalous, given that the two policies are essentially one and the same.) Interest rates to support the dollar contributed to the slowdown in 1987 and perhaps to the stock market crash in October. Following the crash, Greenspan and his colleagues eased decisively and let the dollar fall, with good macroeconomic results.

Dollar defence may be a consideration again now, when domestic demand expansions and tight monetary policies are raising interest rates in Japan and Europe. I see no good reason to oppose a depreciation of the dollar when lower interest rates are appropriate to domestic demand management, particularly when there is room in the economy for more net exports. How will we get the capital inflow that we need to 'finance' our trade deficit if our interest rates are lower than those overseas? If it takes a dollar low enough to make investors around the world believe that it is going to rise, so be it.

As early as the spring of 1982, I suggested a tripartite accord – White House, Congress and Fed – to shift the policy mix to tighter budget and easier money. It was a good idea then, and it has been a good idea ever since.

11. Monetary policies in the 1980s and beyond*

In this *tour d'horizon* I am going to remind you of various important ways in which the environment of central bank policy-making today differs from the environment of ten years ago and 20 years ago. I shall emphasize the United States and the Federal Reserve, but I shall note several points of international similarity and difference. The discussion will naturally lead to some observations about current issues of policy.

As a general introduction friendly to our hosts, I want to pay some tribute to the Fed's policies in this decade.

When Paul Volcker retired he was praised all over the world as the courageous and victorious general in the 1979–82 war against inflation. I think he deserved that praise, as Grant deserved credit for taking Richmond: in both cases, victory came the old-fashioned way, with plenty of casualties. No one doubted that unflinching monetary restriction could bring deep recession and disinflation. It did, and I guess the 'credible threat' strategy of 1979–82 may have speeded the process, compared with those four of the seven previous post-1945 recessions that were also the deliberate consequences of disinflationary monetary policy.

Almost none of the tributes to Paul Volcker gave him credit for knowing when to stop, for following in spirit the wise advice of the late Senator George Aiken of Vermont about the Vietnam War: declare victory and get out. Inflation was still four or five points above zero when, in the fall of 1982, three years after the announcement of monetarist policies and reserve-quantity operating procedures, the Fed reversed course. Volcker took mercy on the world financial system and on the US and world economies.

Since then the Federal Reserve has presided over a long and steady recovery, which has cut the US unemployment rate in half without increasing the inflation rate. The Fed effectively abandoned targets for intermediate monetary aggregates; even though such targets are still announced, no one worries about whether they are hit or not. Policy is instead oriented to macroeconomic performance as indicated by real GNP growth, unemployment,

*First published in *Conference on Monetary Aggregates and Financial Sector Behavior in Interdependent Economies*, Board of Governors of the Federal Reserve System, 1990. The conference was held in March 1988.

prices and inflation, and exchange rates. Likewise, short-term operating procedures aim at targets for the Federal Funds rate, which are changed as seems
necessary to keep the economy on the Fed's desired macroeconomic path.
That, at any rate, is how Fed policy-making appears to me, and that is how I
think it ought to be done.

I could nitpick a little. The Fed was justified in slowing down the rapid
pace at which recovery was proceeding in 1983 and the first half of 1984. But
for the next two years the unemployment rate seemed stuck at 7 per cent plus
some tenths. Since then the Fed has allowed the economy to test gradually
lower and lower unemployment rates, about a tenth of a point a month.

That brings me to the first of the five observations I want to make about
changes in the environment in which central banks are operating. From 1966 to
1982, the unemployment–inflation trade-off appeared to be the major problem
of macroeconomics and of macroeconomic policy, the intractable obstacle to
good performance. Now it seems quiescent, almost eerily so. For 25 years
macroeconometricians and policy-makers had been raising their estimates of
the lowest inflation-safe unemployment rate in the United States – from 4 per
cent to 5 to 6 – and a few years ago many pundits said 7. Now we are at 5.5 per
cent, and pessimists have to strain their eyes to find signs of accelerating prices.
The much maligned short-run Phillips curve seems to be in place again: money-
wage inflation and price inflation fall while unemployment is declining so long
as unemployment exceeds some critical rate or zone.

Why? I see three reasons:

1. The problem was overstated in the 1970s. Stagflationary difficulties due
    to external supply shocks were mistakenly attributed to the structure of
    the economy, particularly its labour markets. The 'natural rate' of oil
    consumption at the time was interpreted to be the natural rate of unem-
    ployment. Moreover, one-shot adjustments in important individual prices
    and in price levels were uncritically extrapolated as signals of changes in
    ongoing inflation rates.
2. Keen international competition finally disciplined industries and workers
    in sectors that had misbehaved in the 1970s; for notable examples see
    automobiles and steel.
3. Trade unions were chastened and weakened, and employers' backbones
    were stiffened, by Volcker's disinflationary recession and by the object
    lesson of President Reagan's tough stand against the air controllers.
    Under credible threats of losing jobs, unions and unorganized workers
    have made concessions unthinkable a decade ago.

While the least inflation-safe unemployment rate has declined in the United States, the prevailing view among policy-makers and economists in Europe is that there it has dramatically risen. The difference is hard to understand, at least for me on this side of the Atlantic. Why should economies that grew rapidly for 20 or 30 years with 2 or 3 per cent unemployment and low inflation suddenly have natural unemployment rates of 8, 9, 10 per cent? What institutional or structural changes, so different from those in North America, could have brought this about?

I am sceptical. On the statistical side, I think that these large increases in natural rates are estimated because inflation rates have not fallen as fast as might have been expected were unemployment much above the Non-Accelerating Inflation Rate of Unemployment (NAIRU). If you think you know the slope of the short-run Phillips curve, then you can explain the observations since 1979 only by concluding that the curve must have moved horizontally a long way in the wrong direction. But in none of these European countries has there been direct evidence in the 1980s that stimulus to demand that reduces unemployment will accelerate prices. (I exclude the ill-starred Mitterand attempt at demand expansion in one country, partly because the policy deliberately raised money wages and prices.) It may well be that in the range of unemployment rates experienced in this decade, the short-run Phillips curve is pretty flat, so that unemployment and price developments are disjoint.

In 1982, I wrote an essay entitled, 'After Disinflation, What?'. I conjectured that after the concerted international monetary war against inflation was won, central banks and conservative governments would be very cautious about recovery. Reluctant to enjoy the fruits of their hard-won victory lest they lose the victory in the process, they would add a few points of risk premium to unbiased estimates of NAIRUs. That is what I suspect has happened in Europe, even in some degree in Japan. Where I was wrong was here at home. Each for his own reasons, Volcker and Reagan both took actions that led to recovery.

The second big change in the environment of the Federal Reserve has been the radical fiscal policy of the federal government in the 1980s. The federal budget has been almost totally disabled as an instrument of macroeconomic stabilization. Fiscal policy had already been partially disabled, just by the shift to floating exchange rates in the 1970s, although Mundell's theorem hardly applies in extreme form, especially to an economy as large as the United States. Reagan's extreme fiscal policy was adopted in 1981 for reasons quite separate from stabilization. Indeed, the official line denounced and eschewed active measures of stabilization, certainly on the fiscal side. However, I notice that the supply-side faithful have had more and more difficulty distinguishing their fiscal measures from demand stimuli.

From 1982 to 1985, as large and growing deficits were stimulating aggregate demand, the Fed's task was to keep the recovery going but not too fast. The result was that real interest rates, although lower than in 1980–82, remained higher than they were in previous periods of cyclical recovery. Now that the focus of budget policy is to engineer gradual decline in the deficit relative to GNP, the burden of stabilization still falls wholly on the Fed. There is no way to adjust fiscal policy to fight recession; even the built-in stabilizers may be annihilated by budget politics. It is even unlikely that fiscal policy could be used against inflationary overheating; taxes and spending are now determined by political and economic considerations divorced from short-run macroeconomics.

In principle, the Fed can handle the task of stabilization by itself. So long as its target is macroeconomic performance, as described above, the Fed will adjust to fiscal policies, as to other events, so as to stay on its desired macro path. It is for this reason that I argue that we could have had, and would have had, the same recovery with the 'middle of the road' mixes of fiscal and monetary policies characteristic of all previous post-1945 recoveries. This faith would not be justified if the Fed still placed important weight on monetary aggregate targets *per se*. Back in 1982, when the magnitude of the Reagan deficits began to become obvious and before the Fed had downgraded the monetary aggregates, I thought it would take a formal Accord among the Federal Reserve, Congress and the President to alter the mix of policies. Maybe that would still have been a wise course for the blue ribbon National Economic Commission to recommend after the 1988 election.

A third change in the environment is a legacy of the 1970s: the hypersensitivity of bond and stock markets to perceived risks of future inflation. It is not just individuals and institutions investing in fixed-dollar securities that are sensitive. Shareowners, even borrowers, also regard inflation news as bad news. What used to be regarded as good news about the economy – increased production, sales, profits, employment, exports and the like – is often regarded as bad news. Why? Because these events might presage tightness in the economy, wage and price pressures, and – most important of all – restrictive monetary policies, leading to higher interest rates and recessions. This perception makes it important for the central bank to maintain its inflation-fighting reputation at the same time it accommodates non-inflationary real growth.

The term structure of interest rates often reflects the expectations and fears of future Fed policies, and thus future short-term interest rates. Sometimes the term premiums respond to hints from the central bank itself. In any case, these premiums are not informed predictions about the markets for goods and services where prices are actually determined, and the Fed should not respond to them as it would to solid forecasts.

I never saw the rationale for the 'bills only' dogma the Fed adopted in 1953. In the 1960s, for a brief period, the Fed did dabble in longer markets. Now operations are concentrated into even shorter-term paper than the bills of the 1950s – 'repos'. I think the Fed should be ready to operate in all maturities of bills and bonds. The same is true of the Treasury. It has not made sense for the federal government to borrow long at rates several hundred basis points higher than its own official forecasts of future rates. If bond-holding institutions are nervous about future inflations and prosperities that borrowing households and businesses do not anticipate, we can have an impasse similar to Keynes's liquidity trap. The Fed and the Treasury could help by weighing in on the side of realistic optimism.

My fourth point is the focus of a number of papers in this volume. The structure of the financial markets in which central banks operate has been changing more rapidly and significantly than it has at any time since World War II, perhaps since the Great Depression. The changes are of several kinds: technological, institutional, entrepreneurial and regulatory – or rather, deregulatory. The effects are not all in the same direction, and their combination has probably increased uncertainties both for policy-makers and for private agents and market participants. Uncertainties about the meaning and behaviour of monetary aggregates doubtless contributed to dethroning them, at least by giving the Fed an excuse acceptable to the markets.

As for the payment of uncontrolled, market-determined interest rates on deposits in M1 and M2, much discussed in this volume, I thought the directions of the effects were pretty obvious. The régime change itself would bring a once-for-all increase in demand for the affected deposits, thus for M1 and maybe for M2 as well (although that depends on a complex of substitution coefficients for the components, with each other and with other assets and debts). At the same time, demands for money would be less elastic than before with respect to general levels of interest rates. The LM curve would be steeper – to what degree would depend substantially on the microeconomics of banks and of other intermediaries. The marginal costs of intermediation may be roughly constant, or they may depend on scales of operation, both of individual firms and of whole industries.

I conjecture that the smaller size and greater stability of the net opportunity cost of holding deposits make the demand for money not only less interest elastic but also more volatile. Why use a sharp pencil in cash management if there's not much in it? For example, consider the Miller–Orr *S,s* inventory model for cash holding. Under the new regime a depositor following this rule would now choose a larger difference between *S* and *s*, and might well not change their values very often in response to transaction volumes, transaction costs and opportunity costs. As Akerlof and Milbourne (1980) have shown, so long as *S* and *s* remain the same, like sluggish rules of thumb, the income elasticity of the demand for money is zero. (They titled their paper 'Irving Fisher on His Head ...'.) Consequently, velocity can vary a great deal in the short run.

Bill Poole's famous analysis (1970) implies that when the demand for money becomes less interest elastic or more volatile, the central bank's supply should be more elastic with respect to interest rates. That is, in the short run, when interest rates are observed but GNP is not, the Fed should be more accommodative than it was in the old régime.

The fifth big environmental change is the internationalization of macroeconomics and macro policies. The technical efficiency of financial markets around the globe, of communications and transactions, has vastly increased the mobility of funds across currency exchanges. All this has happened, by coincidence, under the floating-rate regime. That regime is itself a reason that monetary policy bears most of the burden of stabilization.

In the 1980s, international macroeconomic events responded to policies and other shocks pretty much as our lectures and textbooks predicted – only much more so, and now maybe more slowly than expected. Under floating rates, the current account surplus or deficit becomes an important, perhaps the most important, vehicle of transmission of monetary policy. The central bank has both internal and external imbalances to worry about.

The idea that floating rates would allow each country to forget about external imbalances and disturbances and concentrate on its own domestic objectives was always a non-starter, especially for the locomotives of the world economy. National monetary measures individually tend to export unemployment or price inflation to other countries, via the currency markets. At the same time they collectively determine the macro policy environment of the world economy as a whole. National monetary policies work through differences from other countries in monetary policies and interest rates. But who determines the world level of interest rates?

The issues of monetary macroeconomic management facing the Federal Reserve right now are interesting and instructive. Federal Reserve caution is understandable. Unemployment must be getting closer to the inflation-safe threshold with each month's tenth-of-a-point reduction. It is natural and rational to slow real GNP growth ever closer to its sustainable rate. Both the threshold and the sustainable growth rate are uncertain.

Few signs of increasing inflation are visible. Ongoing inflation – a wage–price–wage spiral – should be distinguished from one-shot increases in prices and price indexes. Depreciation of the dollar, what has already occurred and what may yet occur, is bound to increase some import prices in dollars and accordingly to raise some US price indexes. When we worry about our current account imbalance, we are impatient to see the depreciation of the dollar passed through to the prices of foreign goods in dollars, so that American goods will be more competitive. Without such changes in international relative prices and costs, it is hard to see how our trade balance will ever be righted. Therefore, we have to expect these price changes to show up in price indexes, just as the appreciation of the dollar in 1981–85 assisted our statistical disinflation. Only if increases in the Consumer Price Index (CPI) due to import prices, or to increases in the production of exports and import-competing goods, were to trigger secondary waves of wage and price increases should depreciation be a reason for restrictive macro policy.

As the margin of unemployed resources dwindles, the major macroeconomic strategy in the United States must be the substitution of net exports for government purchases, and for personal consumption, induced by transfers and tax reductions. In other words, we have to substitute net exports for the federal deficit in the use of non-federal saving. We would be lucky, or policy would be unusually successful, if our two deficits, trade and federal budget, were to decline at the same pace. The Fed could operate 'steady as you go'. If net exports improve faster than the budget's contribution to aggregate demand declines, more restrictive policy is needed. If the budget correction cannot be speeded up, the Fed will have to tighten. The markets and the media jumped to this conclusion when the trade statistics (for the first quarter of 1988) were announced, although the hopes for and fears of an export-led boom seemed premature. The opposite possibility, with the opposite moral for monetary policy, is that the federal budget's support of aggregate demand will fall significantly faster than the trade deficit does.

Forecasts of the current account deficit have it declining over the next few years faster than does the Congressional Budget Office baseline structural budget deficit, but slower than do the budget reductions 'mandated' by the Balanced Budget Reaffirmation Act of 1987, the 'Son of Gramm–Rudman'.

Quite a different view of US macro policy would dedicate it to correction of the external imbalance. In this view, the growth of the economy should be made slower than the sustainable rate, bringing a 'growth recession' if not a true recession, in order to diminish domestic absorption. Moreover, this move should be made even if it is not indicated by the inflation–unemployment situation. Europeans and Japanese prefer this recipe to further depreciation of the dollar. (Sometimes this preference seems to have moral content: the United States should experience recession in penance for its fiscal profligacy, as if an adverse change in terms of trade were not penalty enough.) Our economic summit partners are reluctant to accept the other side of the same coin – namely, that their economies should grow faster and that they should increase their domestic absorption and imports, as the US government has chronically urged. The reality Europeans and Japanese do not seem to face squarely is that however the US trade deficit is corrected, the result is not going to be pleasant for their exporters, or for their economies, unless they substitute domestic demand for exports.

Realistically, the trade imbalance is only fractionally remediable by income effects on either side or on both sides. Marginal propensities to import are just not big enough. For example, if the US marginal propensity to import is 0.20, it will take a 15 per cent loss of GNP to eliminate our current account deficit. Adjustments in international relative prices and costs are essential.

A possible conflict between external and domestic objectives arises from the Federal Reserve's role in making effective our Treasury Secretary's agreements on exchange rates with foreign finance ministers. To the outside observer, it is not clear how weighty this consideration is in the minds of the Federal Open Market Committee.

It is commonly said that the Fed has no choice but to raise interest rates if and as needed to keep foreign investors satisfied; otherwise, goes the argument, how can we 'finance' the trade deficit? Economists know this is not true. The balance-of-payments identity tells us that the balancing capital inflow will arise somehow.

Benign neglect is not bad policy. You don't have to talk about it, only to refrain from committing yourself to an exchange rate target. Let the dollar fall – yes, let it 'free fall'! There is some level from which it will be expected to rise, and that expectation will take the place of high US interest rates in holding foreign and American funds. The current international interest differentials indicate that the prevailing expectation is for the dollar to fall. If that is so, it is better that the dollar fall fast so that the expectations are reversed, and so that the level of the exchange rate will be helping to bring about the improvement in the trade balance that will justify the expectation. This argument does not deny that the Fed may need to allow or to engineer increases in US interest rates for domestic macroeconomic reasons.

Some students of the trade deficit believe that the dollar is already low enough or even too low – that it's just a question of time until the trade balance is corrected without further depreciation. If the market believed this, then the exchange rate would already be higher or the interest differential smaller. If the governments believed this and wanted the market to believe it too, they would start making the dollar rise by lowering foreign interest rates further.

How came the mysterious backward metamorphosis of the world monetary system from market floating exchange rates to managed stable exchange rates? With scarcely a raised eyebrow, the financial community and press have accepted the view that the dollar's exchange rates with major currencies are a matter of joint official policy agreement. It is not clear just who has what responsibilities for the maintenance of agreed rates. Official central bank interventions apparently have played a big role. Sterilized or unsterilized? Most economists believe there is not much in sterilized intervention. If so, these agreements may have been a way in which the central banks of surplus countries were pushed into expansionary monetary policies. If stabilization ultimately depends on interest rate differences, who has the responsibility for maintaining differences commensurate with market expectations of exchange rate movements? And how does the general world level of interest rates get decided and established? Agreement on issues of this kind would be true international policy coordination.

Despite economic summits, despite periodic meetings of financial bigwigs at the Plaza or at the Louvre or in Basle – or wherever – we have not developed the machinery for meaningful coordination of macro policies. Agreements to stabilize exchange rates substitute shadow for substance.

In the 1970s, our economies suffered from savage wounds inflicted from the outside. In this decade, while recovering from some of those injuries, we have inflicted new wounds on ourselves.

REFERENCES

Akerlof, George and Ross Milbourne (1980), 'Irving Fisher on his head: the consequences of the timing of payments for the demand for money', *Quarterly Journal of Economics*, 145–57.
Poole, William (1970), 'Optimal Choice of Monetary Policy Instruments in a Simple Stochastic Model', *Quarterly Journal of Economics*, **84**, May, 197–216.

12.   Statement on monetary policy*

I will try to answer briefly the questions posed by the Chairman of the Committee in his letter of invitation.

1. Has monetary policy been appropriate in the light of the credit crunch and the length and depth of the current recession?

I was glad the Federal Reserve lowered its discount rate and the Federal Funds rate on 1 May. However, larger reductions, say 50 more basis points, would have been preferable. The Funds rate, the basic cost of money to the banks, was cut only a quarter-point.

It was important for the Fed to dispel the impression, given during the Group of Seven meetings a few days earlier, that US interest rates could be lowered only in concert with Europe and Japan. Although a generalized cut in rates would be welcome to stimulate global economic activity and trade, it is not the only way to increase foreign demand for US goods. A powerful way, under our control and actually welcomed by our G7 partners, is to lower US interest rates relative to theirs enough to bring down the dollar in the foreign exchange markets, making American goods more competitive at home and abroad. We had further improvement in exports to propel recovery from this recession. It was unfortunate, therefore, that the Federal Reserve allowed the dollar to appreciate so much in the last two months. I attach to this Statement an article on this subject I published in *The New York Times* on 24 March, 'Bring the Dollar Down'.

Monetary policy has, in my view, been too slow and too grudging in lowering interest rates to fight the recession. Real interest rates are extraordinarily high, especially in terms of price movements in producers' goods, capital goods and houses. With nominal costs of capital around 10 per cent and relevant price changes close to zero or even negative, it is no wonder that private fixed investment, residential and non-residential, is a disaster area.

2. Should the Federal Reserve further lower interest rates and, if so, what is the appropriate level of interest rates?

*Presented at Hearing on Monetary Policy at Joint Economic Committee of the Congress, 9 May 1991.

Yes, as I already suggested, the Fed should lower rates further. I do not know the appropriate level. I think it is correct to lower rates in steps while additional information is becoming available on the state of the economy, and on the foreign exchange value of the dollar.

It is important to remember that in this recession, unlike all previous recessions since 1945, monetary policy is the only game in town. Fiscal policy has been incapacitated as an instrument of macroeconomic stabilization by its excesses in the 1980s – fiscal stimulus of aggregate demand was a big factor in the recovery that began in late 1982 – and by the budget compromise of October 1990.

I do not know when the recession will end in the sense that growth of real GNP turns positive, and I do not think that event by itself will merit three cheers. It will be only the possible beginning of a recovery, whose continuation is by no means automatic. The Fed will have to manage, indeed fine-tune, a 1990s recovery as it did the 1980s recovery.

We should not put so much emphasis on whether the quarter-to-quarter change in real GNP is positive or negative. The arbiters at the National Bureau of Economic Research date the recession from July 1990, but the economy has been in a slowdown or 'growth recession' much longer. Right now we are in the eighth quarter of real GNP growth below an annual rate of 2 per cent. Normal growth of labour force and productivity permits the economy to grow at an annual rate between 1 and 2.5 per cent without reducing unemployment rates and other measures of excess capacity. For nearly two years we have been adding to the slack in the economy, raising the gap between actual and potential output to about 5 per cent.

Almost all US recessions since 1945 have been deliberately provoked by monetary policies designed to arrest and reduce inflation. This one is an exception, because inflation had stayed throughout the 1980s in the range the Fed found acceptable when Volcker and his colleagues turned the economy around in 1982. Since wage and price inflation are still well behaved, I see no reason to prolong this recession by a new anti-inflation crusade.

3.   Does the current structure and condition of financial intermediaries impede the transmission of monetary policy to the real economy?

The caution of commercial banks impedes the transmission but does not prevent it. The result is that monetary policy must be easier, and the discount and Federal Funds rates lower, to have the same effects on the availability of credit to business and household borrowers and on the rates banks and other lenders charge. The differentials of those lending rates above the costs of funds to the banks have risen. The prime rate is now 300 basis points above the Federal Reserve discount rate, twice as large a differential as in the late

1980s. The prime rate exceeds the three-month Certificate of Deposit rate by as much as it did in the depths of recession in 1982. Nevertheless, as basic money market rates fall, bank lending rates and long-term bond rates do come down.

As banks seek to raise their capital ratios – and many of them are quite properly under pressure from regulators to do so – they have to increase the margin between their lending rates and the rates they offer depositors. As some of their borrowers and depositors respond by moving to the open market or to other financial intermediaries, the banks shrink their assets and liabilities and improve their capital ratios. The wider margins also give them the opportunity to earn profits and add to their capital. The central bank can mitigate the effects on banks' borrowing customers by providing banks with more reserve funds at lower costs.

It should not be thought that all the borrowers shed by banks as they seek to raise their capital ratios are necessarily deprived of credit. The same process also moves depositors out of banks, and the two sides may get together in the open market or on the balance sheets of non-bank intermediaries.

4. Should the Federal Open Market Committee (FOMC), as currently constituted, be the forum for making monetary policy decisions; if not, what changes, if any, would you recommend in the FOMC or the procedures used by the Federal Reserve to make monetary policy?

I guess the current concern about the constitution of the FOMC is related to recent press reports of dissension between Federal Reserve Bank Presidents and the Board of Governors, its Chairman in particular. I do have serious doubts of the democratic legitimacy of the powers of the Presidents as members of FOMC. But I would emphasize that those doubts are not the consequence of any presumption that the Bank Presidents will be systematically more or less monetarist or more or less hawkish about inflation than the Chairman and other Governors. (Further comment on Federal Reserve governance occurs in Chapter 15 below.)

BRING THE DOLLAR DOWN (*New York Times*, 24 March 1991)

Victory in the Gulf dissipated some of the clouds, but the February jump in unemployment shows that the economy is still in trouble. Can the Government lift the country out of recession?

In recessions, spending by consumers and businesses declines; demand for goods and services falls short of the economy's capacity to supply them.

Businesses lose markets. Workers lose jobs. Normally, federal fiscal and monetary policies can increase demand. Both have been used for this purpose in almost all business cycles since 1945. Why not now?

Fiscal remedies are simple. The Government steps up its own spending, or taxes are cut to enable taxpayers to spend more. Ronald Reagan gave the economy an overdose of fiscal tonic. Ironically, his Administration disavowed such 'demand-side' policies and billed its budgets not as anti-recession medicine but as supply-side incentives to boost long-run growth. However labelled, the military buildup and tax cuts did stimulate demand. But the exploding Federal debt that resulted has virtually ruled out use of anti-recession fiscal measures today.

With fiscal policy sidelined, the task now falls wholly on monetary policy – the province of the Federal Reserve. By lowering interest rates and expanding credit, the Fed can promote recovery. It has already cut the Federal Funds rate (what banks charge one another for overnight loans) by three and a half points since mid 1989. Why not cut it further?

There are three excuses: the abnormal caution of banks, the inflation danger and the need for foreign capital to finance the trade deficit.

To fight recessions, the Fed supplies banks with more cash reserves and cheaper credit; then the banks usually lend more to their customers on easier terms. The present credit 'crunch', it is argued, makes banks unresponsive to Fed policies. Banks are now unusually cautious, troubled by the bad loans on their books and struggling to comply with stiffer capital requirements. This caution shows up in higher interest rates for borrowers relative to market rates on Federal Funds and other safe assets.

The lesson for the Fed is simply to cut the interest rates on safe assets more than usual. There is ample room between today's 6 per cent and zero. Banks will use additional reserves if the Fed supplies them.

Central bankers always fear that excessive zeal against recession will ignite inflation. Their nightmare is a spiral like that of the 1970s, in which increases in wages and prices fed on each other. But the risk of a spiral looks negligible now. Price inflation remains moderate, despite recent wiggles in the indexes. Labour's bargaining position is weak, and wage gains are puny. Inflation is no barrier to a vigorous fight against recession.

A third alleged obstacle to anti-recession monetary policy is concern for the dollar. Pessimists say the Fed is trapped because cuts in US interest rates could lead investors to move funds into foreign currencies with higher rates. We need to keep capital flowing in to finance our trade deficit. If the inflow slows, the dollar falls. The worriers say the Fed must gear interest rates and monetary policy to the foreign exchange rate, not to the American economy.

At the moment, this is no problem. Since the Gulf victory, foreign money has flooded our markets and the dollar has soared. Furthermore, market expectations of increases in Germany's and Japan's interest rates have abated. All the more reason for the Fed to lower US rates further, trying to bring the dollar down.

Dollar depreciation is good medicine for a country suffering from a recession and a trade deficit. It stimulates exports and slows imports. Further declines in the trade deficit would help mightily to arrest and reverse the recession, supplementing traditional channels of monetary influence. Lower interest rates and easier credit stimulate demands for machinery and plants, home-building and consumer durable goods.

A lower dollar will reduce our trade deficit relative to GNP, but not soon eliminate it. What will attract money to finance it if our interest rates are too low? The answer lies in expectations that the dollar exchange rate will rise, relative to what it is.

What would create such an expectation? The dollar would have to fall first, enough to make the market believe it would subsequently rise. This would be a rational expectation, because in response to the low dollar our trade deficit would gradually decline, the more so if at the same time we took fundamental steps to improve our productivity.

The recession can be fought. We are not up a creek without a paddle.

13. Remarks on international considerations for US monetary policy in the near term*

These remarks were made in a panel discussion which was the afternoon session of a Colloquium at the Federal Reserve Bank of New York, 13 October 1989, presided over by the President of the Bank, E. Gerald Corrigan.

The panel discussion began shortly after the onset of a sharp drop in the US stock market, a development mentioned by some of the panelists in their remarks. The market closed that afternoon down 191 points on the Dow Jones Industrial Average, its sharpest one-day decline since October 1987.

In opening the session, Mr Corrigan asked the panelists to answer three questions in the course of their remarks. First, is a current account deficit of two or three per cent of GNP (roughly the range in which the US external deficit has fallen over the last several years) sustainable in the long term? Second, what course for US monetary policy would the panelists choose if they were responsible for that policy? And third, in that context, what should be the longer term goals for US monetary policy?

The topic of this panel, as the Chairman said, is the bearing on current US monetary policy of the country's external finances and the dollar exchange rate. Since I have heard many references to teaching models in this room, I want to admit at the outset that the model with which I think about these things is the model that I teach. It's the only one I know.

I have an old-fashioned preference for economic models over statistical time series models. I do not think of the exchange rate as white noise.

Monetary policy *is* exchange rate policy. It's not just exchange rate policy, because it does a lot of other things. But monetary policy, under the present regime of floating exchange rates and mobility of financial capital, is exchange rate policy. Moreover, nowadays one of the principal channels of transmission of monetary policy to the domestic economy is the trade balance.

*First published in *Colloquium on International Financial Integration and the US Monetary Policy*, Federal Reserve Bank of New York, 1989.

By widening the difference between local and foreign interest rates, the monetary authorities induce a change in the exchange rate. Interest differentials bring short-run movements in exchange rates relative to longer-run expectations of exchange rates, expectations related to the fundamentals of the real exchange rate and the viable long-run imbalance. The latter is not necessarily zero but whatever is consistent with lasting differences among the trading nations in saving, investment and absorption. Normally we count on the policy-induced movements of the exchange rate to set up exchange rate expectations that compensate, at least partly, for interest differentials. For the normal scenario to work, portfolio managers need to have expectations of future exchange rates that are relatively inelastic with respect to the current rate. Extrapolative expectations spell instability and trouble. Even in the normal case, of course, revisions of evaluations of future fundamentals are a source of variations in the current exchange rates, only loosely related to current monetary policies.

Can sterilized intervention work? As a portfolio theorist, I say yes in principle, because the assets that the central bank exchanges for its money in the two open-market operations aren't exactly the same. But they are probably fairly close substitutes, and it may be true, as economists usually say, that the effects are only transitory or episodic. The Group of Seven (G7) often does influence the course of exchange rates. Perhaps the reason is not simply its sterilized interventions but the threat of unsterilized interventions, thus the threat of changing interest differentials.

I do not expect monetary policies and the interest rate changes they bring about usually to make exchange rates 'jump' the way the stock market moved this afternoon. That's unusual for the stock market too. Despite finance theory, financial markets generally take time to absorb news. Consequently, it is always difficult to know where the markets stand relative to their ultimate adjustments. But as I read about the exchange markets from day to day, it seems market participants themselves surely believe that exchange rates are related to interest rate differentials.

The question before us right now is whether international considerations suggest a monetary policy different from one wholly oriented to the American economy. Of course, any monetary policy necessarily takes account of effects transmitted to the domestic economy via the balance of payments. While I do not exclude on principle that the exchange rate or other external variables should sometimes have an independent influence on monetary policy, I don't see that now is one of those times.

Now be prepared, Jerry Corrigan, for praise of Federal Reserve policy from an unusual source. Since 1982 the Fed has fine-tuned extremely well. You kept the recovery going – maybe a little slowly for two years from mid 1984 – and achieved a lower rate of unemployment than almost all economists in this room thought inflation-safe ten years ago. Inflation remains steady at the 5 per cent rate you succeeded in convincing the country is zero. Your success came not from sticking to a rule for any single instrument or intermediate aggregate, ignoring feedback from observations and predictions of the course of the economy, but from eclectic and pragmatic responses to information as it developed and from watching all dimensions of economic performance, prices, real growth and unemployment.

The economy is now in the neoclassical phase of a Keynesian business cycle. The Fed can reasonably regard employment as full, considering the risk that lower rates of unemployment would not be inflation-safe. Your present domestic strategy is doubtless to maintain this equilibrium, avoiding both recession and overheating. 'Steady as you go' may take a lower interest rate and a lower exchange rate, or a higher interest rate and a higher dollar, or sometimes one and sometimes the other.

Unfortunately, the economy has little room for improvement in net exports. The small share of net exports in the extra GNP from 2.5 per cent real growth is not a big improvement in a $100 billion current account deficit. Faster improvement would require curtailment of domestic demands to make room. Reducing our foreign disinvestment would have to 'crowd out' domestic investment or government purchases or private consumption.

The ideal solution would be a miraculous surge in the national saving rate of the United States. Then the Fed could and should ease, lowering interest rates to encourage both domestic investment and, via exchange depreciation, net exports. Tight fiscal policy is, of course, the instrument that might bring an increase in national saving without a spontaneous miracle. But it is still barred by demagogic politics. Indeed, the President and Congress seem more likely to move in the wrong direction in the coming election year. Their competition to lower taxes – déjà voodoo all over again – has probably been deferred, not abandoned.

If the macro climate permitted lower interest rates and dollar depreciation, should the Federal Reserve forgo such a policy on the grounds that depreciation is *per se* inflationary? I think not. The price implications of a depreciation should not be an obstacle to a policy desirable for domestic economic performance. A one-shot increase in dollar prices of internationally traded goods is not a problem in a general climate of stable inflation, where there is little danger of a secondary wave of wage and price increases.

Nor should the Fed be scared of depreciation itself in those circumstances. Indeed a jump down, preparatory to a rise, would be a desirable outcome of a low interest rate policy responding to recession or to fiscal tightening or to increased private saving. While the low level of the exchange rate was improving the trade balance, the expectation of its appreciation would be pulling in the funds to match the continuing, though declining, current account deficit.

Eventually, I suspect, international equilibrium will require a lower dollar. I am alarmed by the combination of political and economic circumstances that traps us into a higher dollar than the likely eventual equilibrium. What could we do if there were a loss of foreign confidence that would require a higher United States interest rate to prevent depreciation? The best of unpleasant alternatives might be to let the dollar fall but be ready to tighten monetary policy if net exports started rising too quickly. Recession provoked by tight money is another alternative, recommended by many critics of American profligacy at home and abroad. But the marginal propensity to import is just not big enough to allow a normal recession to rectify the trade imbalance, especially if it is triggered by an interest rate policy that keeps the exchange rate high.

Many Americans believe the solution to our external deficit is macroeconomic expansion abroad, especially in Europe. Once again, marginal import propensities are too low to enable such expansion to substitute in any large degree for exchange rate adjustment. Even so, it would be a contribution to eventual American and world adjustment. But at present our economy does not have room for expansion of demand for US output from this source any more than from any other.

Our present fiscal policy is not viable in the long run. Both federal debt and the nation's net foreign debt may rise explosively if we continue to have so low a national saving rate and so high a real interest rate relative to our growth rate.

I have spoken of US monetary policy without mentioning any constraints upon it imposed by international coordination of macroeconomic policies. That is not because of nationalistic disdain for policy coordination. Unfortunately, what passes for coordination these days is agreement in the G7 on a range of exchange rates for an indefinite short term. That is putting the cart before the horse. There is no agreement on the various national policies that would support those rates. It may be fruitful to smooth speculative fluctuations and to use sterilized interventions to steer the exchange markets towards equilibrium. But it is certainly not constructive to alter basic monetary policies to sustain non-viable exchange rates.

If there were genuine policy coordination in the G7, then surely for its part the United States would be expected to tighten fiscal policy, increase national saving and lower real interest rates. That is exactly what we should do for our own good anyway. But our President and his Secretary of the Treasury cannot promise it as long as they are prisoners of the nine most momentous words uttered by any US President in the last 20 years: namely, 'make my day' and 'read my lips, no new taxes'.

In the absence of explicit coordination the world average level of interest rates will be left to chance and to the markets of greatest weight. Not every country can gear its monetary policy solely to its interest rate difference with the others. One reason the US monetary policy-making role may still look so much the same as before 1973 is that the Federal Reserve has effectively 50 per cent or more of the powers of the world's central banks. The agenda of policy coordination would include the world level of interest rates and the question whether adjustments to imbalances should be made by raising interest rates here or lowering them there or both.

14. Statement on Federal Reserve reform proposals*

The most important decisions of macroeconomic management in the United States, and indeed the world, are made by the Federal Reserve. For good or ill, its monetary policies determine the path of the American economy and strongly influence other economies throughout the world. Interest rates, stock and bond prices, exchange rates, trade balances, inflation rates, GNP growth and unemployment rates, to mention only the most important variables, depend on the Fed's actions. The meetings of the Federal Open Market Committee (FOMC), held eight times a year, are the world's most decisive regular deliberations on government economic policy.

Of course, many other government policies have substantial economic effects. They concern taxes, regulations, public investments, transfer programmes, commercial policies and other familiar items on the agenda of Congress. For the long run, these may be more substantial than anything the Fed can do. But for management of aggregate demand in the short run, for stabilization of the economy against cyclical fluctuations, for avoidance of recessions and inflations, the Fed's monetary policies are virtually all the federal government has.

In the past, fiscal policies, as embodied in the overall demand-side impact of the federal budget, could be regarded coequal to monetary policies. But the extreme deficit-spending policies of the 1980s have effectively ended the possibility of using the budget as an instrument of short-term stabilization. Instead it has become an unwelcome fixture of the environment in which the Fed makes monetary policy.

The proposed reform legislation, H.R. 3512, raises a fundamental issue of democratic government. The issue is: should the makers of the most important economic policy decisions of the federal government be so far removed from responsibility to the electorate as is the FOMC?

When the Federal Reserve System was founded in 1913, it was envisaged as an important financial reform and as insurance against financial panics, not as an agency controlling the whole economy. Even in 1935, when the cur-

*Presented at House Committee on Banking, Finance and Urban Affairs Subcommittee on Domestic Monetary Policy, 9 November 1989.

rently governing legislation was enacted, no one imagined the decisive economic role the System has now come to play. Indeed in those days the federal government altogether was not assigned the responsibility for macroeconomic performance now taken for granted.

The FOMC has 12 members, seven Governors and five Federal Reserve Bank Presidents. Also present at the meetings and participating in the discussions are the seven Presidents who at the time are not voting members. (Membership rotates among the Banks, although not equally. The New York President always has a vote and the Chicago and Cleveland Banks have votes in alternate years; the others are two years off and one year on.) Nobody besides these Federal Reserve officials and their staffs attends the meetings.

The 14-year terms of the Governors can perpetuate the influence of the Presidents who appointed them long after the Presidents themselves have left office. There may be as few as two appointments in a Presidential term, two of 12 members of the decision-making body, the FOMC. Usually there are more, because Governors resign before their terms are up and the tenures of their replacements are limited to the time remaining in the 14-year terms. A case can be made, I think, for reducing the terms to ten years and the size of the Board of Governors to five. This subject is not addressed in H.R. 3512.

H.R. 3512 proposes to rectify at long last the timing of the four-year term as Chairman of the Governor so designated by the President. The timing is now accidental. No one intended that the President should wait for 30 or 40 of the 48 months of his term before choosing, with the advice and consent of the Senate, a Federal Reserve Chairman. The timing is accidental, because the 1935 Act provides that a new Chairman shall serve for four years from date of appointment. Future accidents might shift the time again, maybe nearly to the end of the Presidential term, maybe to just after inauguration. It is surely a good idea to set the time rationally and permanently, and to allow for some overlap into the new Administration. Six months seems to me long enough, but one year, as the Bill provides, would work well too.

The major violation of democratic legitimacy is the power of the Presidents of the district Federal Reserve Banks. Although they participate in definitive votes on crucial economic policy, they are neither appointed nor approved by elected officials in either executive or legislative branches of government. Technically, legally, the Banks are private corporations owned by the member banks of the district. Thus the Presidents are selected by the Directors of the Banks, subject however to the approval of the Board of Governors. In practice, experience suggests, the Chairman can have considerable influence. In keeping with the legal fiction, the Bank Presidents are paid like private bank executives rather than federal officials. Appointed for renewable five-year terms, they generally have long tenures.

The Bank Presidents should not have it both ways. The regional information and perspective the Bank Presidents can bring to the FOMC doubtless have value. But if they vote like Governors, they should be appointed (and paid!) like Governors. They should be appointed by the President of the United States with the advice and consent of the Senate. The District Bank Board of Directors could make nominations, the Chairman and other Governors likewise. If the Bank Presidents are appointed (and paid) as they are now, then they should be allowed to attend the FOMC meetings but not to vote.

I believe it is important that the Administration has the opportunity to explain its economic strategy and outlook to the Fed. It is important because the President and his Administration have the ultimate responsibility to the nation for economic performance. Direct relationships to Federal Reserve actions arise from the Treasury's responsibilities for public debt management and for international financial and monetary relations. I would go further than H.R. 3512, and provide that the three executive branch officials – Treasury Secretary, Council of Economic Advisers Chairman, and Office of Management and Budget Director – participate without votes in FOMC meetings. There should be communications between them and the whole FOMC, not just the Chairman. These should occur routinely at the regular action meetings of the FOMC, not just three times a year. If the parts of those meetings at which votes are taken exclude non-voting participants, they should exclude the non-voting Bank Presidents as well as the Executive officials.

The proposals of H.R. 3512, and my somewhat stronger proposals, are quite modest. They leave the Federal Reserve with considerable independence of the Executive, much more than most other central banks. Nevertheless they are condemned as bringing politics to bear on monetary policy. Politics? In a representative democracy? Think of it! Economic performance necessarily involves political choices; it is hard to imagine issues of greater moment.

Consider, for example, the two big Federal Reserve policy decisions of the last ten years. In 1979 Paul Volcker and his colleagues decided to restrict money growth and bring about recession in order to overcome the inflation accompanying the second oil shock and the Iranian revolution. That policy eventually brought unemployment nearly to 11 per cent and plunged many firms and financial institutions into bankruptcy. In late 1982 it was the Fed again that decided to suspend the anti-inflationary crusade and promote recovery although the inflation rate was still 5 per cent. I am not arguing here whether either decision was right or wrong. I do argue that policies of such economic and political gravity should not be adopted by the present FOMC all by itself.

Macroeconomic policy-making is a two-way street. Had there been more consultation about the mixture of fiscal and monetary policies between Federal Reserve and Administration in the early 1980s, we might have had a more moderate fiscal policy and a somewhat easier and lower-interest-rate monetary policy. That strategy would have been very advantageous to the nation.

I have little comment on the other provisions of H.R. 3512. I do not favour the provision mandating immediate announcement of Fed policy decisions. There are times, I think, when Fed monetary actions are the more effective for not being announced immediately. Moreover, the fact that every FOMC meeting leads to some action at a known date means that a great deal of speculative attention will focus in advance on those action dates. We know from the speculative frenzy that used to anticipate the weekly release of money stock data that such activity is not necessarily constructive or stabilizing. That is also evident from the continuing speculation on releases of many other macroeconomic data. I would let the Fed decide whether and when to make policy announcements prior to the present 45-day deadline.

I am strongly opposed to Congressional action mandating Fed anti-inflation targets. The country faces no crisis that justifies a new single-minded anti-inflationary crusade. Volcker's decision to declare victory over inflation in 1982 has turned out well, and has been generally accepted by the country. For all practical purposes 4 to 5 per cent inflation has been defined by general consensus as price stability. The Fed has successfully managed a long recovery, which has brought unemployment to lower rates than most observers ten years ago thought possible without triggering an inflation spiral. And now the Fed seems to be managing a 'soft landing', steering the economy between the Scylla of overheating and inflation and the Charybdis of recession. The Fed's successful fine-tuning since 1982 seems to me to be due to the pragmatism and eclecticism of its goals and its instruments. Let well enough alone.

Lowering inflation to zero in five years, as proposed, is bound to sacrifice output and jobs. Experience suggests that it probably involves recession, perhaps as deep as that of 1981–82. The country would enter this period of disinflation with unprecedented public and private debt, bearing interest rates geared to the stable 4 to 5 per cent inflation of recent years. At zero inflation, those debts would become very burdensome to businesses, stockholders and taxpayers.

The proposal relies on the abstract proposition that real economic outcomes – production and employment – are independent of nominal prices in dollars and of their rates of change. Therefore, it is over-confidently argued, disinflation is painless. The same argument was made in 1979, but the disinflation turned out to be quite painful. The proposition might be true in some hypothetical long run, but past recessions and recoveries demonstrate that it is not true in business cycles.

Should another supply shock hit, as in the 1970s, sticking to the commitment would be especially devastating to the economy. If the dollar depreciates further, as seems essential for significant progress on the trade deficit, inflation will appear to rise temporarily, and the Fed would be bound to impose additional monetary restrictions to meet the target.

It is true that the Federal Reserve, like any central bank, needs to maintain credibility that it will not promote or accommodate unlimited inflation, that the monetary system and the value of the dollar are not anchorless. The Fed has already established and maintained such credibility, long since. H.R. Res. 409 is not necessary for this purpose, and it is mischievous to the extent that failure to pass the resolution or to achieve its aims might be misinterpreted as indicative of inflationary policies.

PART III

Fiscal Policy

Part III   Fiscal Policy

In the 1990s the President and Congress are struggling with the fiscal legacies of the 1980s. Reaganomics, political gridlock, demographics and exploding health care costs combined to generate unprecedented and persistent federal budget deficits. Relative to gross domestic product, federal debt to the public doubled between 1980 and 1993 (from 26 per cent to 52 per cent in 1993). Many of the chapters in *Policies for Prosperity* discussed these developments, and here they are reviewed in Chapter 16.

On taking office in January 1993, the Clinton Administration inherited not only deficits and debt but also a weak economy not yet recovered from the 1990–91 recession. Part III discusses the difficulties of meeting these two challenges simultaneously.

One of the economy's two maladies dated from 1973, when growth in the economy's capacity to produce was slowed drastically. The problem was the stagnation of labour productivity, and therefore of real wages, disappointing and alienating American workers. In 1993 the new President sought measures to increase productivity over the long run: investments in public infrastructure, education and skill training, science and technology, and incentives for business investments in plant and equipment.

The second malady was of more recent origin: a large gap between actual and capacity GDP, of which persistent high unemployment was the major symptom. The remedy for that is more spending, whether for investment or consumption.

The coincidence of these two maladies, for which remedial prescriptions are quite different and even contradictory, created confusion and ambiguity in federal policy-making. Federal deficit reduction could contribute to solution of malady number one: inadequate long-run growth. Under favourable circumstances, deficit reduction would channel more of the country's resources into investment for the future. But deficit reduction can only be accomplished by measures that reduce somebody's spending on GDP goods and services, whether spending by government or by taxpayers. Therefore, with respect to problem number two, short-run demand deficiency, deficit reduction works in the wrong direction.

Public opinion and the political process find it difficult to cope with two macroeconomic problems at once, especially when the indicated therapy for one appears to be the opposite of the prescription for the other. The President started with a stimulus-now-deficit-cuts-later programme, but political logic forced him to concentrate solely on deficit reduction, now and later. Fortunately the economy recovered quite satisfactorily anyway. But the five-year deficit cuts in the Clinton budget, opposed by all Republicans in Congress, are only a beginning. Republicans gained majorities in both houses of Congress in the mid-term elections of 1994. They have committed themselves to reach a balanced budget in 2002 – with or without the spur of a Constitutional amendment requiring it (which so far has failed to pass the Senate but may pass later in 1995 or in 1996 before the Presidential election.) Reaganomics lives again, and political gridlock too, with the Presidency and Congress controlled by different parties, both proposing tax cuts and avoiding the daunting arithmetic of budget-balancing without butchering popular expenditure programmes or raising taxes.

In public and political discussion of these issues the relations of fiscal policy to current prosperity and future well-being usually get lost. In Chapters 17, 18, and especially 19, I try to clear the air.

15.   Legacies of Reaganomics*

The election of the Reagan–Bush ticket in 1980 brought drastic changes in US economic policies. By any historic measure, American elections are seldom revolutionary. Despite campaign rhetoric, when a President of the opposite party takes over he usually makes only cautious and gradual alterations in the courses selected by his predecessors. This was true from the election of Franklin Roosevelt in 1932 until 1980. Ronald Reagan's nomination as the Republican candidate in 1980, however, signalled the capture of the 'Grand Old Party' (GOP) by the ideological right wing of the party. George Bush had labelled Reagan's views as 'voodoo economics' as he competed for the 1980 nomination. When Reagan offered him the consolation prize of the Vice-Presidential nomination, Bush, a pragmatist with political ambitions and no strong convictions, was easily converted to Reaganomics and other tenets of conservative ideology.

After nearly three full Presidential terms of Reagan–Bush policies, now is a good time to assess the present state and the future prospects of the American economy. What are the legacies of Reaganomics?

THE 1980s BUSINESS CYCLE RECOVERY

President Reagan was inaugurated during a brief interlude between two recessions, one in 1979–80 (which helped him to win the election) and one in 1981–82. Both were the consequences of a determined crusade by Federal Reserve Chairman Paul Volcker to kill the inflationary dragon. Triggered by the second OPEC shock, which was accompanied by the Iranian revolution, inflation had hit double digits in 1979–80. Volcker's crusade pushed up unemployment to 9.7 per cent for the year 1982 – the highest since 1941 – and succeeded in bringing inflation down to about 5 per cent per year.

The central banks of other major economies were enthusiastic participants in the anti-inflationary crusade of 1979–82. The US recovered more promptly and more completely than either Europe or Japan. The Federal Reserve managed – one could say, fine-tuned – the 1982–89 recovery as it had

*First published in *Harvard International Review*, **XVI** (4), Summer 1992.

managed the prior recessions. Annual average US unemployment rates fell from 9.7 per cent in 1982 to 5.2 per cent in 1989, lower than the 5.8 per cent rate at 1979's cyclical peak in business activity. Eighteen million persons got jobs. By contrast, unemployment in Europe remained high, and even now has not fallen to the rates that prevailed before 1979 or the even lower rates customary prior to the first oil shock of 1973–74.

The deficit spending that resulted from Reagan's 1981 programme of tax cuts and defence buildup became a powerful demand stimulus beginning in 1983. Reagan's fiscal policy helped Volcker get a brisk recovery started – even though demand stimulus had not been a rationale for the Reagan pro- gramme. With Federal budget deficits soon reaching more than 5 per cent of GNP, Reagan budgets were the most massive Keynesian fiscal stimuli ever given to the US economy in peacetime, extending beyond what any con- sciously Keynesian Administration would have done. In effect, the fiscal policy gave the Fed too much help. To keep the economy from overheating, the Fed had to keep interest rates much higher than in normal cyclical recoveries.

Presidents are held politically responsible for poor macroeconomic per- formance during their tenure, even if they are not at fault, so naturally they deserve credit for good performance, even if they did not bring it about. The cyclical recovery of the 1980s was certainly welcome after the deep reces- sion, but it was nothing unusual – definitely nothing that could be attributed to the supply-side policies of Reaganomics. Between 1982 and 1988, just as in the recovery 20 years earlier between 1962 and 1968, non-farm payroll employment increased by 22 per cent. But the 1960s period saw a production increase of 31.5 per cent, while in the 1980s production rose by only 25.5 per cent. To the extent that Reagan fiscal policies contributed to recovery, it was not because they were supply-side measures but because they were demand stimuli. The same recovery could have been achieved by normal fiscal and monetary policies, with lower budget deficits and lower interest rates and without the unfortunate by-products of the fiscal and monetary policies that were actually followed.

VICTORY OVER INFLATION

An important beneficial legacy of the last 12 years is a stable, low inflation rate. The 1979–82 crusade was painful but successful. The subsequent recov- ery was achieved without escalation of inflation, which remained in the range of 4 to 5 per cent per year. In 1979, no economist would have predicted that a 5.5 per cent unemployment rate could be achieved ten years later without spiralling inflation. Like the period 1961–65, the period 1983–88 demonstrates that recovery from recession need not entail increasing inflation. In 1992, after three years of slowdown, recession and stagnation, inflation has fallen further to around 3 per cent per year.

What were the reasons for this achievement? The length and depth of the recessions of 1979–82, the Reagan political climate, the President's stern treatment of striking air controllers in 1981 and the persistent challenges of foreign competition brought important changes to labour relations. Trade unions dwindled in numbers and strength as employers became more assertive. Wage concessions and 'givebacks' of fringe benefits and work rules, which would have been unthinkable in the 1970s, have become commonplace. At the same time, the oil shocks that triggered inflation in the 1970s gave way to oil gluts. Relative to prices in general, gasoline is as cheap as it ever has been since World War II.

ECONOMIC SLOWDOWN 1989–92

George Bush had the misfortune of taking office when the recovery was ending. Again, the major culprit was the Federal Reserve. The Fed was afraid that momentum from the recovery would take demand too far, overheating the economy and causing new inflation. In 1988, Chairman Alan Greenspan and his colleagues began to tighten monetary policy, and it turned out that they overdid it. After the first quarter of 1989, the real growth of the economy fell below its sustainable rate of 2–2.5 per cent (normal labour force and productivity growth) and has stayed below that rate ever since. A 'growth recession' evolved into actual decline in the third quarter of 1990. Apparent signs of recovery in the second and third quarters of 1991 proved to be transient. A more robust recovery may begin in 1992, but this time the first year of recovery is likely to be weaker than usual and reduce unemployment very little.

Although the state of the economy by statistical measures is not nearly as depressed as in 1982, the mood of the country is more pessimistic and much angrier. Compared to 10.7 per cent in the 1982 trough, the current unemployment rate of 7.3 per cent does not adequately measure the degree of distress and discontent. Despite the recovery of the 1980s, workers' real take-home pay has actually been declining throughout the past two decades, not even keeping up with the low rate of productivity growth. Now, in addition, their jobs are in jeopardy.

The Fed did not begin to ease the money supply until the end of 1990, and until December 1991 its actions were consistently too little and too late. The public and private debts inherited from the 1980s today weigh heavily on governments, businesses, households and financial institutions. It is by no means certain that the Fed by itself can promote a vigorous recovery in this environment. Fiscal policy – deficit spending – has in past business cycles helped to stimulate demand and to fuel recovery. An unfortunate legacy of the chronic high budget deficits of the past decade is that fiscal policy is now crippled, virtually immobilized. Neither the President nor Congress wants to increase the deficit – even to get the economy moving again.

THE FAILURES OF SUPPLY-SIDE POLICIES

Reaganomics was supply-side economics. The tax cuts of 1981, sacrificing about 2.5 per cent of GNP, were intended as supply-side incentives that would release the shackled energies of the American people and encourage them to work harder, save more, invest more, start more entrepreneurial businesses and take more risks. The productive capacity of the economy would take off.

Supply side claims have been proven false by experience. The 'Laffer Curve' idea that tax cuts would actually increase revenues turned out to deserve the ridicule with which sober economists had greeted it in 1981. Net saving and investment declined to pitifully low rates. The tax incentives that were supposed to increase them were counter-productive because much of the revenue they gave away was spent in consumption. Tax incentives for real estate developments were disastrous. Coupled with ill-advised deregulation, they contributed to the collapse of federally insured savings and loan associations and commercial banks at enormous costs to taxpayers. Empty office buildings and condominiums will be haunting these markets for a decade. Tax laws, deregulation and the general climate of the era created a mania of corporate mergers, acquisitions and leveraged buy-outs, diverting entrepreneurial talent from production of goods and services to the 'paper economy' and leaving in their wake many dangerously debt-ridden companies.

The Reagan recovery of 1983–89 was largely a consumption and defence spending recovery. Although these uses took 70.2 per cent of real GNP in 1978, they took 73.4 per cent in 1988, a year of comparable cyclical prosperity. Consumption and defence devoured 84.8 per cent of the 32 per cent increment in constant-dollar GNP between 1978 and 1988. Thanks to budget deficits and high interest rates, capital investment was below par. Moreover, high interest rates in the US drew funds into the American financial markets, appreciated the dollar and made American goods uncompetitive at home and abroad. Trade deficits rose to 3 per cent of GNP, and their accumulation year after year made the US a debtor nation. The problem remains although the trade deficit is gradually declining in ratio to GNP.

Low growth in the productivity of labour is the main chronic failing of the US economy. It transcends business cycles and slows down economic and social progress in times of prosperity as well as during recessions, regardless of whether unemployment is low or high. It is, in fact, a much more difficult malady to cure than a cyclical recession. US economy-wide productivity growth is lower than growth in Japan, in Europe and in the rapidly emerging newly industrialized economies of Asia. At 1.0 to 1.5 per cent per year, it is considerably lower than the 2.5 to 3.0 per cent rates experienced in the first quarter-century after World War II.

The bottom line of supply-side policy is productivity growth. Although Reaganomics cannot be blamed for the slowdown that began around 1973, its well-advertised remedies were policy failures. Throughout the 1980s, productivity growth remained disappointingly low for the economy as a whole, though productivity in manufacturing began to revive under the spur of global competition. Overall, the recovery of the 1980s was not a recovery in efficiency, productivity, enterprise or competitiveness.

Growth in real wages cannot exceed labour productivity growth for very long. Recently, real wages have not even kept up. They have been stagnant or declining. The high interest rates resulting from Reagan deficits, paid by corporations on their increasing indebtedness, have apparently cut into the wage share of the national income.

During the last 12 years, consumption and defence commandeered resources that businesses and governments might have used for future investments: modern plants and equipment public infrastructure, research and development, environmental protection and education. Likewise, as a nation the US has acquired large debts to foreigners by importing more than it exported. One consequence of below-par productivity growth is that to be competitive internationally, Americans now must settle for a low value of the dollar and unfavourable terms of trade.

POVERTY AND INEQUALITY

The most ominous threat to the nation's future has been the persistence of poverty and the increasing inequalities of wealth, income and opportunity. Rapid progress in reducing the proportion of the population living in poverty (as measured by constant absolute real income thresholds adjusted for family size) diminished the proportion of persons living in poverty from 22 per cent in 1959 to 11 per cent in 1973. The major factors were the overall progress of the economy and government's 'war on poverty' programmes. But in the prosperous year 1989, the rate was 13 per cent and rising. Twenty per cent of American children, and 45 per cent of black American children, live in poor households. The economy-wide slowdown since 1973 is one culprit; the erosion of governmental anti-poverty transfers and programmes is another.

The increasing poverty of urban neighbourhoods is a national disaster. These neighbourhoods are caught in a vicious downward spiral, in which each of the several pathologies accentuate the others: drugs, guns, homicide, crime, broken families, teenage pregnancies, unemployment and unemploy-ability, ineffective schools, high morbidity and mortality. We are failing in the primary task of a civilized society: to socialize its young so as to perpetuate its civilization.

These problems are formidable, especially because they are bound inextri-cably to the old American dilemma – the status of black Americans. Those of us who do not live in poverty-impacted neighbourhoods or in poverty may well prefer to ignore and to forget the victims, but must not. While 'throwing money at the problems' will not by itself solve them, neither will a failure to provide funds improve the situation. It is really up to the President to make their solution a task of the highest priority, and neither Reagan nor Bush undertook such leadership.

Income inequality has increased since 1980. The income share of the lowest quintile of families fell from 5.1 per cent to 4.6 per cent in 1989, while the share of the highest quintile rose from 41.6 per cent to 44.6 per cent. The income share of the top 5 per cent alone rose from 15.3 to 17.9 per cent. American business executives are paid much more relative to the wages of production workers than their Japanese counterparts. The affluent did ex-tremely well in the 1980s and their taxes were cut at the same time. Their lifestyles are celebrated on TV and paraded before the poor kids who have no hope for their own lives. Can a society with such visible extremes hold together? In America, anarchy and mindless violence are more likely reac-tions than organized political revolt.

THE LACK OF PUBLIC FUNDS

The public sector is impoverished. A principal objective of Reagan and his conservative supporters was to deprive government of budgetary resources. They succeeded. The federal deficits generated by their tax cuts and defence spending still inhibit civilian spending.

Reagan and Bush flourished politically by cutting taxes and by promising never to raise them. They could not quite keep that promise, but they made it politically impossible for Democrats in Congress or Democratic Presidential aspirants to propose tax increases that a Republican President would veto. The American government taxes its people less than any other major capital-ist democracy. 'Peace dividends' made possible by the end of the Cold War might be expected to relax budgetary stringency, but the Pentagon and the Bush Administration resisted substantial cuts in military spending by ingeniously discovering new threats in the world. In these hard times, they gain allies from politicians in the constituencies that are most dependent on defence contracts. In any case, there is great political pressure from the Republican Right to use peace dividends for still further tax cuts, in addition to understandable pressure from financial circles and from economists to use them to reduce the deficit. There may be nothing left for other claims, domestic or international, on America's resources.

After paying for defence, debt interest and veterans' benefits, 1978 federal receipts (other than payroll taxes and contributions earmarked for social insurance) were sufficient to pay for non-defence discretionary programmes equal to 5.4 per cent of GNP. Ten years later this figure had declined to 2.1 per cent. The actual non-defence discretionary outlays were larger by the amounts of deficit spending in the two years: 2.2 per cent of GNP in 1978 and 3.2 per cent in 1988. Current five-year federal budget projections hold little hope for increasing discretionary spending, domestic or international, as a proportion of GNP even though the 1997 deficit is projected to be no lower than 3.0 per cent of GNP and the defence share of GNP is supposed to decline by three percentage points.

The civilian public sector is mainly the province of states and local governments. Their finances are fiscal disasters. National and local economic difficulties have cut their revenues and increased the need for their social services. The federal government has assigned them greater responsibilities while cutting back their grants in aid. Reagan–Bush demagoguery on taxes has infected state and local politics and hamstrings those governments as well. Altogether, this wealthy country pleads 'lack of funds' in the face of the host of domestic needs neglected since 1980. Among them are public investments in education, research, transportation, infrastructure and environmental protection. These are important for future productivity. It is false economy to sacrifice them either to deficit reduction or to the politics of 'no new taxes' or to interest groups benefiting from wasteful government expenditure or tax privileges.

Leadership does not mean being number one in some world economic Olympics. Japan and Germany do not threaten us by competing with our automobile or electronics industry or by having now or in the future (by some measures) higher wages or higher standards of living. Their success should be a matter of pride for us, since it began with the humane and far-sighted assistance we gave them after World War II and continued under the international trading and financial institutions we took initiatives to establish.

America needs to accelerate its productivity, not because other countries have become more productive but because we will be better off ourselves.

Faster productivity growth will make us more competitive, it is true, but we would want it for its own sake even if we were not having problems in foreign trade.

The United States after World War II found the resources to live up to its stature as the leader of the world. Today we are again, geopolitically and militarily, the unchallenged world leader. But our own political leaders, unlike the statesmen of the 1940s and 1950s, have turned this nation economically into a pitiful, helpless giant, incapable of finding the funds needed to help democratic reforms and economic reconstruction in Eastern Europe and the former Soviet Union or to take any other initiatives towards a 'new world order'.

Our country's commitment to free trade has been the casualty of our trade deficits in the last 12 years, thus a casualty of the fiscal and monetary policies that led to such large and persistent deficits. Some Congressional Democrats, abandoning the historical position of their party, became outright protectionists. Presidents Reagan and Bush, while talking free trade, have actually multiplied our non-tariff barriers to imports competing with domestic businesses and our unilateral retaliations and threats against foreign competitors and their governments. We are on the edge of a trade war with Japan and Europe. The United States should instead be leading the world to a new regime of internationally agreed and respected rules of the game.

16. Statement on the federal budget deficit*

The federal budget deficit is by now an old and tiresome subject, on which virtually nothing new can be said. I have organized my remarks as answers to seven questions which frequently come up in current discussions.

1.   Is it really important to reduce the federal deficit? If so, why?

No catastrophe has yet occurred, no day of sudden and final reckoning. Instead we are enjoying a long non-inflationary recovery, which has brought unemployment rates lower than almost all economists thought possible ten years ago. The recovery, it is important to understand, is a *demand-side* success. It has been skilfully managed, one could say 'fine-tuned', by the Federal Reserve. Although the Reagan tax cuts and defence buildup stimulated demand for goods and services and for labour, they were not essential to the recovery. As I shall explain later, the Fed could have managed the same recovery with a more normal fiscal policy implying much lower budget deficits.

The recovery has been a supply-side disappointment. The 15 per cent increase in employment since 1982 did not produce a lot of output, only a 26 per cent increase in real GNP. (In 1961–67 a 13 per cent increase in employment yielded a 33 per cent gain in output.) Productivity growth has not revived from its post-1973 slump; from 1948 to 1973 it was 2.8 per cent per year, and now it remains at 1 or 1.5 per cent. Real wages generally advance with productivity, but lately they have not even done that well. Productivity growth is the bottom line of supply-side policies, and so far they have failed this test.

Chronic large budget deficits, run in prosperities as well as in recessions, are bad supply-side policies. They work against the productivity growth this country needs to compete in world markets while yielding the steady gains in real wages and living standards that Americans expect from their economy.

That is why I continue to say that deficit reduction deserves highest priority. I say so not because I expect the growth of federal debt to bring a

*Presented to the Ways and Means Committee of the House of Representatives, 7 February 1989.

147

disastrous financial and economic crash like 1932–33. The consequences are gradual and insidious, an erosion of the growth of the productivity of American labour. The costs fall on our children and our children's children more than on us. Our fiscal profligacy means that they will be able to produce and consume less.

The reason is that our rate of national saving and investment is pitifully and shamefully low. I refer to *net* rather than gross saving and investment and compare them to net rather than gross national product. The net figures exclude capital consumption, depreciation and obsolescence, which any prudent business or household would leave out in estimating its income and saving. National saving consists of non-federal (household, business, state and local) saving plus federal saving (a negative number when the federal government is running a deficit).

Non-federal net saving is roughly 6 per cent of net national product (NNP) nowadays; before this decade, the post-war norm was 8 to 9 per cent. When federal dissaving of around 4 per cent is subtracted, we have an overall national saving rate of 2 per cent. The pre-1980 post-war norm was 8 per cent. Domestic capital investment is down from 8 per cent to 6 per cent. It is as high as 6 per cent, while national saving is only 2 per cent, only because we have been borrowing 4 per cent of NNP from foreigners.

Between 1978, a normal prosperous year, and 1987, real NNP (in 1982 prices) increased by $597 billion – 22 per cent. Personal consumption and government purchases rose by $736 billion – 29 per cent. Real net domestic and foreign investment, the remaining major categories of uses of national product, actually declined. The increase in personal consumption alone was 94 per cent of the increase in net output. In a similar comparison for the previous decade, consumption took only 87 per cent of a (larger) increase in output, and consumption and government purchases combined only 91 per cent, leaving 9 per cent for net domestic and foreign investment.

I shall not rehearse the dreary international comparisons which show how low United States national saving and investment rates are relative to those of our major allies and competitors in Japan and Western Europe. Here is one dramatic figure to bear in mind: While US and Japanese fiscal deficits are about the same proportions of NNP, ours takes nearly two-thirds of the net saving of the rest of the economy, the Japanese only one-fifth.

Our profligacy is depriving future Americans of tools and technologies that could augment their productivity, while saddling them with onerous obligations to foreign creditors and owners.

2.   But isn't the deficit overstated?

There are various ways of calculating the deficit, and some of them would give lower figures in dollars. My friend Robert Eisner and Northwestern University is even able to find the federal government in surplus. He also defines private saving and investment in ways that increase their amounts.

I believe these questions of definition and measurement are mostly irrelevant to the issues of fiscal policy before the Congress, the President and the people today. My reason is this: whatever measure you use, there has been a big decline in both federal and national saving in the 1980s. Whatever measure you use, United States saving and investment is extremely low relative to other advanced capitalist democracies.

There may be merit in capital budgeting, although the treatment of land, military capital and depreciation present formidable problems of estimation and interpretation. There is merit in inflation accounting, although recent experience can give us scant confidence that bondholders automatically save extra amounts to make up for erosion in the purchasing power of their bonds. But whatever merits there are, these same points had equal or greater merit before 1980. They cannot erase the fact that the federal government became much less thrifty, much more profligate, in the 1980s.

In one important way the federal deficit is *under*stated today. The 'unified deficit', on which official attention is still focused, does not count the increase in Treasury obligations to social security beneficiaries. I shall return to this matter later.

3.   The federal debt now is smaller relative to GNP than it was after World War II until 1963, but those were years of prosperity and rapid growth. If we could handle a debt of that magnitude then, why not now?

There are three big differences. First, in 1946–62 deficits were much smaller and the growth of GNP much greater. The debt/GNP ratio was steadily declining. In the 1980s, for the first time in peacetime, the ratio has been rising. Second, non-federal savings were much more plentiful. There was lots of room in the economy for investment, without resorting to foreign borrowing. We had export surpluses; our overseas wealth was increasing. It is now declining. Third, interest rates, both nominal and real, were low. Service of the debt was a smaller burden, even though the debt itself was relatively bigger.

4.   Why are interest rates higher now?

First let me just establish the fact that they are. As we have often been told, interest rates have come down dramatically in the 1980s. They were sky high in 1980, when the Federal Reserve, determined to subdue inflation, drasti-

Fiscal policy

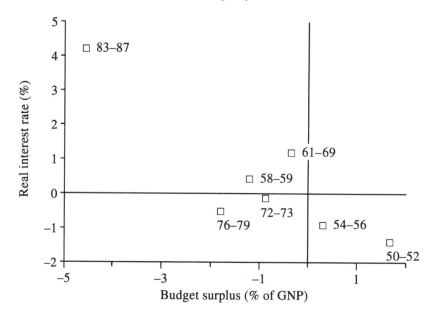

Figure 16.1 Budget surplus and real interest: seven recoveries, 1950–87

cally restricted the supply of money and threw the economy into recession. That brief episode is not relevant to our analysis of fiscal policy. The revealing comparison is of real interest rates in the recovery 1983 to date and in previous business cycle recoveries. This is shown in Figure 16.1, where it is clear that the 1980s recovery stands apart, with outsize deficits and outsize real interest rates.

The mechanism is clear. The Federal Reserve has been trying to keep the economy on a track of non-inflationary economic growth. After the 1979–82 recessions, this meant growth of aggregate demand enough to keep up with the annual increases in the labour force and its productivity (together about 2.5 per cent these days) *plus* enough to reduce unemployment and excess plant capacity at a prudent pace. Now that unemployment and excess capacity are close to their inflation-safe minima, that second, recovery, component of demand growth is no longer available. (For that reason, Reagan Administration budget projections that contemplate real GNP growth in excess of 3 per cent, combined with 200 basis points declines in interest rates, are not credible.) In any case, since high-deficit fiscal policy has been contributing a big push to demand, via high defence spending and low taxes stimulating consumption, the Fed has had to keep interest rates high in order to avoid overheating the economy.

High interest rates feed back into higher deficits. That can turn into a vicious circle. If debt interest rates exceed the growth of the economy, the debt will grow faster than GNP even if the budget is balanced on non-interest transactions. Right now we are close to this threshold. With real growth confined to 2.5 per cent and inflation at 5 per cent, GNP in dollars can grow at 7.5 per cent, about the same as the interest rate on government obligations net of taxes paid on such interest. By the same token, substantive cuts in the deficit would be rewarded by a bonus in savings of debt interest. Contrary to the wishful thinking we sometimes hear, the bonus has to be earned by tax increases or cuts in non-interest expenditures.

5. Would cutting the deficit now cause recession?

No, it certainly need not have that result. Given reasonable notice, the Fed can offset with lower interest rates withdrawals of demand due to budget cuts or tax increases. New demand would come from domestic investment and from greater exports and/or lower imports. Improvements in the trade balance may already be in the cards, lagged responses to the substantial declines in the dollar since 1985. Eventual trade balance will probably require further dollar depreciation, which could be a natural result of the reductions in US interest rates that would be the welcome by-product of serious deficit reduction.

The economy and its helmsman, Alan Greenspan at the Fed, face greater hazards if nothing is done about the deficit. Given the low dollar and the possibility that markets will push it lower, production of exports and import-competing goods should be increasing. Given the high degree of capacity utilization, domestic investment should be strong. But now there is not much room in the economy for these desirable claims on resources. In the absence of fiscal measures to lower private and public consumption, the Fed is likely to see overheating and inflation as the principal danger. Monetary restriction, if overdone, could lead to high interest rates, recession and an uncompetitively appreciated dollar. Our adjustment to the imbalances of the 1980s would be further postponed.

6. Do we need new taxes?

Yes, definitely, in my opinion. I say 'yes' for two reasons. One is to lower the deficit. The other is to finance essential and desirable expenditures not now in the budget.

It is still unreasonable to count on growing out of the deficit. The 'total deficit' for fiscal year 1989 is projected by the Congressional Budget Office (CBO) to be 3 per cent of GNP. Even if real outlays (inclusive of interest) are held to increases of 2 per cent per year while real revenues and GNP grow at the economy's sustainable rate of 2.5 per cent, the deficit/GNP ratio will decline only by one-tenth of a percentage point per year.

It is especially unreasonable in view of the compelling new claims on the budget now being recognized: the rescue of the Federal Savings and London Insurance Corporation, burdened by epidemic failures of insured thrift institutions; the repair of nuclear weapons facilities; deferred maintenance and expansion of the nation's infrastructure in transportation and public health; education from infancy to graduate training and research; the 'war' on drugs; day care; the homeless and the shortage of low-cost housing; welfare reform and provision of the associated jobs and training; rehabilitation of pathological urban neighbourhoods; foreign policy; environmental protection; health insurance, and so on.

It is true that 1988 federal revenues, in total, are the same percentage of GNP (19) as in 1979, and total outlays (22.3) are 1.7 percentage points higher. The compositions of both sides of the budget have changed drastically. Social security tax revenues have increased 1.3 points, while regular income tax revenues have declined a similar amount. Defence has increased 1.3 points, interest 1.5 points and entitlements 0.9 points. Leaving social security to one side, in 1979 the excess of regular income taxes over defence and interest outlays was 5 per cent of GNP. In 1988 it was only 1 per cent of GNP. Essentially, any excess of civilian discretionary spending over 1 per cent of GNP now has to be met by borrowing. In fact such spending was 3.7 per cent of GNP in 1988, down from 5.5 per cent in 1979.

7.   Should social security surpluses be counted as deficit reductions?

The social security surplus, officially called 'off-budget', is projected by the fiscal year CBO to be $56 billion (1 per cent of GNP) this fiscal year and to rise to $68 billion in 1990 and to $117 billion (1.6 per cent of GNP) in 1994. These figures include as off-budget revenues both payroll taxes and interest payments from the Treasury to the Old Age and Survivors Trust Fund, just as if the Fund were a non-federal entity holding federal debt.

Clearly, if attention remains focused on the 'total deficit', the growing social security surpluses make a big contribution to deficit reduction. But Congress had good reason to provide in the compromise legislation of 1983 for the growth of reserves in the Trust Fund, and likewise for moving the Trust Fund off budget.

In the past retirement insurance benefits were met on a pay-as-you-go basis from the contemporaneous revenues of payroll taxes. The big demographic changes now anticipated will reduce the number of workers per retiree from five in the 1960s to two in the middle of the next century. The reserves in the Trust Fund, both interest and principal, will enable benefits to be paid until 2060 in spite of the decline in the number of contributing active workers.

For this solution to work in the real economy, not just on paper, it is necessary that the nation save extra amounts and invest them in extra productive capital yielding the returns that will be credited as interest to the Trust Funds for the benefits of future retirees. That will not happen unless Congress and the President firmly resolve not to use the social security surpluses as an excuse for higher 'on-budget' deficits. The debt to the Trust Fund must be regarded as debt to the general public. Federal fiscal policy should see to it that federal debt, including debt to the social security Trust Funds, will in future be declining relative to GNP.

At the beginning I argued that the saving of this nation is woefully low, in relation to the nation's needs and to the obligations of present generations of Americans to their successors. The demographic transition and its implications for social security are a special addition to our saving requirements. The Trust Fund surpluses are a way of meeting that additional need, not a way of ameliorating the shortage of saving due to the declines in non-federal and federal saving rates during this decade.

17.   Policy for recovery and growth*

The United States suffers simultaneously from two macroeconomic maladies. One is short run and cyclical; the other is long run and secular. The first is demand-side; the second is supply-side. The first is that spending on goods and services currently falls well short of the economy's capacity to produce them. The second is that productive capacity itself has been falling behind the needs and aspirations of the nation. The first has resulted in a shortage of jobs. The second is eroding the quality and real wages of jobs.

The great challenge of the Clinton Administration will be to provide remedies for both maladies. It won't be easy. The key to job creation in 1993 and 1991 is more spending: private or public, domestic or foreign, consumption or investment. The key to better real wages over the next two decades is faster growth of productivity, requiring greater national saving and investment.

Growth of the capacity of the economy determines the trend of real gross domestic product (GDP) over the decades, across business cycles. Potential GDP at full employment – now about 5.5 per cent unemployment – grows nowadays at about 2.5 per cent per year. Half of that is due to the normal increase of the labour force, the other half to productivity. Productivity is growing much more slowly than before 1973, and more slowly than in other economies today. This is the long-run, supply-side malady. We need to raise productivity and the speed of its growth for the benefit of future Americans.

The short-run demand-side problem is that we haven't even kept up with the growth of capacity. Two and a half per cent is the sustainable growth rate. If GDP rises at that pace, it will just absorb the influx of new workers and the unemployment rate will remain constant. If GDP grows more slowly or actually declines, the unemployment rate will increase. The 2.5 per cent sustainable rate, not zero, is par for the US economy. Relative to that par, we've been in recession – call it 'growth recession' – for nearly four years; although GDP change was positive in most quarters, growth was usually slower than the 2 per cent annual rate. That is why unemployment increased by two percentage points, about 2.5 million workers. As a result, GDP has by now fallen 5 or 6 per cent below capacity.

*Presentation at President-elect Clinton's Economic Conference, Little Rock, 5 December 1992.

To catch up in four years, we have to grow faster than the sustainable rate, indeed on average 1.5 percentage points faster. GDP growth averaging 4 per cent will be needed to bring the unemployment rate back down to 5.5 per cent in 1996, by creating 8.5 or 9 million jobs – for roughly 5 or 5.5 million new workers, 1 million persons re-entering the labour force, and the 2.5 million now unemployed.

Will this catch-up recovery occur on its own? Or do we need fiscal stimulus to pep up demand for goods and services and for labour? There is, I believe, a strong case for stimulus. The labour market is weaker than the unemployment rate suggests. The number of employed workers involuntarily confined to part-time jobs is abnormally large. Job vacancies, as indicated by the Help Wanted Index, are extraordinarily scarce. Defence cutbacks and corporate downsizings are destroying jobs irreversibly; to an unusual extent hirings in this recovery will have to be truly new jobs.

Although some recent macroeconomic numbers – notably, third quarter GDP – are encouraging, recovery is by no means in the bag. Typically growth spurts in the first year and then tapers off; no such spurt is now evident or forecast. Among other unpromising demand prospects are the slumps in Europe, Japan and throughout the world, which, together with the appreciation of the dollar, curtail US exports; the forced belt-tightening of state and local governments; and the sluggishness of business and household investments.

The improved productivity growth recently reported, if not transitory, means that potential GDP is higher and growing faster than estimated above. That would be good news for the long run. But its flip side would be that extra demand expansion would be required to achieve full recovery in four years.

Why can't the Federal Reserve do the job by itself, without fiscal help? One impediment is the banks' 'credit crunch'. Short-term interest rates are already very low. It may be that the Fed acted so little and so late from 1989 onwards that, as in 1930–31, they destroyed business and consumer expectations of recovery and let the economy slip out of their grasp. And after all, in virtually every previous cyclical recovery since World War II, monetary policy has had active fiscal help.

Nevertheless, the Fed still has 300 basis points between here and zero, and they should lower rates further. The new President and Treasury Secretary will want to do their best to induce the Fed to be accommodative and to help reassure the bond markets. After all, no inflation cloud darkens the sky, and congestion of the capital markets is at least as distant as full recovery. Also, we may hope that Secretary Bentsen will not let his debt managers supply the markets with any more long-term high-interest bonds.

Fiscal policy for recovery is bound to raise the budget deficit temporarily. (Among the virtues of an Investment Tax Credit is that it delivers a big bang of demand stimulus per dollar of lost tax revenue.) I recommend stimulus of $60 billion a year for the two years 1993 and 1994, about 1 per cent of GDP, capable thanks to secondary 'multiplier' effects of adding 1.5 per cent to GDP demand, a modest amount relative to the 6 per cent shortfall of GDP from its potential. The ratio of federal debt to GDP, which has risen from 25 per cent to 50 per cent over the past 12 years, would be about one percentage point higher than otherwise. That price is worth paying for assuring a vigorous recovery.

Fiscal stimulus for recovery should be combined with credible deficit reduction policies to be phased in later, so far as possible enacted in 1993. For deficit control as well as for its own sake, nothing is as important as health care reform. Otherwise federal outlays for Medicare and Medicaid will bust the budget throughout this decade, in particular rising by nearly 2 per cent of GDP from 1996 to 2002.

In today's weak economy, immediate fiscal austerity would be counterproductive. It would raise unemployment. It would actually reduce investment for the future, thus doing harm rather than good to coming generations. The story will be different in robust prosperity three or four years from now. Once the economy is again producing at capacity, there will be no room for additional productive investment unless other demands on GDP are reduced – that is, unless the country saves more. Federal deficit reductions are the prime way to raise national saving – provided they occur at the expense of private and public consumption, and provided that the Fed lowers interest rates enough to channel saving into investment rather than going to waste in unemployment.

In the meantime the Clinton Administration has the opportunity to provide in constructive ways the fiscal stimulus needed for recovery. The much-touted 1980s recovery, fuelled by the most massive deficits in peacetime history, were incurred for defence buildup and for tax cuts for affluent consumers. Those deficits had no lasting pay-offs in productivity and growth. In admirable contrast, Clinton programmes of private investment incentives and public investments in infrastructure and human capital would leave behind them important permanent gains.

18. Thinking straight about fiscal stimulus and deficit reduction*

On 17 February President Clinton presented to a joint session of Congress, which was televised to a nation-wide audience, a fairly detailed economic programme that is to be the central work of his Administration.

This article is based on a memo prepared in November 1992 for the Congressional Budget Office panel of economic consultants. It has been modified only slightly to reflect subsequent events prior to President Clinton's 17 February address.

The purpose here is not to present a policy proposal that in any way competes with President Clinton's proposed plan, but rather to indicate how professional economists should analyse our current budget problems and fiscal corrections.

PUTTING FIRST THINGS FIRST

Deficit reduction is not an end in itself. Its rationale is to improve the productivity, real wages and living standards of our children and their children. If the measures taken to cut deficits actually diminish GDP, raise unemployment and reduce future-oriented activities of governments, businesses and households, they do not advance the goals that are their *raisons d'être*; rather, they retard them.

This perverse result is likely if deficit reduction measures are introduced while the economy is as weak and as constrained by effective demand as it is now and will be in 1993, and quite possibly in 1994 as well. Moreover, if public sector future-oriented expenditures are the victims of such mistimed and misplaced fiscal austerity, the contradiction between rationale and actual consequence is compounded.

By the same argument, it does not make sense to oppose, on the grounds that they will raise the deficit, fiscal measures which would stimulate demand, reduce unemployment, raise the GDP and very likely raise private investment too. It is especially illogical to do so if the measures in question

*First published in *Challenge*, March–April 1993.

are themselves future-oriented, public sector investments and tax incentives for private investment.

Keeping ends and means straight may be too much to ask of politicians and pundits, but it is not too much to ask of economists and policy wonks.

ISN'T RECOVERY ALREADY IN THE BAG?

That's what some critics asked when Bob Solow and I, and 100 or so like-minded business and academic economists, tried to advance the idea of investment-oriented fiscal stimulus last March. Some of those critics later repented. The current signs of macroeconomic improvement are more credible. However, it is too soon to bet that the growth recession that began in the second quarter of 1989 is over.

So far, what is heralded as recovery is two quarters of growth above the sustainable growth of potential output. The third and fourth quarters were comfortably above the sustainable rate, but still two percentage points below usual performance in the first year of recovery. If, on its own, the economy grows faster than its sustainable rate in 1993 and 1994, the consensus is that it will do so by much less than has been normal in post-war cyclical recoveries.

While the unemployment rate has declined seven-tenths of a point from its peak, employment growth remains sluggish. The number of new jobs has not been quite enough to absorb the labour force growth expected in prosperity. We need 8 or 9 million net new jobs in the next four years to keep up with the labour force and productivity, and bring the unemployment rate down to 5.5 per cent.

At present the economy is producing real GDP 5 or 6 per cent below its potential capacity anticipated with 5.5 per cent unemployment. Closing this gap in four years requires exceeding the economy's sustainable growth rate by 1.25 to 1.5 points on average. The sustainable growth rate is estimated to be 2.25 or 2.5 per cent per year. Thus recovery over four years requires average growth of the order of 3.5 to 4.0 per cent.

Recent good news about productivity suggests that the gap may be larger and the sustainable growth rate higher than the estimates used above. It is too soon to tell if the good productivity numbers are just cyclical and transitory, as has happened in the early stages of many recoveries. But they may reflect the success of the competitive adjustments, downsizing and lay-offs of American businesses in improving efficiency, productivity and productivity growth. If so, it will take bigger gains in GDP in the next four years to achieve the same gains in employment.

The outlook for stable price inflation, with or without a catch-up recovery, is extraordinarily favourable. In these circumstances, the risks of overheating the economy by modest deficit-increasing fiscal stimulus – say, of the order of 1 per cent of GDP for both 1993 and 1994 – are minimal. With the help of the multiplier, that would raise the level of GDP by 1.5 or 2 per cent (if the Fed is accommodative), and raise its rate of growth by 0.75 or 1.00 percentage points. The inflationary risks are minimal relative to the downside risks to GDP and employment of doing nothing. Anyone who used to believe in well-behaved cycles, in which well-defined recession troughs automatically turn into monotonic and accelerating recoveries, must be considerably chastened by now.

CAN'T THE FED DO THE JOB?

Evidently the Fed can't or won't. I still think that, with 300 basis points between the Funds rate and zero, the Federal Open Market Committee can, and should, try harder. But there are reasons why monetary policy has been less potent than usual – the weak balance sheets of banks, the overhangs of debt among potential borrowers, the stickiness of long-term interest rates. Moreover, the growth recession lingered so long and the responses of monetary policy were so grudging that businesses and households lost the confidence in future prosperity that has historically facilitated most post-war recoveries. The 1990s slowdown, moreover, has been accompanied by unusually large downward structural adjustments, to defence cutbacks and to global competition. As James Medoff has been pointing out, vacancies – as proxied by the Help Wanted Index – are extraordinarily scarce relative to current unemployment rates. In addition to the direct contractionary effects of irreversible lay-offs, these adjustments have generated pervasive feelings of insecurity, which also inhibit spending.

WON'T THE FED OFFSET FISCAL STIMULUS?

My guess is that the Fed, while unable or unwilling to take the initiative to generate or accelerate recovery, is willing to allow and accommodate one driven by 'natural causes' or by moderate fiscal stimulus. Given the outlook for recovery and for inflation, there is little likelihood of a sudden overheating beyond the capacity of the Fed to arrest. Certainly the new President and his team will make every effort to persuade the Fed of the prudence of its policy and the reality of its commitment to deficit reduction once prosperity is restored.

In 1960–61 the Fed checked the predictable fall in interest rates in recessions because it was worried about outflows of short-term funds to higher-interest-rate European markets, and the losses of gold that might result. For this reason, monetary policy could not be an active agent of recovery. But the Kennedy Administration was able to persuade the Fed to lean only gently against the wind, as aggregate demand recovered for other reasons, including fiscal stimulus.

WON'T THE BOND MARKET OFFSET FISCAL STIMULUS?

I don't really believe in some super-central-bank whose mandarins pass judgement on policies and control the macroeconomic path of the nation by moving long-term bond rates. If these omnipotent governors existed at all, I suppose their policy objective would be to maintain a slack economy with negligible risks of inflation or capital market congestion, like the one we've enjoyed the last four years. They would render ineffectual any monetary or fiscal policies aimed at recovery.

Actual bond investors are institutions, insurance companies and pension funds, that manage growth portfolios on behalf of policy-holders and future beneficiaries. Those funds have to go somewhere, and if the alternatives to long-term bonds offer unattractive returns, they will go into long-term bonds even at lower yields. That's why it is important for the Fed to keep short rates low. One of the fruits of that policy has been the bullish stock market, which has made the cost of equity capital to non-financial corporations low even though the decline in long-term bond rates has been disappointingly small. Presumably, low prospective returns on stocks bring downward pressure on bond rates; interactions between the markets occur in both directions.

High bond rates in foreign markets are another alternative to dollar-denominated bonds. While the dollar was steadily falling against the Deutsche mark, the likelihood of capital gains in the currency market was compounding the interest rate attraction of German and other European bonds. But this could not be sustained. Apparently, the dollar fell far enough that dollar appreciation could be expected to compensate for the interest differential.

The federal government itself is the principal heavy long-term borrower. The Treasury should stop adding to the supply of long-maturity bonds. The Fed should, when its monetary policy involves supplying more bank reserves to the money market, remove long-maturity bonds from the market. No law of man or nature requires that all central bank open-market interventions occur in the shortest possible instruments.

Naturally, the new Administration will do its best to explain to the 'bond markets' its strategies for short-run recovery and long-run fiscal discipline. One hopes that the Federal Reserve will join in this effort of persuasion and reassurance. But there is no getting around the fact that the kind of economy those mythical mandarins prefer is one that will make President Clinton run for re-election in 1996 not as the 'failed governor of a small state' but as the failed President of a great nation.

IS LESS MORE?

Some financial pundits and some economists say that fiscal austerity is actually expansionary because it reduces long-term interest rates. As a proposition regarding fiscal policy in 1993, with given monetary policy, this is surely a fallacy. If the problem with fiscal stimulus is that it increases aggregate demand and thus raises interest rates, then fiscal austerity cannot at the same time raise aggregate demand and lower rates. It can lower rates only by curtailing demand and economic activity.

Deficit reduction expected in the future, inadequately offset by easier monetary policy and lower interest rates, could be unfavourable to 1993 investment and economic activity by perpetuating expectations of weak demand and low economic activity. However, deficit reduction expected in the future, during prosperous times, would be quite favourable to aggregate demand and economic activity in 1993, provided that the Federal Reserve's monetary policy was expected to ensure interest rates sufficiently low to make up for the future demand lost by fiscal austerity. A scenario that generates 'model-consistent' expectations, expectations supporting the scenario itself, consists of expansionary fiscal policy and accommodative monetary policy for recovery, followed by deficit reduction and appropriately easy monetary policy in prosperity.

WILL IT EVER BE TIME TO REMOVE THE FISCAL STIMULUS NEEDED NOW?

If the economy can't generate enough demand at today's low interest rates without a bigger deficit, what reason is there to think it will be able to do so in 1995 or 1996? The question is reminiscent of the old debate about pump-priming. It is a vulgar error to think that a burst of spending turned off after a few months would jump-start the economy into vigorous self-sustaining growth of demand. It is likewise an error to think that the present situation is an equilibrium, in particular that investment demands by business, households and state and local governments are permanently as low relative to national saving as they are currently. Recovery itself will revive those demands once economic agents regain confidence in a viable path of recovery and growth.

Then, judging from the 1980s, interest rates will be higher than they are now in the absence of deficit reduction, and a correction in the mix of fiscal and monetary policies will be possible and desirable.

CAN FUTURE FISCAL AUSTERITY BE MADE CREDIBLE?

It's never possible to make wholly credible guarantees of future policies in a democracy. Yet somehow the republic has managed to muddle through. Some deficit reduction measures can be legislated in 1993 to take effect in later years. It would then take both Congress and the President to reverse them, assuming vetoes are sustained. This should certainly be done for tax increases. A phased-in carbon tax or gasoline tax increase would be an excellent, though not politically popular, idea. Cuts in defence expenditures can be credibly budgeted for years ahead. In other cases, the new Administration may be able to do no more than state reasonably realistic intentions.

The most important budgetary area is health care reform, a critical item on the legislative agenda for its own sake. Unless federal net health care costs are brought under control, their explosion later in the 1990s will bust the budget for sure.

THERE AIN'T NO JUSTICE!

The new President faces a large chronic budget deficit bequeathed to him by the unparalleled, irresponsible fiscal policies of his two predecessors. It is ironic that people who displayed remarkable tolerance of those policies for 12 years now insist that the highest and most immediate priority of the new President, the very test of his statesmanship, is to solve this deficit problem in the face of the stagnant economy he has also been bequeathed, at the sacrifice of his own programmatic priorities.

Recoveries from almost every previous post-war recession have had the help of fiscal stimulus. The much touted 1983–88 recovery was driven by fiscal demand stimulus massively greater than any previous peacetime fiscal expansion. It took two main forms: consumption by affluent taxpayers enjoying lower tax rates and a rapid buildup of defence spending. Neither of these uses of resources left in its wake lasting gains in future productivity and growth; Clinton's spending and tax-cutting initiatives, in contrast, are tilted towards investment, public and private.

During the past 12 years, the ratio of publicly held federal debt to GDP has increased by 25 percentage points. The future of the United States surely does not hinge on whether it increases by a couple of extra points in the next few years, in the interest of an economic recovery that would make the economy strong enough to allow serious deficit reduction.

PART IV

International Economic Relations

Part IV   International economic relations

The biggest world event of recent years was of course the end of the Cold War. The Berlin Wall fell; the Soviet Union and the Warsaw Pact broke up; communist dictatorships gave way to democratic and capitalistic institutions. Within the capitalist democracies conservatives proclaimed ideological victory over liberals and social democrats. On both sides of the former Iron Curtain, free market enthusiasts expected that the citizens of the ex-communist republics would quickly enjoy the fruits of 'invisible hand' efficiency. In Chapters 19, 20 and 21 I threw some cool water on these claims and expectations. I made three points:

1.   Our triumph in the Cold War was not a victory of societies with extreme *laissez-faire* institutions and policies, but of diverse countries with active governments, mixed economies, welfare states, progressive taxes and a variety of economic regulations. Moreover, the victory did not belong solely to the governments in power in 1988–89, but to Western governments and policies from 1945 onwards.
2.   Western advisers did formerly communist countries no favours by encouraging their policy-makers just to destroy the institutions of central planning and watch entrepreneurs and free markets rise spontaneously from the ashes. That was not the way economies destroyed in World War II recovered and prospered.
3.   The democratic capitalist nations of Europe, North America and Asia should not be complacent in their hours of victory, because their economies, individually and collectively, have not been doing very well since 1973. European unemployment, stagnant productivity and wages, increasing inequality, social pathologies, ethnic conflict, poverty within advanced countries and in the Third World – these are plagues we are far from conquering.

Chapter 22 explains why, in my opinion, trade conflict with Japan is misguided, inconsistent with the America's 60-year tradition of liberal trade policy. Chapter 23 argues that we cannot expect national currencies to give way to a single world currency, or even to multinational regional currencies, for many decades. There is not sufficient harmony of economic institutions and social values among nations to allow any one of them, except possibly for a few small dependent countries, to surrender irrevocably the possibility of changing its exchange rates with other currencies. At the same time, the immense growth in the quantities of private funds that can move quickly and cheaply across currencies means that governments can no longer defend adjustable pegs of exchange rates from speculation against those parities. When changes in exchange rates are unavoidable, it is much less traumatic to let markets make the changes rather than to repudiate prior solemn commitments and devalue to a new commitment at a lower parity. But market-determined floating exchange rates also can be moved by speculation and interest rate arbitrage, frequently in ways that limit the autonomy of national central banks and governments to follow policies appropriate to their own economies. For this reason I have advocated an internationally agreed tax on foreign exchange transactions, to discourage short-horizon speculations and to create a wedge between interest rates in different currencies within which central banks could pursue policies appropriate to their different circumstances.

19. One or two cheers for the invisible hand*

THE INVISIBLE HAND – RIDING HIGH TODAY

Adam Smith's 'invisible hand'[1] is surely one of the genuine Great Ideas of history, both for its intrinsic intellectual content and for its durable influence on ideologies, politics and public policies. The proposition that the alchemy of market competition transmutes the dross of personal selfishness into the gold of social welfare is still a powerful message in economics classrooms and in political debates. To be sure, since 1776 the doctrine has experienced ups and downs in popularity. At present, it enjoys one of its strongest and most widespread prosperities.

The symptoms can be seen throughout the world. In almost all the advanced democratic capitalist nations, conservative governments committed to *laissez-faire* rule the roosts: notably in the USA and Canada, in the UK and the Federal Republic of Germany, in the other major countries of the European Community (even in France, where the socialists were forced to fall in step) and in Japan. In the communist countries – China, Eastern Europe, now even the Soviet Union – the new vogue is the promotion of private enterprise and market-pricing. The main ideological adversary of the tradition of Adam Smith for the past 140 years, Marxism–Leninism, stands discredited before the world. As a principle for the organization of society and economy, it is a failure. Now it is an admitted failure. Likewise in the 'Third World', the success of the economies of Taiwan, Korea and of other NICs is attributed largely to free markets and free enterprises, while in contrast stagnation is observed in countries where governments intervene with heavy hands. The official policies of international agencies, the IMF and the World Bank, make adoption of market-oriented reforms conditions for their aids and credits.

These developments follow and reverse a long period of scepticism and doubt about the Smithian message, even among those who always firmly rejected Marxism and other extreme alternatives. Fifty or 60 years ago the depression in the fortunes of the invisible hand was related to the Great

*First published in S.G. Rhee and R.P. Chang (eds), *Pacific-Basin Capital Markets Research*, Amsterdam: North Holland, 1990.

Depression of the world economy, and then to the pragmatic compromises of market capitalism with social democracy, welfare state institutions, trade unionism and state planning that flourished before and after World War II. Even governments which by traditional doctrine had eschewed responsibility for fluctuations in economic activity – international, national, regional, sectoral, personal – began to assume more and more responsibilities for them and to be held to account by democratic electorates.

Disenchantment with government interventions has spread contagiously in the last 20 years. There were two main reasons. One was the disappointing performance of the world economy in general and of most national economies in the 1970s, in contrast to the quarter century of unparalleled growth, prosperity and stability before 1973. Whether justifiably or not, the disappointments of the 1970s were blamed on the economic doctrines and policies adopted and often praised during the preceding decades. The other reason was the growing disillusionment and cynicism about politics and governments – legislatures, executives and bureaucracies – fuelled by obvious and perceived failures of policies and their execution and, worse, by endless revelations of venality, hypocrisy, deception and mendacity.

Professional – shall we say scientific? – economics and the economic ideologies of public and political debate are always intertwined. *The Wealth of Nations* itself was both a tract of political economy and a scientific – or, as the author would have put it, a philosophical – treatise. The Great Idea has led parallel lives in the two arenas: public and professional. In the professional arena, the invisible hand eventually came to be formalized as the basic theorem of welfare economics – that a competitive market equilibrium is Pareto-optimal and that every Pareto-optimal allocation can be supported by a competitive equilibrium with a suitable arbitrary allocation of endowments among agents. This is a very precise and refined distillate of the sweeping conjectures of Smith himself and of hordes of his successors, especially those in the public arena of ideologies. In any event, the appeal of the invisible hand within the profession shares the cyclical fluctuations of its popularity in the wider arena. The same dialectic of revolution, counter-revolution and synthesis has been repeating itself in economic science and in economic politics.

It is not surprising, therefore, that the popularity of the invisible hand in our profession has revived strongly in the past 15 years. The main target has been Keynesian macroeconomics, as it developed in the first 25 years after the publication of *The General Theory*.[2] During that time the mainstream consensus of the profession came to support a synthesis of Keynesian macroeconomics and neoclassical microeconomics. Theoretical misgivings about this compromise burst into full-scale counter-revolution in the 1970s, called by its protagonists the 'new classical macroeconomics'. This new old macroeconomics, fortified by Rational Expectations, extends the pretensions of *laissez-faire* to macro theory and policy and undermines the case for monetary and fiscal stabilization policies that most economists, even those opposed to microeconomic interventions, had previously come to accept.

On the micro side, too, the invisible hand was gaining professional as well as public adherence. Supply-side economics, fortified by this new label, greatly magnified previous estimates of the deadweight losses attributable to taxes, transfer payments, subsidies, quotas, price controls, tariffs and regulations of all kinds. Economists, especially theorists, became much readier to take the theoretical optimality of a free market solution as a reference point, placing the burden of proof on anyone who would defend or propose a government intervention.

These are influential ideas. Given the overhang of regulations and other micro interventions and the vested interests they serve, it is, of course, difficult even for conservative free market governments to dismantle them. Nevertheless, the spirit of the invigorated invisible hand certainly makes a difference. And in macroeconomics it has become quite decisive, especially in Western Europe, where established doctrine among policy-makers and business and financial leaders is that governments should never actively stimulate aggregate demand, whatever the circumstances of their economies.

EXAGGERATIONS OF EXUBERANT IDEOLOGY

Yet there are large divergences of intellectual substance between Adam Smith's invisible hand thesis and modern scientific proofs of the optimality of competitive market solutions. Consider several of them:

1.　First, careful economists know that Pareto optimality, which is all the fundamental theorem of welfare economics can claim for competitive equilibrium, is not necessarily maximization of social welfare. We know there are trade-offs between 'efficiency' and 'equality', to mention just one important kind of distributive issue. Maybe real GDP could be maximized by allowing free rein and untaxed gain to the enterprising, the talented, the ruthless and the lucky, and by leaving the weak, the ignorant, the shiftless and the unlucky to their own devices and to private charity. I doubt it, but even if it were true it is an unpleasant caricature of a 'good society'. A system with zero distortionary fiscal or regulatory interventions is a chimera. The question is always the one Arthur Okun posed so effectively:[3] The bucket carrying goodies from rich to poor is always leaky. How leaky does it have to be before the transfer is not worthwhile?

　　Even so good a cause as free trade is, in my opinion, exaggerated when it is argued, as it generally is in public debate even by economists, that free trade is obviously welfare-improving. I am not referring to the slim possibility that a country has some market power in international trade that can be exploited by an 'optimum tariff' or by strategic gaming in commercial policy. Assuming that free trade is efficient and maximizes the consumption opportunities of a society as a whole, it still can change – relative to any alternative status quo – the internal distribution of these opportunities, not only among persons, sectors and regions but also as between broadly defined factors of production: labour, capital and land.

2. Smith says, and his latter-day adherents repeat, that selfish motivations and local information suffice to guide individual economic decisions in ways that aggregate into social optima. Modern theory requires much more: simultaneous clearing of a complete set of markets, including those for future and contingent commodities; globally complete information available to all agents. Economic theorists may take methodological refuge in the assertion that every model, including general equilibrium theory itself, is a simplifying metaphor or reality, to be judged by congruence between its implications and predictions and real-world observations. So far there is no convincing evidence of such congruence, certainly nothing that entitles anyone to accept and assert literally the formal propositions of the model.

3. The invisible hand, especially in the general equilibrium version of formal theory, requires that agents lack market power and take parametrically the prices determined for a predetermined list of commodities. The looser ideology makes a big logical jump in extending the invisible hand proposition to all market structures and to competition in products and other non-price dimensions. The recent complacency in my country about mergers and conglomerations, the atrophy of anti-trust policy to apply only to overt conspiracy, reflect the broader and looser *laissez-faire* zeitgeist.

PRAGMATISM IN REGULATION AND DEREGULATION

These considerations counsel against uncritical acceptance of 'free market' and 'supply-side' arguments in every application, and suggest that economists adopt more cautious, pragmatic and discriminating approaches than their ideological and political counterparts.

Of course, a discriminating and pragmatic approach is double-edged. Theory may not be able to prove that a particular intervention is injurious to welfare, but that failure of proof does not justify the intervention. One should be suspicious of advocates of, let us say, lower taxes on capital incomes on grounds of incentives and efficiency when the advocates stand to gain without making any new risky investments. (And likewise of professors who want to raise their own salaries on the grounds that higher pay will attract better talent in the future.) We should be especially suspicious of interventions that seem both inefficient and inequitable, for example rent controls in New York or Moscow or Mexico City, or price supports and irrigation subsidies benefiting affluent farmers, or low-interest loans to well-heeled students.

I myself think that invisible hand theory is mostly irrelevant to macroeconomic stabilization policies. The business fluctuations that give rise to those interventions play no role in the writings of Adam Smith, Leon Walras and Arrow–Debreu. Whether active counter-cyclical demand management brings better macro performance than stable policies blind to economic conditions is an empirical question that cannot be settled by pure economic theory.

One thrust of *micro*economic deregulation is justified in almost all countries: the dismantling of institutions that protect privileged individuals from competition. Everybody would like to own a toll booth and grow rich collecting tolls from the multitudes who pass by. As the point is sometimes expressed, people are rent-seekers. Sometimes the bottlenecks and scarcities that yield tolls or rents are natural. Sometimes they are the pay-offs of Schumpeterian innovations. Sometimes they arise without government help and are maintained by restraints of trade. Sometimes both the scarcities and the rents are artificial results of government interventions, made-to-order for political deals and too often irresistible invitations for corruption. In the US, flagrant examples have been on the hit lists of economists in all Administrations, liberal and conservative, Democratic and Republican. Even when it can be argued that some deserving low-income persons are beneficiaries of rights to buy or sell at subsidized prices, economists can often show how equal gains could be provided to them in a more efficient manner.

GOVERNMENT AND FINANCIAL MARKETS

Undiscriminating and thoughtless deregulation can misfire. As examples I refer to financial markets and institutions. You probably have heard of the epidemic insolvencies of Savings and Loan Associations in the USA. In the last ten years, under great political and economic pressure, the regulations of these institutions were substantially relaxed. Originally these were mutual associations attracting savings in the form of 'shares' for the purpose of financing mortgages in their communities, but later they were allowed to convert to stock companies managed for profit. In the 1980s they were allowed to broaden their asset menus to compete with commercial banks.

They were allowed to convert savings shares into checkable deposits and to pay market interest rates to attract them. They were allowed to seek deposits and lending opportunities nation-wide. Their supervisory agency, following the spirit of the times, became less strict and less diligent. Yet their deposits were still federally insured, in principle only up to $100,000 per deposit but in practice 100 per cent. Thus the institutions, whether sound or unsound, cautious or reckless, honest or corrupt, solvent or insolvent, could always attract deposits by offering high interest rates. If the deposits were invested in risky loans that went bad, no losses fell on the depositors. Losses were borne in part by other insured institutions, whose insurance premiums would have to be increased to help pay off the depositors, and by federal taxpayers, the ultimate guarantors. The Federal budgetary cost is likely to exceed $200 billion. The moral is that you can't apply free market principles to an industry that deals in contingent obligations of the central government.

The fad of deregulation has led serious economists, as well as exuberant ideologues, to propose free competitive enterprise in the creation of money. The idea that 'private money' could supersede government money is a ridiculous one. Someone's IOUs have to be those in which clearings take place among banks and other transactors. Someone's IOUs have to be those the government itself will accept in payment of taxes and other obligations, and those the government regards as legal tender in the satisfaction of private debts. Once the government guarantees the value, in the country's unit of account, of any private IOUs, then it cannot allow the private issuers completely free choice as to the assets that stand behind them.

Should government take an 'anything goes' attitude towards the financial structure of non-financial corporations? At the moment, US corporations are being rapidly, drastically and spectacularly restructured. Firms whose assets were covered 60–100 per cent by equity, are moving to 10 per cent equity, 90 per cent debt. Some of this refinancing arises from a reduced assessment of the disadvantages and risks of debt obligations, in part because the tax-deductibility of interest was enhanced in value by the 1986 increase in the effective corporate profits tax rate. In some respect, the corporation as restructured is simply renaming, as 'interest', income that formerly was called 'profits'. The surprising thing is that such restructurings are the immediate sources of such large increases in the value of the assets over the previous market value of the equities, even after the very considerable deadweight losses of the transactions, the fabulous fees of investment bankers and lawyers. Much of the best talent of the country is engaged in transactions of this kind, and their imminence or possibility preoccupies the managers of companies who should be trying to make better mousetraps and compete with Taiwan, Korea and Japan.

Our federal Administration is quite complacent about these activities, and it is indeed hard to see why shareowners of companies with lethargic or inefficient managements should be deprived of the capital gains takeovers might bring them. On the other hand, the wholesale replacement of equity by debt makes companies individually more vulnerable to adverse business developments and the economy collectively more vulnerable to deflationary or recessionary shocks. Monetary policy may be crippled as a result. If the government is going to take responsibility for ensuring the survival of non-financial companies – individually like Chrysler or Lockheed, or collectively – then perhaps it should limit their permissible debt/equity ratios, just as it does for financial institutions. As a minimum, of course, the government should make the tax liability of companies neutral with respect to their debt/equity structures.

A disquieting implication of the large premiums in takeover values is to confirm failure of ordinary market prices to reflect long-run fundamental values. The long-standing suspicion of this failure was expressed eloquently by Keynes when he likened the stock market to a beauty contest in which the contestants' prizes depend on voting the same as other contestants. The quest for short-run profits, 'day trading', stresses the ability to gauge the immediate impacts of news events on other speculators rather than their long-range effects on earnings. In the last ten years, the excess volatility of stock market prices relative to dividends and earnings has been ingeniously documented econometrically by Robert Shiller.[4] Despite their best efforts, the finance intelligentsia who espouse efficient markets theory have not been able to refute Shiller.

Errors in market valuations have further negative repercussions. Managers of corporations may be short-sighted in their outlooks and investment decisions, believing they get points and bonuses for the performance of their companies' stocks in a quarter, a year or four years. If the stock market gave them reliable signals of fundamental values, short-horizon managers would be making good decisions. But if the stock market signals are speculative noise, the managers are making bad decisions. Whether the newly structured high-debt firm, in which managers have considerable stakes in highly leveraged shares and stand both to lose much more and to gain much more than under the old structures, will be more efficient remains to be seen. The unrelenting pressure of debt service may force managers to be more efficient, but it might also force resort to short-term expedients to maintain cash flow at the expense of longer-run values.

One way to encourage fundamental investing and to discourage short-horizon speculation is to tax financial transactions. Keynes tentatively suggested this tax, and I favour it today. With international agreement a transfer tax could also, in my opinion, diminish speculation in foreign exchange markets and allow larger differences among currencies in short-term interest rates, permitting somewhat greater autonomy in national monetary policies.

I think developing countries should go slow in copying the financial institutions and markets of the US and the UK, or of Japan for that matter. When I
read that Wall Streeters are visiting Beijing to help the People's Republic
establish a stock market, I shudder. It is far from clear that the proliferation of
financial instruments, markets, arbitrage opportunities and paper transactions
in advanced countries has created social product to justify the high-quality
human capital resources it devours. Business schools are beginning to wonder if they shouldn't be teaching students how to make products and manage
workers rather than how to shuffle paper. David Halberstam's *The Reckoning*
tells how the famous financial Whiz Kids of the Ford Motor Co., many years
ago, lost the ball game for Ford.[5]

The major purpose of financial markets and institutions is to channel the
excess savings of some agents in the economy to the excess real investments
other agents are prepared to undertake. There are many ways to organize such
flows, and they do not all require speculative markets.

Developing countries should not be in a great hurry to free capital movements into and out of their currencies of all controls and central bank super-
vision. Remember that much of the rapid growth of European countries and
Japan after World War II occurred before the full dismantling of exchange
and capital controls. It is important even for small countries to maintain some
degree of autonomy in monetary policy, so that local interest rates are not
wholly determined by foreign markets. The foreign exchange transactions tax
is one way to do that. Third World countries seeking developmental investments from overseas companies should avoid competitive scrambles with
each other. Such competition can easily transfer the lion's share of the gains
from the investments to the multinational companies, at the expense of the
countries themselves. In the USA, states and cities are engaged in unsavoury
bidding for locations of new business installations, and the result is mutually
destructive of their tax bases and reasonable regulations.

CRITICAL PROBLEMS ON WHICH THE INVISIBLE HAND NEEDS A HAND

Intensified confidence in the invisible hand – among economists, politicians
and the general public – comes at a time when more and more reasons for
doubt are arising. It is not easy to discern how *laissez-faire* unaided, unguided
and uncontrolled can handle the big new challenges of the 21st century. Let
me mention several examples:

1. At a time when long-range decisions are essential and myopia is espec-
    ially dangerous, private markets evidently have great difficulty focusing

on long horizons. If anything, they seem to be becoming shorter in their orientations. Business managers, especially in the United States, are criticized, even by themselves, for their preoccupations with quick pay-offs. Financial markets are untrustworthy guides for managers, as I argued above, because they are dominated by speculators. Much activity of financiers and managers is devoted to the thriving markets in whole businesses: takeovers, leveraged buyouts, mergers, break-ups of previous mergers. A disproportionate number of the brightest and most enterprising youth is devoted to the churning and shuffling of paper, in search of quick wealth rather than production of goods and services.

Speculative frenzy is not confined to the United States. Consider the fabulous booms in real estate values in Japan, beyond what could be justified by rents, and in related stock market prices as well. These booms generate prices that do not guide allocations of land to economically rational uses.

2. In the 1970s the world was jolted to a sudden realization that its economies were dependent on exhaustible sources of energy. When oil became plentiful again in the 1980s we seemed to forget the lesson. Energy prices reflect transient demand/supply conditions in disproportion to inevitable future scarcities. Perhaps because capital markets are short-sighted, investments to develop energy resources and to conserve energy use are abandoned or ignored when current prices are low, even though they would be justified by probable future prices. Commodity and capital markets together do not seem to have long enough horizons to give dependable signals. Nevertheless the thrust of energy policy in the United States these past eight years has been to rely wholly on private markets.

3. Economic theory has always recognized externalities as exceptions to invisible hand propositions. Externalities are non-market effects of economic activities on other economic activities. When agents receive no price signals to deter them from activities damaging to other agents or to encourage them to engage in activities useful to others, the market by itself fails to allocate resources optimally among activities. Generators of electricity in Ohio acidify lakes in the north-east United States and in Canada. Neither the Midwest utilities nor their customers consider the acid rain costs their electricity is imposing on their north-east neighbours when they decide how much to produce and consume, or whether and how much to invest in anti-pollution technology. Likewise, the driver considering going on to a busy highway or city street thinks of his own convenience but not of the extra delays and inconveniences the additional congestion will cause others.

Belatedly, awkwardly, erratically and often inefficiently, governments have been trying to deal with environmental damage, the health and safety of workers, customers and neighbours, and other external effects. The affected industries chafe under the regulations and costs imposed upon them. Unfortunately the conservative fashion of deregulation has sometimes been blindly extended to these measures, along with the anti-competitive 'toll booth' interventions that deserve to be dismantled.

Ronald Coase did both Adam Smith and Dr Pangloss one better by suggesting that the parties to negative externalities on the delivering and receiving sides could and would get together and contract with each other to eliminate or limit them, if the social gains were worth the trouble.[6] In the case of positive externalities, similarly, the generators and beneficiaries would bargain to bring them to an optimal level. Thus would externalities be internalized. The Coase theorem seems to be a rationale *for* government rather than against it. It is precisely to handle situations where markets have difficulties reaching agreements and contracts of this kind that societies utilize governments.

Paradoxically, free market doctrines are more uncritically accepted just when externalities appear to be more serious than ever before. It's hard to maintain the pose of old welfare economics textbooks, that externalities are the exceptions that prove the invisible hand rule. Current problems are all the more complex because the adverse effects are cumulative but delayed, and because they are intrinsically difficult to evaluate. Many technologies that are efficient contributors to the welfare of individual consumers today spin off side effects that will be costly or disastrous in the future: ozone depletion, greenhouse effects, toxic and radioactive wastes, receding water tables, and many other environmental and ecological dangers. As my acid rain example illustrates, these hazards do not respect international boundaries.

4. In the background of all our ecological problems is the excessive growth of the world population relative to the sustainable expansion of the planet's capacity to support human life, let alone to support it at standards of living to which all peoples aspire. No market miracle brings population and resources into balance and keeps them there. The only invisible hands are the cruel Malthusian checks. The hope of avoiding over-population is that fertility will spontaneously decline as standards of living rise. Over the past two centuries this mechanism worked successfully for the now advanced countries. For the poorest countries today the catch is that their rates of natural increase prevent the very progress in living standards that might diminish fertility. Modern medicine can keep people alive longer but it does not add space for them to live or resources to feed them. The rich countries of the world have obligations to help the poorer nations develop, yes even to help the workers of those lands to compete with their own high-paid workers. They are much less

likely to offer assistance, markets for products and privileges of immigration if it appears that the consequences are not to raise living standards but to foster still higher rates of population growth.

5. The invisible hand, as exaggerated and glorified in free market ideology, has several unfortunate social externalities of its own. It is a rationale for unabashed and unmitigated individualistic selfishness. It assures those who seek, above all else, to accumulate material wealth that they are patriots doing Adam Smith's noble work, promotion of the wealth of nations. Indeed nowadays there are numerous right-wing preachers, 'televangelists', telling them they are doing God's work.

One message they get is that their obligations to others are just those specified in the literal language of previous contracts and written laws. All too frequently another one is that disobedience of those rules is worthwhile and even legitimate if the personal benefits exceed the costs. Many ordinary good people do not put quarters in parking meters if they calculate that the probabilities of being ticketed and fined $5.00 are less than one in twenty. That transgression of civic virtue may be innocuous. But if everyone behaves like that in all aspects of life, the social order breaks down. The burdens on police and courts are intolerable; law and litigation absorb the best minds of the society.

Competition is supposed to make self-interest work for the best. But competition itself cannot function without a clement political and legal framework, and competitive markets will not survive the efforts of competitors themselves to eliminate them without the unceasing vigilance of governments. And if governments, elected officials and civil servants are constantly denounced as wasteful and worthless, as foreign bodies in a Utopian organism of private markets, the central institutions and essential infrastructures of economy and society decay and wither away. Taxes are, according to Mr Justice Oliver Wendell Holmes, the price of civilization.

6. Finally, there are limits to the extremes of inequality that a democracy can tolerate, especially when television incessantly parades the luxurious life styles of the rich before poor youth who can never expect to taste them. Materialism, hardheartedness and incivility are, according to many observers, by-products of the Reagan revolution in the United States. President George Bush himself is calling for a kinder, gentler America.

NOTES

1. The famous paragraph containing these words and summarizing the basic thesis of the book occurs in Book IV, Chapter II, on page 423 of the Modern Library Edition of Smith's *The Wealth of Nations* (1776) edited by Edwin Cannan and published in 1937.

2. J.M. Keynes (1936), *The General Theory of Employment, Interest and Money*, New York: Harcourt Brace.
3. A. Okun (1975), *Equality and Efficiency: The Big Tradeoff*, Washington: Brookings Institution.
4. R. Shiller (1981), 'Do Stock Prices Move too Much to be Justified by Subsequent Changes in Dividends?, *American Economic Review*, **71**, October, 421–36.
5. D. Halberstam (1986), *The Reckoning*, New York: Morrow.
6. R. Coase (1960), 'The Problem of Social Cost', *Journal of Law and Economics*, **3**, October, 1–44. See also R.D. Cooter (1987), 'The Coase Theorem', in J. Eatwell, M. Milgate and P. Newman (eds), *The New Palgrave. A Dictionary of Economics*, Vol. 1, London: Macmillan, pp. 457–60.

20. Nation states and the Wealth of Nations: challenges and opportunities in an ever more interdependent world*

1. Post-Cold War euphoria has given way to pessimism. The triumph of democracy and capitalism over communism was sweet. But the difficulties of transforming the political and economic systems of ex-communist societies are much greater than anticipated. And Western nations cannot be proud or complacent about their own recent economic performance.

We in the West confidently expected the ex-communist countries to become democratic and to prosper under free market capitalism. The Walesas and Havels would take over. After all, it could only be the disastrous economic and political system that kept the living standards of Soviet citizens and East Europeans so far below those of their Western neighbours. Once the Berlin Wall fell, East Germans expected soon to enjoy the affluence of West Germans, and we naive Cold War victors did not find those hopes unreasonable. Released from thralls to Moscow and Comecon, other Warsaw Pact nations would soon prosper too. The same optimism extended even to Western hopes for the transformations of the former republics of the USSR, notably Russia itself.

Unfortunately, Westerners offering professional advice on the management of transitions to market capitalism – economists, financiers, business executives, politicians – encouraged high expectations. Their confidence in free markets and private enterprise had been reinforced by the political and ideological success of conservative anti-government movements in their own countries. Their advice was in that same spirit: dismantle your communist controls and regulations, privatize your enterprises, stabilize your finances, get governments out of the way, and just watch a new market economy rise from the ashes. It turned out not to be so easy.

In the euphoria of the moment, Western advisers all too often forgot that the economic victory in the war of systems was not won by ideologically pure free market regimes but by 'mixed economies' in which governments played substantial and crucial roles. They forgot too that elaborate structures

*Presented at XIX International Conference, Pio Manzu Research Centre. 'The Third Round' Rimini, Italy, 17 October 1993.

of laws, institutions and customs, which evolved over centuries in existing capitalist countries, are essential foundations and frameworks for market systems. At a minimum, property rights must be defined and contracts must be enforced.

In Western countries themselves right-wing anti-government politics had gained in strength even before the end of the Cold War. Thatcherism and Reaganomics stand out, but the Right had come to dominate G7 governments and those of most other advanced capitalist democracies. The collapse of communism increased the confidence and conservatism of these movements, and they cited the failures of extreme *dirigiste* regimes behind the Iron Curtain to promote their political agenda at home. Milton Friedman, for example, wondered out loud why the US was veering towards statism just when statist failures had been so dramatically exposed and rejected in the East. (We weren't.)

At the same time as the Cold War was ending, however, it was becoming painfully apparent that Western economies had less to brag about than previously thought. Their performances in the 1980s, indeed in the 1970s too, were definitely not licences for complacency. Europe never really recovered from the oil shock recessions of 1974–75 and 1979–82, and now is in recession again. Unemployment, chronically high in most European countries, has been rising in the 1990s. The United States had recovered during the 1980s, but after 1988 slipped into what turned out to be a fairly shallow but terribly stubborn slowdown in economic activity and growth. Even before unemployment began to rise in 1990, Americans were unhappy with the declines in real wages they had been suffering since 1973. Even Japan, the admired and feared *Wunderwirtschaft*, turned out not to be immune to cyclical reverses.

2. The central economic problem of the day is to reallocate labour and other productive resources from activities no longer of social value to uses that satisfy current and future human needs and priorities. Economic progress always requires reallocations, painful as they can be to individuals directly affected. Today the main opportunity and the main problem, especially in Russia and other ex-Soviet republics, is reallocation of resources long devoted to military purposes. At the same time, rapid changes in technology and the globalization of competition necessitate other reallocations. To expect free markets to engineer these reallocations by themselves is a fantasy, especially in societies where the markets scarcely exist.

In Russia, other ex-Soviet republics and Eastern Europe, workers and other productive inputs must be substantially reallocated – shifted from activities where they are no longer needed to activities of social value. Immense reallocations are both today's necessities and tomorrow's hopes. Resources released from obsolete activities must be redeployed – into new industries, new technologies and new products. Swords must be beat into plowshares, guns must be supplanted by butter. The winding down of military production is not the only reallocation required. As the civilian sector grows, its composition will be quite different. The goods and services freely chosen by consumers will diverge radically from the menu offered by communist planners.

It is a fallacy, a tragic fallacy, to expect this reallocation to occur on its own, at least to occur quickly enough and reliably enough to satisfy the aspirations of an impatient public. That doesn't happen even in Western countries, with well-established capitalist and democratic institutions. Redeployment may be of immense social value eventually, but its initial impact is devastating to the many people who depend on the old activities for their livelihoods.

The United States also faces difficult and painful reallocations, though by no means as severe as those of Russia. We have political trouble shutting down the production of nuclear submarines, stealth bombers and aircraft carriers. We have similar troubles making trade agreements with our neighbours, Mexico and Canada, because freer trade might cost some jobs, even while it generates others.

The local pains, vested interests and political perils that obstruct such reallocations must be even greater in the ex-communist countries. Shock therapy strategy would suddenly create mass unemployment and leave it to spontaneous private enterprise to create new enterprises and new jobs. The new jobs wouldn't happen very fast, and meanwhile the depression in aggregate demand would discourage potential entrepreneurs and investors. The scenario is not politically viable. In the absence of positive programmes to provide jobs for displaced workers, it is not surprising that workers continue to be employed and paid in obsolete and unproductive activities.

3. To effect reallocations, governments must provide some leadership. The example of Jean Monnet's 'indicative planning' in economic reconstruction after World War II is instructive. It is dangerous to apply indiscriminately anti-government sentiments and ideologies so popular today.

Consider what Jean Monnet did for France, Germany and Western Europe immediately after World War II. Devastated by the War, their economies were in shambles. For the most part they hadn't been doing very well before the War either. To revive the crucial industrial complex straddling the French–German border, Monnet conceived and organized the Coal and Steel Community. Industries and governments cooperated on concerted consistent plans to expand peacetime production capacities. These plans envisaged optimistic but feasible levels of demand for coal and steel products, which the expansionary activities of those very industries would help bring about. To put the matter simply, simplistically, coal companies were induced to invest in expanded production capacity because they became confident the steel industry would buy more coal; steel companies similarly raised their capacity because they became confident the coal industry would buy more steel. All the firms raised their sights above what they would have expected without coordination.

In the same spirit, Monnet developed for France itself a system of 'indicative planning'. Private industries and public sectors worked out mutually consistent plans of production and investment. These then could serve as wholly voluntary guides for individual industries and enterprises. As in the coal–steel case, each sector could expand without fearing it would be overextended because the rest of the economy would lag behind. Periodic exercises in indicative planning were useful in concertedly lifting the sights of French entrepreneurs for two decades after the War, but the device became unnecessary later.

Monnet's institutional inventions could be useful in transitions from communist to market economies. But the animus against communist controls is so strong that anything that involves government participation and seems to be 'planning', however indicative and powerless, is rejected out of hand.

The anti-government sentiment of the era, in both East and West, is counter-productive if carried too far. Governments have often done economic harm by misguided interferences with markets for the protection of particular interests and for the benefits of politicians and bureaucrats themselves. But governments have also always played important and essential roles in economic life, even in capitalist societies. Modern technologies are making constructive public sector activities more essential than ever. Public education has to train workers literate in the skills needed in high-tech industries and in the uses of computers and modern communications networks. Public infrastructure is necessary for up-to-date national and international systems of transportation and communication.

Many economic activities have important third-party effects, 'externalities' in economists' jargon. These are costs or benefits that businesses and individuals do not consider in deciding what and how much to produce. Environmental damage incident to production processes or to the use and disposal of products are well-known examples. Often these consequences cross national borders. On the other hand, businesses that train workers or invent new techniques or products may spin off valuable by-products for which they cannot enforce payment. It is an important function of governments to manage these external costs and benefits.

Blind campaigns for retrenchment of government expenditures and taxes can be very damaging. Disasters of this kind are occurring in my own country, as visitors to our cities can testify. Wholesale destruction of the public sector in Russia and other ex-Soviet republics, however understandable as a reaction to communism and its privileged bureaucracy, could be catastrophic.

4. Industry, not finance, produces the wealth of nations. Financial markets and financial institutions are exciting and important features of capitalism. But they are not ends in themselves. Their purpose is to make the allocation of real productive resources – land, capital and labour – efficient in the production of goods and services of value to individuals and to society. Likewise financial stabilization, important as it may be, is an instrumental goal, not in its own right the proper primary priority of government fiscal and monetary policies.

A mature capitalist economy contains an immense variety of markets, some well organized and others quite informal. Some are for goods and services, others for paper assets and debts. These financial markets are very exciting. They attract many of the best brains. The fantastic development of computer and communications technologies has multiplied the speed, scope and sophistication of financial transactions. The sun never sets on trading in currencies, equities and bonds. Derivative instruments, offering new opportunities for arbitrage and speculation, are invented, it seems, almost every day. Developing countries once regarded steel industries and national airlines as symbols of economic manhood. Now the prestigious symbol is a stock exchange.

The 1980s were the decade of the paper economy, encouraged by deregulation of both domestic financial institutions and cross-border financial transactions. Speculators and deal-makers who hit jackpots came to rival multimillionaire sports stars as heroes to college students. It is no wonder that Russian youths equate capitalism with the paper economy – with finance, deals, speculation, brokering and consulting. Western advisers to countries in transition from communism stress the creation of competitive financial institutions and unregulated markets, open to foreigners as well as to residents.

Foreign advisers and lenders also insist upon government policies of financial stabilization. In practice, this means balancing government budgets, restricting central bank credit and currency issue, deregulating financial transactions, and stabilizing the foreign exchange value of the local currency. It certainly is important to prevent or bring to an end hyperinflation. But the faith that monetary stability is a sufficient condition for reviving production, re-orienting industry and achieving the essential resource reallocations is a dangerous fallacy. The Russian central bank has been deservedly condemned for fuelling hyperinflation by exorbitant printing of rubles. The purpose of its unrestrained issue of currency is equally deserving of condemnation. It is to enable old state enterprises to meet their payrolls even though they are now producing little of social value. The result is that Russia manages to maintain full 'employment' while producing less and less gross domestic product. The bank should be, directly or indirectly, channelling credit to promising new ventures.

We should never forget that the overriding purpose of economic activity and of markets is to produce goods and services of value to individuals and to society. Financial markets are means to that end, not ends in themselves. The title of Adam Smith's 1776 book, *The Wealth of Nations*, conveys its principal message. Wealth does not consist of paper claims or even gold and silver *per se*, but of commodities useful to consumers or capable of producing consumer goods and services. Smith sought to overcome the mercantilist instincts of sovereigns who geared their nations' economies and foreign trade to maximize accumulations of precious metals. Excessive emphasis upon finances can be counter-productive, especially in adolescent capitalist economies. Ex-communist economies need entrepreneurs who will produce real goods and services and develop markets where they can sell them. The weakness of privatization voucher markets suggests that it's too early for stock exchanges.

5. The invisible hand deserves two cheers, not the three or four proposed by its zealot ideologues. Individual self-interest can be a motivation for actions of great benefit to society, but only if disciplined and channelled.

Adam Smith's most famous passage is this:

> As every individual ... endeavours ... to employ his capital in the support of domestic industry, and so to direct that industry that its produce may be of the greatest value ... [he] necessarily labours to render the annual revenue of the society as great as he can. He ... neither intends to promote the public interest, nor knows by how much he is promoting it. ... [He] is in this, as in many other cases, led by an invisible hand to promote an end which was no part of his intention.

The invisible hand is certainly one of history's Great Ideas. Competitive markets in which prices, rather than queuing or rationing, equate demand to supply are marvellous mechanisms of social coordination. Like the wheel, the market is a widespread ancient human invention.

But as I noted above, the invisible hand theorem has to be modified by recognizing externalities and public goods, where individual and societal interests diverge. These require treatment by governments to protect collective interests. Adam Smith himself was quite aware of government's role.

A moral philosopher first and a political economist second, Smith was also aware of the perils of counting too heavily on the beneficent results of unmitigated self-interest. It's easy to see the powerful energy of self-interest working for the best when Henry Ford mass-produces cars, Edison lights the world and Bill Gates designs computer operating systems. The social benefits are well worth the fortunes these inventor–entrepreneurs garnered along the way. But the invisible hand depends on competition as the discipline that converts self-interest into socially optimal outcomes. Undisciplined self-interest impels individuals and businesses to seek and protect monopolistic positions. Who would not like to control a toll booth through which economic traffic has no choice but to go? Maintenance of competition requires eternal vigilance in enforcing 'anti-trust' laws.

Smith's system works only within social institutions that channel and guide self-interested energies into constructive activities. Without those institutions – which can never be perfect – we are stuck with Hobbes's war of every man against every other, with outcomes quite different from Smith's invisible hand. Recent events in Italy and Japan, even more than in America, show how easily those institutions may be weakened and perverted by crime and corruption. Enterprise can take the form of extortion by threat of violence or political and bureaucratic persecution. Alas, this appears to be the kind of capitalism flourishing in Russia.

Laws and police can never be complete answers in any society. A civilized society cannot survive if obedience to laws and other social norms becomes a matter of self-interested calculus, where most people obey laws, for example pay taxes, only if hedonistic calculus reveals that the probability-discounted penalty of being caught exceeds the probability-discounted gain from the violation. The glorification of self-interested behaviour and the denigration of government in recent years bear some responsibility for recent trends. The mentality, 'anything goes if you can get away with it' is a recipe for anarchy.

6.   Are today's leaders of major capitalist democracies, the world's economic locomotives, up to the challenges and hazards confronting the world economy? The record of the last 20 years is discouraging. G7 policies have not sustained full employment, potential growth in living standards or liberal foreign trade. Nor do they meet the challenges of helping the economic transformations of the ex-communist countries and their integration into the world economy, and of promoting peaceful economic development in the Third World.

The first quarter-century after World War II was a period of unparalleled world-wide prosperity and growth. The major capitalist democracies, the G7 countries, indeed the more inclusive group, the OECD, followed enlightened fiscal, monetary and international trade policies. The International Monetary Fund, the World Bank and the General Agreement on Tariffs and Trade

(GATT) were established to promote orderly commercial, financial and monetary relations among nations. Consider the results:

First, these policies and institutions achieved and sustained high employment and production. Business cycles, the plague of the capitalist world before 1940, were dramatically moderated. Second, high investments in new capital, technology and education by households, businesses and governments led to rapid growth in productivity, real wages and standards of living. Third, world trade and international capital investments grew at unprecedented rates, both among the big industrial countries and between them and the poorer nations. As the advanced economies prospered and trade barriers were reduced, they served as locomotives of the world economy. Smaller, poorer and less developed countries could rely on expanding markets in Europe and North America.

Unfortunately, developments since 1973 have been much less salubrious.

G7 governments and central banks were traumatized by the inflations of the 1970s, triggered by the Vietnam War and the two oil shocks. They engineered three increasingly severe recessions to overcome these inflations. They succeeded, but the costs in lost output, lost employment, and lost capital investment were high.

G7 policy-makers are still fighting the war they won. As a result, Europe has inflicted upon itself chronically high unemployment and slow GDP growth. Persuaded by monetarist theory, European makers of monetary and fiscal policy, led by the inflation-paranoid Bundesbank, reject the use of fiscal or monetary demand stimuli to restore or maintain full employment – no matter how depressed their economies. In Japan the same doctrinaire policies have converted a minor hiccup in growth into a serious and prolonged recession.

On this score, the United States did better than its G7 partners in the 1980s. Federal Reserve Chairman Paul Volcker led the 1979–82 anti-inflation crusade and was deservedly acclaimed for his success. But he was not doctrinaire, and under his leadership the Federal Reserve terminated its monetarist policies in the fall of 1982 and managed a successful recovery. President Reagan's fiscal policy was expansionary too. Indeed, it was too much so, and Reagan bequeathed intractable high deficits to his successors. Volcker's successor at the Federal Reserve, Alan Greenspan, allowed the US economy to slip into stagnation and recession beginning in 1989. President Bush's complacency about weak economic performance cost him the 1992 election. President Clinton and his Administration are struggling, against formidable economic and political obstacles, to cope with the multiple fiscal and economic maladies they inherited. The US may be on the way to joining its G7 partners as an under-achieving economy, beset by chronic job shortage and a large corps of permanently unemployed workers.

The integrative internationalism of 1946–73 is giving way to disintegrative nationalism. Its most virulent and destructive manifestations are in the ex-communist countries. The euphoria of 1989–91 obscured the strength of long suppressed ethnic enmities within Yugoslavia and the USSR. Ethnic and religious conflicts, events show once again, are clearly a more important cause of war than economic interests. Even without the tragic violence, these fragmentations are economically disastrous. The breakdown of established patterns of specialization and trade in the former Soviet Union and Comecon have been very costly to all parties. As we economists insist, there really are mutual gains from trade. Certainly there is no invisible hand that guarantees that any state with ethnic boundaries will be viable, let alone self-sufficient. Indeed trends of technology, especially in communications, enhance the gains from trade and specialization. If these are absent, people seeking escapes from poverty will vote with their feet as much as they can, regardless of ethnic or national identities. Europe and America are familiar with the policy dilemmas resulting from hordes of would-be immigrants and refugees.

Even in the Western World, the internationalism of the golden quarter-century has given way to national and regional conflicts. The prolonged difficulties of the Uruguay Round, even now not sure to be consummated, are one symptom. The European Community has achieved remarkable integration, but sometimes acts in a disturbingly protectionist manner *vis-à-vis* the rest of the world. The opposition to the North American Free Trade Agreement (NAFTA) in the US and Canada is disheartening. At the same time, if NAFTA is ratified, the rest of the world deserves assurances that it will be more trade-creating than trade-diverting. The proclivity of the United States to arrogate to itself judgement on whether its trading partners are guilty of unfair practices that merit retaliation is an unfortunate departure from commitments to GATT rules and GATT procedures for orderly dispute resolution. Likewise, US steps now underway to 'manage' bilateral trade with Japan by insisting on specified quantitative outcomes, exports and imports of particular products and trade surpluses, both overall and bilateral, are deplorable.

Protectionism is a natural political result of the frustrations in economies beset by high unemployment, job shortages and declining wages. Our economies are increasingly interdependent. Our opportunities are increasingly worldwide. Our maladies are contagious and intertwined. The leaders of the G7 countries have yet to show appreciation of the seriousness of the problems they jointly face, let alone enough imagination and initiative to seek joint remedies. In comparison with their predecessors who confronted the tasks of world economic recovery after World War II and responded with the Marshall Plan, the Bretton Woods institutions and the GATT, our present leaders are pygmies.

21. Prospects for prosperity and growth in democratic capitalist economies*

INTRODUCTION

G7 governments and central banks are, in varying degrees, fighting the macro-economic wars of the 1970s, indeed fighting misinterpretations of those wars. The lesson they have drawn is that inflation and stagflation in the 1970s were the result of over-stimulative macro policies, especially of extravagantly expansionary monetary policies. They forget the effects of the two OPEC oil shocks, brought on by Mideast realpolitik rather than by indulgent Western central banks. In Europe and in Japan they have adopted the view, popular in the monetarist and new classical wings of the economics profession, that deliberate government policies to stimulate demands for goods and services are at best ineffective in raising economic activity and at worst inflationary, no matter in what economic circumstances they are undertaken, and that market economies will on their own find the optimal rates of employment and production.

As a consequence, the advanced capitalist democracies are forfeiting favourable opportunities for prosperity and growth. Oil prices, the culprits in the 1970s inflation and stagflation, have declined radically since 1980 and are no obstacle to economic expansion today. Inflation in general is quiescent, for example declining in the United States even as unemployment dwindles. This is particularly true of wage inflation, in the past the stubborn core of inflationary pressures. The full-employment unemployment rate, the lowest inflation-safe amount of unemployment, appears to be lower than it was thought to be in 1980. Trade unions have lost power and have learned that excessive wage demands cost jobs. International competition, both within the developed world and from the emerging industrial economies elsewhere, is strong discipline for wages and prices in North America, Japan and Europe.

*Presented at Barcelona Economic Forum, 12 May 1994.

190

THE GOLDEN ERA: FROM WORLD WAR II TO OIL SHOCK I

The first quarter-century after World War II was an era of unprecedented prosperity, growth and stability for the economically advanced capitalist democracies of Western Europe, North America and Japan. They quickly overcame the immense wartime damage and surpassed their pre-war national outputs. They grew rapidly in per capita income and material well-being. Business cycle recessions were short and shallow, in significant contrast to pre-war experience. Unemployment was kept very low, and inflation, like unemployment, contained at low single-digit rates. International trade grew even faster than production.

The success of that golden quarter-century can be summarized in terms of the following framework. The trend of an economy or group of economies can be represented by real (inflation-corrected) potential gross domestic product (PGDP), the output capable of being produced when the economy is at full employment, defined by the lowest inflation-safe unemployment rate, often called the natural rate of unemployment. Actual GDP moves around PGDP, more often falling short than overshooting. The gap between the two, potential minus actual, is the business cycle. If an economy's potential trend is steep, it may seldom, if ever, experience a big enough gap to suffer an actual arithmetic decline in GDP. This was the good fortune of Japan until very recently. Unemployment of labour and excess industrial capacity move up and down with the GDP gap. However, overt unemployment is more sensitive to GDP in some economies than others, much more sensitive in the US than in Japan, where much redundant labour is kept on payrolls. The summary of OECD macroeconomic performance in the golden quarter-century is this: PGDP was growing fast, and GDP gaps were kept small. On both counts performance deteriorated in the subsequent 25 years.

Successful macroeconomic performance between 1945 and 1970 had many favourable by-products, notably in public investments, social legislation, reduction of poverty and assistance to less developed countries. Cooperation among these democracies, led by the United States, had established new international institutions that helped to shape the post-war world economy: the World Bank, the International Monetary Fund, the General Agreement on Tariffs and Trade and the OECD. The OECD became a facility for international coordination of macroeconomic policies among the major powers themselves. In 1961, for example, the Finance Ministers of the OECD agreed to pursue, individually and jointly, growth of real output in the OECD area of 50 per cent (averaging 4.1 per cent per year) over the decade of the 1960s, a target that in the event was surpassed. Not only is it inconceivable that the OECD Ministerial Council or today's G7 would set so ambitious a target, it is even inconceivable that they would set any target at all for this central measure of their countries' economic performance.

STAGFLATION IN THE 1970s AND ITS LEGACY

A decisive historic break in the performance of G7 and OECD economies occurred around 1973. There were three main symptoms, related to one another.

First, growth of PGDP slowed appreciably. Part of the slowdown was demographic, reflecting the decline in labour force growth as the 'baby-boomer' bulge receded. By itself this was no particular cause for concern, although the consequent ageing of the population is now bringing difficult adjustments in social insurance and medical care. The great cause for concern was the other factor in the PGDP slowdown, the slump in the growth of labour productivity. In the long run, growth in labour productivity pays off in higher real wages, per capita consumption and social well-being. Without productivity growth, those outcomes, too, will be stagnant. This decline has been general throughout the G7 area, while productivity has risen sharply among the Asian tigers and other newly industrializing countries.

The productivity slowdown in advanced economies is a mystery whose solution still defies scholars and econometricians. Its timing suggests that it must have been somehow related to oil shock I in 1973–74, OPEC's embargo of exports and its quadrupling of world petroleum prices. The necessity to pay more for imported oil, to adjust to less energy-using technologies, and to replace energy-intensive installations was a blow to the potential output capacities of oil-importing countries, a shock that was to be repeated in oil shock II at the end of the decade. These shocks were reinforced by the coincidental surge of conscious environmental concerns, leading to regulatory pressure for cleaner production processes, often entailing new equipment and technology. While these events could have lowered productivity, at least temporarily in some industries, this is hard to confirm and even harder to blame for failures of productivity trends to recover in the 1980s.

The second dimension of the 1973 break was the emergence of inflation as a threat preoccupying central banks and other makers of macroeconomic policies. This concern antedates the first oil shock. The United States economy was overheated in 1966–69 by piling the expanded military demands of the Vietnam War on to an already fully employed economy. American inflation rose from 2 per cent per year to 5 per cent, and inflationary pressures spilled into the rest of the world. When a recession deliberately engineered in 1969 to cool off these pressures worked disappointingly slowly, the Nixon Administration in 1971 adopted price controls, and the Federal Reserve pumped up demand to lower unemployment and the GDP gap in 1972. President Nixon also forced Germany and Japan to appreciate their currencies against the dollar. He abrogated the Bretton Woods treaty by abandoning the United States Treasury's commitment to redeem in gold all dollars presented by foreign governments. The gold-dollar Bretton Woods system was probably doomed anyway. The economic rise of Europe and Japan ended American monetary hegemony and made it essential that the US should have the same possibility of depreciating its own currency as other countries had. Moreover, as exchange controls were abandoned and major currencies became freely convertible, the volume of private capital movements made the maintenance of fixed exchange rates by central bank interventions increasingly problematic. At the time, Nixon's move resulted in monetary expansions by countries which were accumulating dollars but were reluctant to appreciate their currencies to stem those inflows.

Oil shock I came on top of these inflationary developments. Inflation shot up, and central banks cracked down on their economies. Nixon's price and wage controls crumbled.

That brings us to the third decisive development of the 1970s, stagflation – the combination of high inflation and high unemployment. Anti-inflation monetary policies generated in 1974–76 the most serious cyclical recessions and the highest unemployment rates since the immediate post-war years of the 1940s. Large gaps between potential and actual GDP were superimposed on the negative shocks to PGDP itself. Thanks to expansionary fiscal policy and accommodative monetary policy as inflation subsided, recovery occurred in America during 1976–79. Japan was especially successful in quick anti-inflation therapy and in recovering growth momentum. But no major economy restored its earlier prosperity, and European governments and central banks seemed content to settle for higher unemployment rates and slower growth, without significant recovery from the 1974–76 recession. At a 1978 G7 summit, Germany reluctantly agreed to the modestly expansionary policy desired by the United States. The dollar was under attack in the exchange markets because the US had been ahead of the pack in recovery since 1975. Chancellor Helmut Schmidt's view, shared by other European leaders, that high unemployment and slow recovery, if any, were needed to guard against inflation was, he thought, vindicated by the new bout of stagflation associated with oil shock II, triggered by the Iranian revolution, the curtailment of Gulf oil supplies and another big boost in oil prices. But it was hard to attribute either oil shock and its stagflationary results to the fiscal and monetary policies of the G7 governments. In any event, those governments and central banks jointly adopted even more determined and severe anti-inflation policies than in 1974–75, resulting in a still deeper and longer recession during 1979–82 and in the highest unemployment rates since the Great Depression of the 1930s.

EUROPE: UNDER-ACHIEVEMENT SINCE 1980

From 1982 on, the macroeconomic policies and performances of the United States have diverged sharply from those of its European and Japanese partners.

Europe has continued its cautious and complacent macroeconomic policies. Having failed to recover from the first oil shock recession, Europe did not recover from the second one either. Instead, Europe accepted quantum jumps in unemployment rates and GDP gaps and described as recovery GDP growth barely adequate to keep unemployment from rising further, and in the 1990s inadequate to that modest task as well. The rationale has been the belief that, even at unemployment rates far above those that were compatible with stable inflation 20 years ago, European economies are on the brink of explosive inflation. The idea is to take no risk at all of higher inflation, but every risk of higher unemployment. A high proportion of European unemployment, much higher than in the United States, is long term. Whole generations of school-leavers are simply not participating in the economy.

The German Bundesbank became essentially the arbiter of macroeconomic policy for all of Europe. The European Monetary System (EMS) became a regional Bretton Woods fixed exchange rate system, with other currencies pegged to the Deutsche mark. The other members of the EMS lost monetary autonomy; they could not move their own interest rates relative to those for Deutsche mark assets without risking an outflow of funds forcing them to devalue their currencies, a traumatic and debasing process. Thus Bundesbank policy set the economic climate for the European Community – and beyond, as non-members chose to join the Deutsche mark area. The Bundesbank tends to see imminent hyperinflation all the time. Often the authorities in both member and non-member countries welcomed Bundesbank discipline, seeing it as a politically painless way of ending or preventing local inflation. But in recent years several affiliates have felt the economic pain of overvalued currencies and have had to devalue and withdraw from the Exchange Rate Mechanism.

Fiscal policy is also immobilized. The dominant ideology in European officialdom advocates low budget deficits, preferably balanced or surplus budgets, in all kinds of economic weather. That doctrine allows no scope for countercyclical expenditure or tax policies. This position is reflected in the strict limits on public debt and deficits set in the Maastricht Treaty.

European officials, supported by many academic and business economists, diagnose their continuing high levels of unemployment as structural. That is to say, the natural rate of unemployment has risen by several percentage points. Macroeconomic policy to expand demand will just push up money wages and prices, without anything more than a transient cut in unemployment. Why has this happened? There are several theories. Real wages – not just money wages – cannot be reduced as would be necessary to induce employers to hire more workers. Unemployment insurance benefits and other subventions of idleness are too generous. Unions are too unreasonable, interested only in an ever narrower group of insiders, to the exclusion of jobseekers. Chronically unemployed persons lack essential work skills and work habits.

Structural diagnoses of unemployment always flourish when unemployment is high. Officials of governments and central banks do not wish to entertain the Keynesian diagnosis that the reason is insufficiency of demand for goods and services and thus of job opportunities, and the Keynesian prescription that government spending or inducements for private spending would create jobs. Structural diagnoses are frequently falsified by events. This was true in the United States in the Great Depression, and again in 1960 and 1980.

Robert Solow has investigated the structural diagnosis of European unemployment today, in greatest detail for France. He concludes that no more than half of the increase in unemployment over pre-1973 levels is structural, while the other half is susceptible to Keynesian therapy. A recent instance of the proclivity to find structural reasons for unemployment was the recent international 'jobs summit' in Detroit, where G7 Cabinet Ministers exchanged information on various remedies for structural unemployment and never even mentioned the possibility that pepping up demand in the economy might be an alternative, or at least a necessary complement, of structural nostrums.

Two other points are worth making. First, some unemployment that was originally Keynesian could, if allowed to persist year after year, become structural, in the sense that the unemployed worker loses or fails to obtain needed skills and habits. In such cases, the structural diagnosis could be self-fulfilling. Second, excessive unemployment, much of it long term, has been a problem for most of two decades. If the solution lies in welfare state reforms, new arrangements in industrial relations and collective bargaining, and various labour market innovations, there has been plenty of time to find and implement such remedies.

AMERICA UNDER REAGAN, BUSH, CLINTON, VOLCKER AND GREENSPAN

Paul Volcker was appointed Chairman of the Federal Reserve System in 1979 to cope with the inflation and dollar depreciation that accompanied oil shock II. He presided over two and a half years of unrelenting monetary restriction that produced double-digit interest rates and double-digit unemployment. His recession succeeded in reducing inflation from 11 or 12 per cent to 5 or 6 per cent. In the summer of 1982, with business activity steeply falling and financial institutions facing insolvency, Volcker reversed field, declared victory over inflation, lowered interest rates, expanded credit and money supply, and started the American economy on the road to recovery. The recovery went on for six years, reduced unemployment from 10.5 per cent to 5.5 per cent, and closed the 12 per cent GDP gap. During most of this recovery both interest rates and inflation were gradually declining.

Volcker turned the economy around and managed the recovery, but much of the fuel for demand expansion came from President Reagan's fiscal policy. His massive tax cuts and buildup of defence spending generated federal budget deficits as high as 5.5 per cent of GDP, unprecedented in US peacetime history. The Reagan Administration was not consciously following Keynesian fiscal policy, which they abhorred on principle. They intended their tax cuts not as stimuli of private consumption spending but as supply-side incentives that would boost PGDP. In their more enthusiastic moods, they held out the hope that tax collections from these gains in production would exceed the initial tax cuts, so that the net effect would be to reduce the deficit, not to increase it. This didn't happen, of course, but recovery did. In this respect American macroeconomic policy in the 1980s was much more successful than European policy. (In recovery from the 1979–82 recession Japan did better than Europe but not as well as the United States.)

However, Reagan fiscal policy tilted American recovery strongly towards consumption and defence spending, at the expense of investment, private and public. The supply-side initiatives did not have their intended productivity-increasing effects, and the sharp decreases in saving deprived future PGDP of some productivity gains greater investment might have generated. Moreover, the decline in national saving meant that much of the investment that did occur was financed by capital inflows from the rest of the world, of which the counterparts were foreign trade and current account deficits, also costly to future Americans.

Unfortunately, Volcker's successor, Alan Greenspan, and Reagan's successor, George Bush, did not succeed in converting the 1983–89 recovery into steady growth at full employment. The Federal Reserve properly slowed the pace of recovery as full employment was approached, but then acted too little and too late as the economy slipped into stagnation in 1989 and actual recession in 1990.

The 1992 Presidential campaign focused on the two major public complaints about the economy: 1) the recession, high unemployment and scarce jobs: and 2) the post-1973 slowdown in productivity growth, bringing stagnation in real wages and actual declines in take-home pay for many wage-earners. Combined, these two developments were devastating for many American families. Their discontents elected Bill Clinton. Unfortunately, the remedies for the two complaints were quite different.

Clinton tried to prescribe for both maladies at once. He was willing to add to federal spending in 1993 even if it temporarily increased the deficit, while asking Congress for austere deficit reduction measures to take effect later in a five-year period.

The stimulative spending he advocated was for investment in education, infrastructure and technology, good for the long run as well as the short run. This sophisticated macroeconomic plan was beyond the intellectual capacity of Congress, TV commentators and reporters. They forced the President to sacrifice his public investment programmes, even though they might contribute more to future generations than either a reduced deficit or lower taxes would.

Clinton's five-year budget programmes squeaked through Congress in August 1993 by the narrowest of votes. This programme is reducing the annual deficit to less than 3 per cent of GDP, a small enough fraction to keep the federal debt from growing faster than GDP. However, the future of the federal budget is threatened by the exploding costs of federal medical care programmes for the elderly and the poor. Health care reform is the biggest issue on the Congressional agenda this year, and the outcome will be crucial for the budget and the economy.

All in all, the President and the country were lucky in 1993. He made progress on malady 1) without doing anything about it. Deprived of its fiscal stimulus package, the Administration hoped that its programme of five-year budget austerity would lower long-term interest rates, and consequently boost investment by businesses and home-builders. The Federal Reserve cooperated to the extent of holding short interest rates at the 3 per cent level set in December 1992. Long-term interest rates did decline sharply, and the stock market boomed, contributing to significant revivals in business spending on plant and equipment and in residential construction.

However, in the wake of the strong fourth quarter of 1993, Alan Greenspan's Federal Reserve broke the spell. Beginning on 4 February the Fed raised the Federal Funds rate in three instalments to 3.75 per cent. Another move, to 4 per cent is expected at the next Fed meeting on 17 May. This drastic shift in monetary policy deranged the bond and stock markets, evoking an irrational melange, fears of future Fed policies, inflation and recession. Long-term interest rates shot up, and the stock market fell, damaging the prospects of strong recoveries in investment and GDP in 1994. The Fed's moves were premature and gratuitous, unprovoked by any inflationary developments or prospects or any other worrisome economic news.

A hopeful piece of good news is that labour productivity has been improving; perhaps its future rate of growth will be higher than in the past. That's good for problem 2), but maybe not good for 1). It means there is more GDP capacity, requiring faster demand growth for recovery: all the greater reason for the Fed to hold interest rates down.

Full recovery is by no means in the bag. The American economy is still one percentage point of unemployment and a GDP gap of 2.5 per cent away from full employment, which the Clinton Administration does not expect to reach until 1998, nearly ten years after the economy was last there. The Federal Reserve is the key player. They have always argued for the kind of deficit-reducing fiscal policy the President and Congress are now committed to, and inflation is quiescent. The Fed's principal task in 1994 is to keep this recovery going, even if that should require later this year a reversal of their recent restrictive moves.

Short of domestic macroeconomic options, the Administration looks to trade policy as the source of job creation for the US economy. The President successfully adopted as his own crusades both the North American Free Trade Agreement (NAFTA) and the Uruguay Round of the General Agreement on Tariffs and Trade (GATT). Their hope for gaining jobs from trade policy makes no sense for reciprocal agreements, like NAFTA and GATT, which increase both exports and imports – good for social welfare on balance but not for total demands for US labour.

Sometimes Clinton and his advisers take off their free trade hats and adopt their trade-war stance. The President hopes pressure on Japan to open its markets will increase US exports without raising imports, thus generating net gains in American jobs. But even if the Japanese agree to aim at the targets we are urging on them, the overall effects on American jobs would be slow and small.

America's trade deficit and Japan's surplus are mainly macroeconomic problems. They are appropriate subjects for G7 economic summits and ministerial meetings, whose central agenda is supposed to be coordination of macroeconomic policies in the interests of global prosperity. Both Japan and Europe should be adopting more stimulative macroeconomic policies, especially expansionary low-interest-rate monetary policies. These are appropriate for the depressed macroeconomic conditions in those economies, and they will indirectly increase demands for exports from America and the rest of the world. Japan in particular is a macroeconomic disaster area, and deserves to be pressed hard to adopt strong fiscal stimuli, with both new public investment spending and tax reductions (not offset by other tax increases now or scheduled in future).

The G7 and OECD economies have been under-achieving – Western Europe for a decade or more and Japan more recently. The United States has been lagging in productivity growth and is in danger of joining its European partners by suffering chronic job shortage and a large corps of permanently unemployed workers.

Protectionism, including trade-diverting regionalism, is a natural political result of the frustrations in economies beset by high unemployment, job shortages and declining wages. Our economies are increasingly interdependent. Our opportunities are increasingly world-wide. Our maladies are contagious and intertwined. The leaders of the G7 countries have yet to show appreciation of the seriousness of the problems they jointly face, let alone enough imagination and initiative to seek joint remedies. Our present leaders do not compare with their predecessors who confronted the tasks of world economic recovery after World War II and responded with the Marshall Plan, the Bretton Woods institutions and the GATT.

22.   On living and trading with Japan: United States commercial and macroeconomic policies*

It's a special honour to be your Adam Smith Lecturer in 1990, 200 years after the death of the man we revere as the founder of the discipline of economics. In July, I participated in a symposium in Edinburgh to mark the anniversary, and in a wreath-laying ceremony at his grave. History also will credit this year with the victory of Adam Smith's political economy over Karl Marx's, the triumph of Western capitalism and democracy over Soviet communism and dictatorship. Especially here in America, these dramatic events have been jubilantly hailed as conclusive vindications of our economic and political institutions.

Yet we Americans are much less sure of the strengths of our system and the virtues of our way of life when we turn our eyes to the Orient and observe Japan's economic success. We do not regard it, as we might, as spectacular evidence of the superiority of 'our system'. We seem to view 'Japan Inc.' as still another alien economic order, one that succeeds not by following our principles but by violating them, a system with which our businesses and workers cannot be expected to compete on their own.

Largely because of the frustrations we feel in our economic relations with Japan, the United States is deliberately flouting the canons of foreign commerce set forth in *The Wealth of Nations*. The book is, after all, a tract arguing for free trade over mercantilism, and we are going for mercantilism.

A *New Yorker* cover this summer depicted New York City as a metropolitan Japanese garden. Robert Reich of Harvard reports an informal poll he takes of many American audiences: which of two scenarios, A or B, do you prefer? In Scenario A, US real GNP is 25 per cent higher in the year 2000 than in 1990, while in Japan real GNP is 75 per cent higher. In Scenario B the figures are 8.0 per cent for the US and 8.3 per cent for Japan. All kinds of audiences prefer B, with only one exception: economists.

Like Reich, I am deeply disturbed by the proclivity I detect, among intellectuals as well as plain Americans, to put Japan in the slot of America's prime nemesis now vacated by the Soviet Union. Japan is seen to be as

*First published in *Business Economics*, January 1991. (Adam Smith address at the National Association of Business Economists, September 1990.)

determined to conquer us by economic clout as the Soviet Union was to subdue us by force, and more likely to succeed. Japan's threat is apparently perceived to be to displace us as Number One in the world economic Olympics, to outcompete us in manufacturing industries and technologies we regard as our rightful domain, to take over our real estate, corporate industries and banks – and, evidently, to flood our homes, roads and shops with machines, gadgets and toys of high quality and reasonable price, taking in return our paper IOUs denominated in a currency we ourselves print.

I am old enough to remember times when we Americans scorned Japanese products as cheap, low quality imitations of the real things made at home. Some crafty Japanese businessmen established in Japan a manufacturing centre named 'Usa' so that they could put 'MADE IN USA' labels on their products. Now American consumers pay a premium just for 'made in Japan'; the Chevy Nova, now Geo Prizm, produced by the joint General Motors–Toyota venture in Fremont, California, is the same car as the Toyota Corolla and sells for $1000 less.

Our ambivalence extends to the growth of Japanese ownership of properties in this country. It's a source of black humour and resentment. Yet governors and mayors eagerly solicit Japanese firms and investors to locate in their jurisdictions, and workers queue up for the jobs. Foreign direct investment positions in the United States amounted in total to only $328 billion in 1988, 2 per cent of the $15 trillion value of land and tangible reproducible capital. Of that $328 billion, Japanese ownership was $53 billion, barely half the British stake.[1]

Has Japan overtaken us? Japan is ahead of us in GNP per capita if conversions are made at exchange rates, but not if they are made at purchasing power parities.[2] Our non-tradeables are much less expensive. Japanese graduate students at Yale in spring 1990 estimated the purchasing power equivalent of their consumption bundle at about 250 yen per dollar overall, more than 300 yen for food, more than 1000 yen for housing. The exchange rate was 140. But if the differential trends in productivity and capital accumulation continue, Japan will pass us in any measure of per capita production and consumption. And so will the major countries of Europe.

If I were a Japanese citizen and economist, I would object to many government policies and business practices, including ones that bother American business and government, on the grounds that they are bad for Japanese consumers. The cliché is that Japan systematically favours producers over consumers. That doesn't make sense, because the same people are both. What it is supposed to convey is that policies and customs promote and protect influential sectoral interests. The main gainers from reforms would be the majority of the Japanese themselves.

As endless incidents and anecdotes attest, Japanese households, businesses and government agencies favour local products, even when foreign-made goods and services have advantages in price and quality. Penetrating these markets takes patience and investment. When home preferences are matters of consumer tastes and traditions and entrenched customer relationships, they are exasperating. When they reflect official policies of discrimination, as often reported (for example, in telecommunications and computers), they are also objectionable. Our own governments have followed 'buy American' procurement policies, and many other governments also systematically discriminate in favour of local suppliers, at considerable expense to their taxpayers.

Notorious Japanese agricultural and land use policies make rice and other food prices sky high, and raise land prices too. On similar grounds, economists oppose the dreadful agricultural policies of the United States, the European Community and most other countries. The Uruguay Round is supposed to be negotiating them away, to the benefit of consuming majorities everywhere.

Reforms of these policies, in Japan and elsewhere, would probably have little effect on country rankings in GNP per capita.

ECONOMIC THEORY AND FREE TRADE

Adam Smith was pretty much a unilateral free trader, to use Jagdish Bhagwati's terminology.[3] That is, Smith's advice to his nation was to allow unrestricted access to its markets regardless of the practices and policies of foreign exporters and their governments. Likewise, he would neither impede nor subsidize his nation's export trade. If the Japanese sell goods to us cheap, whether because they are very efficient or because they choose to sell below cost, let us enjoy our fortune:

> Whether the advantages which one country has over another be natural or acquired, is ... of no consequence. As long as the one country has those advantages, and the other wants [that is, lacks] them, it will always be more advantageous for the latter, rather to buy of the former than to make (Smith 1776).

If the Japanese persist in growing rice at a greater cost to their consumers than importing from us, Smith would say, let us not punish ourselves further by forgoing their bargains in video games. Let us simply allocate to other activities the land and other inputs that would be used to produce rice exports.

Only in Victorian Britain, 70 years after publication of *The Wealth of Nations*, was unilateral free trade official policy and ideology. It is still popular with economists, but more as a pragmatic choice over likely unpleas-

ant alternatives than as a theorem. Adam Smith himself grudgingly acknowledged two reasons that might justify discrimination against imports: national
security and effective retaliation.[4] Smith did not allow, as later theorists did,
an infant industry case; he evidently thought that long-horizon decisions
could be entrusted to the invisible hand.

The model for unilateral free trade is the following: Foreign trade is a set
of activities by which a nation's labour and other resources can earn consumption goods. Other activities involve direct production for domestic use;
they too transform factor inputs into consumption. Resources should be deployed on that set of activities of both kinds that yields maximum consumption. Neoclassical economists would say maximum utility, but the essential
point remains. The free market will solve the activity analysis problem;
interventions in international trade, as in domestic trade, only reduce the
wealth and welfare of the nation.

The theoretical trouble is that a nation's terms of trade, the yields in
consumption or utility of resources devoted to buying foreign goods with
exports, are not wholly exogenous. Unlike domestic production activities,
trade activities are not completely defined by technology. It is not just that
their productivities may change because of external events, but that their
terms may depend on volumes of goods traded, and on foreign responses to
our exporters' offers and our government's policies.

At least a half-century ago economists perceived the possible opportunity
for a big country to act like a monopolist facing a downward sloping demand
curve rather than an exogenous price. The country might then calculate and
set an 'optimal tariff', to get the most import value for the resources it
devotes to exports. Some British economists and Labour intellectuals after
World War II seized upon this argument to oppose liberalization of trade and
currency transactions. But there was never any evidence that they knew how
to find the optimal tariff, or its equivalent in quantitative controls. Probably
Britain did not have all that much monopoly power anyway.

Of course, individual firms or national cartels of firms may have some
monopoly powers in the particular commodities they produce and trade. The
'optimum tariff' argument assumes that the nation in aggregate may be able
to collect rents from foreigners more fully than decentralized private firms.

WHY IS THERE TRADE?

Recent international trade theory has gone far beyond the 'optimum tariff',
applying more sophisticated models from modern microeconomics and industrial organization. These too are being used in opposition to unilateral free
trade and in support of strategically 'managed trade'. To understand the

background of these developments, it is necessary to review briefly economic doctrines on the reasons for international and interregional trade.

The principle of comparative advantage is one of the few things you can teach students that is at the same time a simple idea and a great revelation. (It is due to Ricardo rather than to Smith. Smith speaks of 'advantages', but if he had the 'comparative' idea he didn't expound it clearly.) In Ricardo the comparative advantages are largely due to geographical differences in natural endowments. In the Heckscher–Ohlin theory, which most of us were taught and some of us have taught, they also arise largely from differences in relative factor endowments, as determined by natural resources, population growth and capital formation.

I used to sit on doctoral oral exam committees. Often one of the candidate's fields was international trade, the specialty of one of the other examiners. In that field, the candidate was always asked the ice-breaking question: 'Why is there trade?'. Almost always the candidate took the question as the expected cue to expound Heckscher–Ohlin. I couldn't help asking if factor endowments explained the trade between Boston and New York or Ontario and Michigan. It was hard to extract Adam Smith's answer, and rare.

Smith's answer was, of course, the division of labour. He did not neglect natural advantages, but he stressed the mutual economies to be gained by specialization and trade, whether among artisans in a village or among nations and continents. Modern theorists have rediscovered these major sources of trade. They would add economies of scope, noting complementarities in joint production as well as increasing returns in volumes of outputs.

Economies of scale and scope lead to trade, even in the absence of differential factor endowments. They introduce arbitrary historical determinism to the location of activities. Why should New Haven be an educational centre and Hartford an insurance centre? Why make movies in Hollywood, corn flakes in Battle Creek, beer in Milwaukee, cars in Detroit? Comparative advantages do not seem to be so natural and inevitable as Ricardo and Heckscher–Ohlin made them appear. Economies of scale and scope are also likely to lead to imperfect competition, in which individual producers have some control over prices and product specifications.

THE NEW TRADE THEORY AND MANAGED TRADE

So-called new international trade theory (see the seminal essays of Paul Krugman collected in his 1990 book) casts doubt on the traditional case for free trade, and indeed on the optimality of free market competition in general. Thus it opens the door for strategic gaming in commercial policy. The literature consists mostly of parables in which protectionists or export-promoting interventions could produce gains for the economy undertaking them and perhaps for its trading partners as well.

Imperfect competition itself is a possible source of inefficiency in the allocation of resources. It may, for example, make the marginal productivity of capital or labour or land higher in some uses than in others. Such inefficiencies might be remediable by government intervention.

A good example is the model of Katz and Summers (1989). They argue that most high-wage industries are inefficiently small; the wage differentials they pay are rents to their workers rather than compensations for skills or for non-pecuniary disadvantages of the jobs. Efficiency would be enhanced by subsidizing those industries, to induce them to draw workers from employments where wages and marginal productivities are lower.

The correction of this market failure need have nothing to do with managing foreign trade, but that is one possible way to go. Katz and Summers provide a rationale for the arguments of some trade union economists and other advocates of managed trade, who say that the US should seek comparative advantage in high-wage activities. Since high-wage labour characterizes export industries much more frequently than import-competing industries, the authors' model favours export promotion rather than protection.

The proposition that the wage differentials are rents to workers is essential to the argument. Otherwise it is fallacious to think that society can freely choose to locate its comparative advantages in high-wage or high value-added activities. To expand such activities it would be necessary to find, train and recruit workers with suitable skills. The hope that subsidies, protection and managed trade can enable us to recapture lost comparative advantages in the automobile and smokestack industries is ludicrous. High wages contributed to those debacles.

New trade theory more typically takes off from dynamic scale and scope economies, which could conceivably afford opportunities exploitable by optimum tariffs or other nationalistic interventions. 'Learning by doing' is a favourite dynamic ingredient. It has two important attributes. First, the value of current production exceeds its immediate sales proceeds by the contribution of the 'doing' to the efficiency of future production. Experience matters, and head starts are advantageous. Secondly, the value of the learning is not wholly capturable by the producing firm; it generates 'externalities' of benefit to its workers, suppliers, customers and competitors.

The first attribute by itself is no reason for government help unless capital markets are unduly short-sighted and risk-averse. Start-up losses that will be justified by future cash flows are like any other investments; the capital markets should be able to appraise them and finance them. Externalities, the second attribute, are essential to make a strong argument. Cases of this kind, like those arising from labour market imperfections, need not have anything to do with foreign trade; they could arise in closed economies.

In open economies, protection from foreign competition could enable domestic producers to exploit all the scale and scope economies and learning opportunities of the home market, at least for a while. This is an advanced version of the old 'infant industry' argument, which also depends on irreversibilities and/or deferred gains that would be excessively discounted by capital markets. Alas, the practical record is full of infants who never learned to walk and of senile senior citizens in prolonged second childhoods.

Irreversibilities associated with learning by doing have been strongly emphasized in discussions of Japanese–American electronics competition, in particular in semiconductors, where it is argued that a lead in one product will be a decisive advantage in developing and marketing the next product in the same line, for example, the next multiple of four in memory chips. However, since memory chips of each generation are mass-produced standard products, the ease of entry or re-entry into chip production would seem to be a protection against monopolies created by head starts and 'predatory pricing'. After all, the Japanese were able to learn enough from what American producers were initially doing to enter the field and gain leadership. For that matter, it is from us that the Japanese learned how to make motor vehicles. In these and other cases, an important element in Japanese success was willingness to accept large losses through periods of adversity. American firms have not shown similar patience.

Although new trade theory casts doubt on unilateral free trade, it does not do justice to strategic interactions among rival nations. The examples of potentially welfare-improving interventions do not account for responsive and retaliatory moves of trading partners. Theories of games and strategic interactions are the modern techniques for analysing such situations.

Managed trade could be regarded as a game among competing nations behaving like giant oligopolists – Japan Inc., US Inc., Europe Ltd, etc. (This is close to the Marx–Lenin view of national capitalist governments as rival imperialists.) The gains from trade make it a positive-sum game. Unfortunately the prisoners' dilemma applies: grasping greedily for lion's shares of the gains from trade, the players impose losses on all.

The strategies of the rival nations would have to be incredibly complex. They would involve calculations and forecasts of dynamic economies of scale and scope, complementarities across industries and regions at home and abroad, rates of learning by doing, future technologies and externalities of various kinds. If the managers of Japan Inc. – government, MITI, *keiretsus* all together – made successful decisions of this kind, they dealt with easy cases where experience in the US could guide them. Imagine making similar decisions completely from scratch: centrally planning the railroad–coal–steel developments of 19th century America or the automobile–petroleum–roads complex of the early 20th century.

In summary, new trade theory says managed trade might work in some concrete cases. To escalate that possibility into wholesale advocacy of a new policy is logically unjustified.[5]

TRADING WITH OR WITHOUT INTERNATIONAL RULES

The United States has never subscribed to unilateral free trade, in principle or in practice. Our official policy since Cordell Hull's initiatives in the first Franklin Roosevelt Administration has centred on reciprocity in the reduction of tariffs and, lately, other barriers to imports. We have put great stress on the Most Favoured Nation (MFN) principle, extending 'concessions' negotiated with any parties to all parties who do the same.

Since the General Agreement on Tariffs and Trade (GATT) came into effect in 1946, multilateral negotiations for reciprocal liberalizations have taken place in successive 'Rounds' under its aegis.[6] The treaty binds GATT members to MFN and to 'national treatment' of imports, that is, no local taxes or product standards that are not also imposed on similar domestic products. The general objective can be described as a 'level playing field' for products of different national origins. Trade liberalization under the GATT deserves some credit for the rapid post-war growth of world trade, even faster than the growth of world incomes over the first post-war quarter-century. The erosion of GATT principles deserves some of the blame for the fact that world trade has grown more slowly than world incomes since 1970, and perhaps for the general slowdown in economic growth.

The very idea of reciprocity does accept the mercantilist attitude that country A is doing B a favour by allowing its residents to buy B's goods. In the same spirit, 'concessions' are matched by equating the additional dollar amounts of exports on both sides. Gary Hufbauer (1989) calls the GATT a 'system of managed mercantilism'. (The bias for exports over imports does not, of course, extend to essential goods they cannot supply on their own; the main anxiety of countries that do not produce oil or do not produce enough is that foreign supplies may be cut off.)

In a different and better light, the GATT might be viewed as an attempt at a cooperative solution of the game of nations described in the section above. It is true that the GATT brought some law, order and peace into international commerce. But it is not true that the member nations are playing the economists' game. They are not trying to maximize collective or individual gains from trade. Rather each government is representing parochial and sectoral interests. Or, as might be said of US Presidential Administrations *vis-à-vis*

Congresses, the government is seeking to liberalize trade as much as possible subject to political constraints. GATT Rounds have the virtue of so bundling the outcomes as to provide credible excuses for failures to protect every internal interest.

Still another interpretation of the GATT might be that its internationally agreed rules protect citizens everywhere against governments everywhere, that is, against political proclivities to favour special interests. In this respect the GATT would be similar to international agreements on human rights. Today the GATT is in serious trouble.

1. As tariffs have been lowered over the past 40 years, non-tariff barriers have proliferated. Quantitative restrictions on agricultural imports have long been tolerated, initially at the insistence of the United States. Now there are quotas on many other imports, notably Japanese motor cars and textiles and apparel (under the Multifibre Agreement). In spite of the Reagan Administration's support of free trade in principle and of the Uruguay Round, 28 per cent of US imports were subject to restraint in 1988, compared to 13 per cent in 1980. (Hufbauer, 1989, p. 42).

    Quantitative restrictions are more pernicious than tariffs. They lack automatic flexibility in response to demand and supply shocks. They hand over cartel rents to producing firms on both sides of the barriers. Japanese auto firms have good reason not to be very unhappy about the 'voluntary' limits on their shipments to America. As for American auto firms, they took obscene advantage of import quotas to raise prices, profits, dividends and executive pay. Tariffs have the merit of capturing part of such rents for taxpayers.

2. The MFN principle has been eroded by the formation of free trade areas: the European Community, the United States and Israel, the United States and Canada, and perhaps in future the United States and Mexico. Maybe, as US policy-makers believe, the gains in trade liberalization and creation more than offset the losses in trade diversion. Much will depend on the behaviour of the EC after 1992, and on what happens to the countries of Eastern Europe.

3. Retaliations and threats of retaliation have greatly increased, usually in response to local competitors' complaints of dumping, and now also in response to local exporters' complaints of difficulties in selling abroad. In the United States, complaints to the federal government have become easier to make and to make successfully. The only definition of dumping that makes economic sense is selling goods in an export market at lower prices than at home or in other export markets. This might be predatory pricing preparatory to raising them once competitors are driven out, but that would be only a short-term problem in activities where monopoly

positions would be readily contestable. Effective criteria of dumping in the US are now so loose that relief is granted if the imported goods are sold below American producers' full costs, or in effect below their prices! Most retaliations do not meet Adam Smith's criterion, often claimed as a rationale by advocates of managed trade, namely that the tactics successfully pry open markets and generate net gains from trade.

4. The GATT procedures of adjudicating trade disputes have fallen into desuetude. The US simply arrogates the right to judge and to punish. The major purpose is to get more sales for American industries, and in spite of our pious disavowals these often come at the expense of other nations' exporters. Retaliations actually carried out can deprive American businesses of the cheap imported inputs they need to be competitive. Our attempt to make Japanese computer manufacturers buy more American memory chips backfired when the chips needed by American computer makers became scarce and expensive.

Aggressive retaliation by the United States has accelerated since 1986, especially under the impetus of The Omnibus Trade and Competitiveness Act of 1988. Japan is the principal target. Larger US exports to Japan are the main objectives. Threats of retaliation against Japanese exports are the main instruments. 'Super 301' indictments put Japan in the dock, with the United States Trade Representative (USTR) as prosecutor and judge and with Congress looking over her shoulder. The proceedings completely ignore the GATT, its rules and its procedures of dispute resolution. Other countries deeply resent American arrogance; they know that we assume the role of virtuous policeman with a long record of crimes and misdemeanors.

Japan does not have many tariffs or formal trade barriers of which we can complain. The USTR's complaint covers a remarkable range of internal economic, social and political institutions, which we now apparently regard as germane to negotiations over commercial policy. These include: the inadequacy of Japanese government public works expenditures; the weakness of anti-trust legislation; the prevalence of small shops, rather than supermarkets and discount stores, in distribution networks; the strength of traditional customer ties in Japanese commerce, the inefficiency of reserving land use for agriculture; and other agricultural policies, including the national attachment to local rice production. Together with mot economists in both countries, I believe that Japan would be better off if reforms of this kind were made. But I doubt our right to impose them.

In reply, one might say in rhetorical retaliation, the Japanese submitted a long list of recommendations to American governments, businesses and households, designed to improve US competitiveness and to reduce our trade deficit overall and with Japan. Almost all of them are points commonly made by American observers of the current scene. But don't expect them to be acted upon. Nobody in Washington takes them seriously.

There has to be some line between those social institutions and cultural customs that must be respected by other countries and those features of a nation that are fair game for commercial negotiation. The line may not be easy to draw. Hard cases are agricultural subsidies designed to sustain 'family farms', and government deficits or surpluses that amount to macroeconomic policies affecting interest rates and exchange rates. But surely we have crossed the line. We're coming close to insisting simply that Japanese develop greater tastes for American goods.

THE FOLLY OF BILATERALISM

A disturbing feature of recent US trade policy is its trend towards bilateralism. At the same time that we are engaged in the final negotiations of the Uruguay Round, we are seeking *ad hoc* bilateral agreements, especially with Japan and also with the European Community, Brazil, India and other countries.

Countries with which the US has large and persistent trade deficits are vulnerable to US insistence that they take actions to reduce them. On this score Japan is the principal target, but Korea, Taiwan and other 'NICs' feel similar pressure. We ask for unrequited 'concessions' on the specious ground that our trade gains from previous reciprocal liberalizations did not live up to expectations. Language in early drafts of the 1988 trade legislation would have compelled the USTR to go after countries whose trade surpluses with the US exceed specified numerical thresholds. This language fortunately did not survive, but its spirit lives on, particularly in Congress.

Sometimes distinction is made between 'rules-oriented' and 'results-oriented' trade policies.[7] Economists and others who believe in GATT principles favour the former. Critics of 'free trade' and GATT want to gear trade policies to numerically defined results. Results-oriented policies naturally lead to bilateralism, to targets for overall bilateral imbalances, and to specific commodity targets and quotas.

As we all know, multilateral trade is incomparably more efficient than bilateral clearing. None of us would want to have to balance our purchases and sales with every other individual. As Adam Smith wrote: 'What is prudence in the conduct of every private family, can scarce be folly in that of a great kingdom' (1937, p. 424). The establishment of multilateral trading and monetary institutions after World War II was a major reason for the growth of world trade. In contrast, Comecon, the system of bilateral trade the Soviet Union established in Eastern Europe, failed.

Overall trade imbalances mean something. Measured correctly, the imbalances of all countries add up to zero. Bilateral balances mean little. We could have a zero trade deficit and still have a deficit with Japan. Or we could balance our trade with Japan and still have an overall deficit, while Japan still has an overall surplus.

Here are some illustrations of the meaninglessness of bilateral trade balances. Suppose Japan exported to China automobile parts and the Chinese assembled them into cars exported to the US. Japan's surplus with the US would fall and China's would increase. Suppose the US exported Alaskan oil to Japan – such exports are now prohibited by Congress but would be a good idea because of savings in transport costs. The US deficit to Japan would fall, but replacement of exports from the West Coast by imports to the East Coast would increase our deficit to oil-exporting countries. A somewhat different example is Taiwan's import of gold from the US. It lowers Taiwan's apparent trade surplus with the US, but of course the US does not mine the gold but imports it. Taiwan disarms some pressure from Washington and converts some of its massive monetary reserves into gold.

DID TRADE BARRIERS CAUSE OUR TRADE DEFICIT?

The large and stubborn deficit in America's trade with the rest of the world that arose in the 1980s has been a major motivation for the new look in United States commercial policy. About a third of it has been our persistently high deficit with Japan. Japan's share in the total is not very different from ten years ago, when the overall deficit was much smaller. The $50 to $60 billion deterioration of our trade balance with the European Community was as large as the increase in our deficit to Japan, but it did not arouse popular hostility or provoke a diplomatic crisis.

No doubt the competitive difficulties of various industries would bring political pressures for relief even if our aggregate trade were in balance or surplus. But our overall deficit and our attainment of the position of the world's largest debtor nation made the political climate more receptive than usual to the complaints and claims of sectoral interests. Otherwise I doubt that the Omnibus Trade and Competitiveness Act of 1988 could have been passed and forced down the throat of a reluctant President.

Without flourishing exports, few producing interests are supportive of 'free trade'. The decline of 'smokestack' and automotive industries, historically exporters, cost 'free trade' influential business support and shifted the trade union movement to the side of protectionism. The political parties have in some degree shifted sides, with Democrats abandoning their historic anti-protection tradition and Republicans verbally supporting trade liberalization.

However, politicians of both parties are vulnerable to trade-related pressures from their constituents; the issues divide Presidents and Congresses more than Republicans and Democrats.

The generic deficit made many Americans fear that we would lose out in one line of production after another, until our only jobs would be waiting on each other in fast food restaurants. The remedy seemed obvious. By protecting the industries that provide, or used to provide, good high-wage jobs, we would preserve our standard of living. The Japanese must be cheating, subsidizing exports to America. We let their goods in, but they keep ours out. By restoring 'fair trade', we can eliminate the big trade deficit.

As economists we know that this popular diagnosis of the trade deficit is mistaken and that the Congressional remedy is misguided. The deficit is an overall balance-of-payments problem, not the summation of difficulties in specific industries. The solution is to be found in macroeconomic policy, not in commercial policies and negotiations. It is always possible to treat symptoms industry after industry. But if these are symptoms of a deeper general malady, they will just be shifted to new locations.

What could have happened in the 1980s to raise our deficits in merchandise trade from 10 per cent of our imports in 1980 to 39 per cent in 1986 and 1987 – still 24 per cent in 1989? What could have turned our current account from a small surplus in 1980 to deficits exceeding $100 billion? What could have raised our deficit with Japan from $10 billion to $50 to $60 billion and reversed the net asset position of the US *vis-à-vis* Japan, which remained positive until 1986? How come our net trade position with the European Community worsened by about the same amount? Adverse microeconomic events specific to industries and countries just don't come close to accounting for these changes.

Probably the most important adverse change in the overseas trading environment was that the burden of debt payments cut the demands of our traditional customers in Latin America for US exports by about $12 billion a year. On the other hand, the decline in petroleum import prices actually helped our balance by $35 billion. Hufbauer (1989) estimates that new non-tariff barriers introduced since 1980 by the United States cut our imports by $17 billion, while those installed by other countries against our exports cost us only $6 billion. The Japanese obstacles to our exports that outrage us today were in place long before 1980. During the past decade Japan has reduced both tariffs and non-tariff barriers. My point is not to justify long-standing barriers in Japan or elsewhere, only to question whether the dramatic deterioration of our trade balance in the past ten years can be explained by barriers new or old.

Hufbauer also estimates that non-reciprocal elimination by other industrial nations of *all* their tariffs and non-tariff measures would be worth to us only

$20–30 billion annually. The specific structural impediments we ask Japan to remove are generally admitted to be worth only 10 to 20 per cent of our bilateral deficit.

THE MACROECONOMICS OF THE US TRADE DEFICIT

The trade deficit is largely a macroeconomic phenomenon. What were the macroeconomic mechanisms at work? They were the consequences of two big institutional changes, on which was superimposed the new and extreme macroeconomic policy mix in the 1980s. One institutional change was the floating of exchange rates in 1973. The other was the vastly increased mobility of financial capital across countries and currencies. The second was, in turn, the consequences of the deregulation of financial markets and the remarkable technological developments in world-wide telecommunications. The new Reagan policy mix was budget looseness combined with monetary tightness.

Previous 'Mundell–Fleming' economic theories of macro policy effects in a floating-rate mobile-capital world were qualitatively correct, but the size and persistence of trade and current account imbalances in the 1980s surprised both economists and central bankers.

What do economists know that other people don't? Identities are the first thing, I tell my students. How not to misuse them is the second. Supply equals demand? The *post hoc* equality of amounts supplied and demanded is an identity, reflecting the fact that every purchase is also a sale. In Economics 101 – in pre-inflation days Econ 1, the first course – price is the endogenous variable that keeps the amounts supplied and demanded equal, whatever shifts may occur in supply and demand curves.

Likewise we know that a country's current account deficit is equal to its net inflow of capital – equal *ex post*, that is to say. We know that the current account deficit is also identically equal – again *ex post* – to the excess of domestic investment over national saving, equal in turn to the excess of domestic absorption over home production. Identities by themselves don't tell us anything about causation, although sometimes even economists forget that.

Macroeconomic theory, balance-of-payments theory in our present context, consists in specifying variables that affect one or both sides of such identities and in explaining how the movements of those variables maintain the essential equality of the two sides. Here the endogenous variables may include exchange rates, interest rates, national incomes and wealth, commodity prices and official reserves. When exogenous shocks occur to export and import demands and supplies, to portfolio choices among assets of different nations, and to the savings and investments of nations, the endogenous variables will respond and modify the impacts.

Therefore, to understand US trade deficits of the 1980s, we must also understand capital inflows to the US and the deficiency of US production below domestic absorption.

In a floating exchange rate régime, a scenario in which capital movements drive the current account is quite understandable. Here is how it happened in the 1980s. Financial deregulation in Japan through 1980 freed insurance companies and other intermediaries to invest some of their immense and rapidly growing funds in foreign securities. The US government had urged Japan to make these reforms, presumably not anticipating the consequences. There were two reasons that these Japanese funds flooded into American bond markets. One was simple portfolio diversification, and the other was the yield advantage of US over Japanese interest rates. (More recently, the composition of Japanese flows of capital to the US has shifted from securities purchases towards direct investments. Direct investments, motivated by long-run calculations of market share and profit, are not so sensitive to financial market interest differentials.)

From 19.9 to 1982 high US interest rates were due to the Federal Reserve's anti-inflationary monetary crusade. After the Fed shifted from recession to recovery mode in 1982, Reagan's fiscal policy was giving such a stimulus to aggregate demand that the Fed kept interest rates abnormally high compared to previous recovery periods. The objective was to keep the economy expanding but not so fast as to re-ignite inflation. The inflow of Japanese and other foreign funds appreciated the dollar against the yen and other currencies, with devastating results for American net exports; the trade deficit became 3 to 4 per cent of net national product.

In the 1980s US private saving declined relative to national income. The federal government dissaved on a large scale; its deficits absorbed more than half of net private saving. The deficiency of national saving from domestic net investment was 3 to 4 per cent of net national product. This was made up by the capital inflow.

The story of Japan is the mirror image. Saving significantly exceeded domestic investment opportunities, even though interest rates were low and the government was running a deficit comparable in per cent of GNP to the United States. The outflow of capital made the yen inexpensive, and its real exchange rate was further depreciated by Japan's relatively low inflation rate and rapid advances in productivity.

These stories explain America's overall trade deficit and Japan's overall surplus. They do not specifically explain the bilateral imbalance. There is no identity that says our capital inflow from Japan must equal our trade deficit with Japan. The pattern of bilateral capital flows can be quite different from the pattern of trade deficits and surpluses.

As economists, our trained instincts are to believe that nature's remedy for excess demand for anything is to raise its price, for excess supply to lower its price. America has excess demand for foreign goods? Make them more expensive for Americans. America fails to sell much in foreign markets? Make our exports cheaper for foreigners. A decline in the value of the dollar, in yen or marks, does both tricks. So it is hard for me to imagine a solution to the trade deficit that does not involve depreciation of the dollar. After all, it was the spectacular appreciation in 1982–85 that brought the trade deficit in the first place.

Lay men and women are sceptical of depreciation, as of all price effects on demand and supply. The depreciation 1985–88 did not lower the deficit as quickly as it had risen, for several reasons:

1. After depreciation the same large quantities of imports cost more in dollars. Good results require big enough 'substitution effects' in export and import volumes to offset that initial 'income effect'.
2. American exporters once bitten were twice shy, reluctant to re-enter foreign markets even after depreciation improved their competitive positions.
3. Foreign firms, in particular Japanese firms, did not raise dollar prices in proportion to the depreciation, preferring to absorb large fractions of the higher yen costs of their dollar sales to hold market shares for the long run. This is the kind of calculation American exporters were unwilling to make when the shoe was on the other foot. As both Japanese and American critics say, American businesses have short horizons, especially in international trade.
4. Some imports into the US, notably cars, were restricted by quotas. Their dollar prices were already well above their costs, a margin that would make them insensitive to the exchange rate as long as the quotas were effective constraints.

In spite of these obstacles, our trade balance has steadily improved, thanks especially to exports of manufactures, where strong productivity growth is combining with the lower dollar to make American goods competitive. The United States has not ceased manufacturing. Manufacturing is the same share of national product as it has been for many decades, namely about one-fifth. What has declined is manufacturing's share of the employed labour force, to 17 per cent from 29 per cent in 1953. That's progress.

Of course, we can't expect to bring back all our lost industries. In this decade and future decades the set of export- and import-competitive industries will be quite different from the 1960s and 1970s. The nightmare that America will find no competitive lines of work is, of course, an illusion. The rest of the world is not going to sustain us on the dole. We will have to work for our living, and for our imports. That is both bad news and good news.

If further depreciation is needed, how can we obtain it? The current growth recession, perhaps soon to become technical recession, allows the Fed room to lower interest rates and diminish the attractiveness of dollar assets. At the same time, German and Japanese macroeconomic conditions and policies seem to be raising rates. The dollar has been falling and could well fall further. At present there is room in the American economy for the expansion of net exports that a lower dollar would stimulate, along with the increase in domestic investment that lower interest rates would induce. But the room is limited, because we are not far below full employment.

Of course if police action or war in Arabia brings additional expenditures for several quarters or years, the slack in the economy will be taken up pretty quickly. This will be true even if the Administration succeeds in getting foreign governments to pay the costs. That will make the federal budget look better. But the extra demands for goods and services are the same whether they are government purchases or exports of the services of our armed forces.

Borrowing from others is not necessarily a bad practice, either for individuals or for nations. It's a good idea when the borrowing costs are less than the returns to the projects in which the resources bought with borrowed funds are invested. That's not the case for the net foreign borrowing of the American nation over the past decade. The funds did not go into high-return investment projects, and the terms of trade on which interest and principal payments will be made are likely to be unfavourable.

Borrowing for consumption is sometimes defensible, in order to spread burdens over time and over generations more efficiently and equitably. It makes sense for young workers to borrow for education, housing and consumption, paying back from the higher incomes they expect in future. It makes sense to finance a big war by borrowing, so that its burden doesn't fall wholly on the generation that fights it. Are the last two decades of the century a time in which borrowing to finance a national consumption binge makes sense? I have some colleagues in the academic economics profession who say in effect: 'If we're doing it, it must be the right thing'. They call themselves new classical macroeconomists and take Adam Smith's invisible hand with literal seriousness.

In their view, America has rationally chosen, with eyes open, to consume now and save sometime later. The Japanese are making the opposite choice. International capital markets accommodate both preferences, at interest rates and exchange rates that appropriately provide the excess saving of the one to finance the consumption and investment of the other.

I don't remember hearing Ronald Reagan, Arthur Laffer and David Stockman telling the American public that is why we are cutting taxes and crippling civilian government. They promised a free lunch for all generations, present and future.

THE MORALS OF THE STORY

The extreme tight-money-easy-fiscal-policy mix of the past ten years has been extremely costly to the American economy. Real net national product grew 27 per cent from 1979 to 1989, some $783 billion 1982 dollars. Of the increment 95 per cent went into private consumption and federal defence purchases. Net private investment, domestic and foreign combined, *declined* by $68 billion 1982 dollars, 27 per cent. Public civilian investment declined also. In short, we have not been putting our resources into uses that will add to the economic opportunities of future years and future generations. Those uses are domestic investments of businesses, households and governments, and accumulations of assets abroad in excess of foreign accumulation of American assets.

The immediate priority is to reverse the 1980s macroeconomic policy mix and to restore the normal fiscal and monetary policies of the previous 35 years. One legacy of the extreme policy mix of the Reagan–Bush era is our unusually high real interest rate. In previous recovery periods, when federal deficits were generally less than 1 per cent of GNP instead of 4 or 5 per cent of GNP, real interest rates were four or five points lower than in the 1980s recovery. High interest rates deter all kinds of domestic investments, and by keeping exchange rates high they depress exports, encourage imports and raise the trade deficit and foreign borrowing. Moreover, the short-horizon syndrome of American management may to some extent simply reflect high discounts of future returns and costs.

To make more room, more permanent room, in the economy for investment, foreign and domestic, we need to increase the national saving rate. The most obvious way to do that is to eliminate federal dissaving – by taxes that hit consumption and by cutting Cold War defence outlays. Since the whole purpose of raising national saving is to increase society's provisions for its future, it does not make sense to cut the federal deficit by curtailing public investments in education, health, infrastructure and environmental protection.

The long-run purpose of raising national rates of saving and investment is to advance the growth of productivity. It is commonly said that America's prime challenge is to become more competitive internationally. That is essential, but it could be fairly easily done by sufficient depreciation of the dollar. The true challenge is to become competitive by improving productivity, so that we do not have to sacrifice real wages in order to bring our trade into reasonable balance. Accelerating productivity would be no less a worthy objective if the US were a closed economy.

US macroeconomic policies of the past decade bear indirect guilt for the trends in this country towards protectionist politics and aggressively nationalistic commercial policies. The United States, instead of exemplifying confrontation and retaliation, should be on the side of the rule of law – in international economic relations as in other contexts. If commercial policy becomes an uninhibited game of strategy among nations, everyone is likely to lose, ourselves included.

International differences in saving rates are something of a mystery. Although Japanese–American differences may eventually diminish, they will probably persist for a long time ahead. Consequently neither Japan's trade surplus nor our trade deficit is likely to vanish completely in this decade. Nor is it likely that the US can catch up with Japan's rate of productivity growth before the turn of the century. So we will probably fall statistically behind in the world economic Olympics. We will have to reconcile ourselves to that fate, and to the fact that the fault is not in the rising sun but in ourselves.

Anyway, what do we really mean by being Number One? World military and geopolitical power? The US has no rival, given the disintegration of the other superpower. Whatever else the Middle East crisis has shown, it has made clear that the US is the world leader and that none of our prosperous allies, neither Japan nor Europe, is prepared to share leadership, much less to take it. Cultural dominance? For better or worse, American music, cinema, TV, fashion sweep the world, especially the youth of all countries. Science? Our universities and laboratories lead in research and teach the whole world. Opportunity? America is the mecca for refugees everywhere, and our doors are the most open to immigrants. Our nationhood is not defined or restricted by race or religion. Democracy and individual freedom? Nowhere are they more robust.

Instead of worrying about statistical comparisons of material well-being, we would do well to consider some negative aspects of quality of life where we are Number One or shamefully close to it, at least among advanced industrial countries. I have in mind homicides, firearms in private hands, infant mortality, drug abuse, homelessness, urban decay, mathematical incompetence, scientific, geographical and historical ignorance, energy waste and inequalities of wealth and income.

The main continuing challenge to any society is to socialize its young – barbarians at birth – in its civilization, culture, traditions and values. America is not meeting this challenge at all well right now. The best industrial policy, the best recipe for productivity, the best competitive strategy this country could have right now is to reform the upbringing, education, health and motivation of children and youth. As workers, managers, scientists and entrepreneurs, they will need to be knowledgeable, resourceful and flexible over the coming decades.

In our international relations, in commerce as well as in other intercourse, let us not be tempted by xenophobia and envy but remain true to our liberal principles and best traditions.

NOTES

1. US Bureau of the Census 1990, p. 794, Table 1392, gives foreign direct investment positions, Commerce Department estimates. The $15 trillion estimate of total tangible wealth is due to the Federal Reserve Flow of Funds section.
2. US Bureau of the Census 1990, pp. 840–41: Table 1446 gives GNP per capita, using exchange rates in 1987, as $19,410 for Japan and $18,570 for the US. Table 1447 estimates the same concept in 1988 as $23,255 for Japan and $19,813 for the US. These two are from different sources. Table 1448 gives 1987 purchasing power parity comparisons of GDP per capita as $13,182 for Japan and $18,338 for the US; calculations due to OECD, Paris.
3. Bhagwati 1989, Chapter 2. I am greatly indebted to this book and also to Bhagwati's 1990 paper.
4. Smith, 1937, pp. 429–39. On retaliation, he says: 'There may be good policy in retaliations ... when there is a probability that they will procure the repeal of the high duties or prohibitions complained of. The recovery of a great foreign market will generally more than compensate the transitory inconvenience of paying dearer during a short time for some sorts of goods'. But Smith warns that these reasons can easily be exaggerated and misused. Richard Cobden, the successful promoter of free trade policies in the middle of the 19th century, was more purely unilateral than Smith. See Bhagwati, 1988, Chapter 2.
5. Although Paul Krugman is the acknowledged guru of new trade theory, it is interesting to note that he signed the 'free trade' report rather than the 'managed trade' report in the Twentieth Century Fund's task force debate on commercial policy, 1989.
6. Bhagwati, 1989, Chapter 2, terms the conception underlying official US policy and the GATT *cosmopolitan* free trade, in distinction to unilateral free trade. He describes the GATT as a 'contractarian' institution whose 'essence is a concept of systematic rights and obligations for member states'.
7. This line is sharply drawn between the two sides of the Twentieth Century Fund task force on trade policy (1989). The 'free traders' stress rules, the 'managed traders' results.

REFERENCES

Bhagwati, Jagdish (1989), *Protectionism*, Cambridge: MIT Press.

Bhagwati, Jagdish (1990), 'Aggressive Unilateralism: An Overview', forthcoming as Chapter 1 in Bhagwati and Hugh Patrick (eds), *Aggressive Unilateralism: America's 301 Trade Policy and the World Trading Regime*, Ann Arbor: University of Michigan Press.

Hufbauer, Gary (1989), 'Background Paper', pp. 37–232 in Twentieth Century Fund. Task Force on the Future of American Trade Policy, *The Free Trade Debate*, New York: Priority Press.

Katz, Lawrence F. and Lawrence H. Summers (1989), 'Can Interindustry Wage Differences Justify Strategic Trade Policy?', Chapter 3 in Robert C. Feenstra (ed.), *Trade Policies for International Competitiveness*, Chicago: University of Chicago Press.

Krugman, Paul (1990), *Rethinking International Trade*, Cambridge: MIT Press.

Smith, Adam (1776), An Inquiry into the Nature and Causes of the Wealth of Nations, ed. Edwin Cannan, New York: Modern Library, 1937.

Twentieth Century Fund (1989), *The Free Trade Debate*, New York: Priority Press, pp. 1–36.

US Bureau of the Census (1990), *Statistical Abstract of the United States*, Washington: Government Printing Office.

23. The international monetary system: pluralism and interdependence*

Robert Triffin is my dear friend and long-time colleague, at Harvard, mainly at Yale, and in Washington. He is a few years my senior, and although that difference seems to diminish with time, I still look up to him as a fount of experience, judgement and wisdom. He tutored me, informally and irregularly to be sure, in international economics and finance. Like all the world, I marvelled at his prescience in the 1950s and 1960s about the gold exchange standard. At my urging, he became a consultant to the Kennedy Council of Economic Advisers, and together we sought to advance the cause of internationalized liquidity in the US government. We did not achieve our goals, but we did nudge developments somewhat in a Triffinesque direction.

The world has changed radically in the last two decades. It seems to me that financial innovation and deregulation have outpaced the world-wide integration of markets for goods and labour, to such an extent that a Triffin-type international monetary system is not yet viable for the advanced capitalist democracies. It may work for cohesive regional groupings of nations as we will probably see in Europe post-1992. I am afraid that for larger groupings, the Group of Three or Seven or the OECD as a whole, we will have to be content for some time with some compromise between national autonomies and monetary integration. I therefore look for arrangements that will preserve national pluralism of policy and institutional structure in our increasingly interdependent world economy.

Since the terminal illness of Bretton Woods in 1971–73, exchange rates among major national currencies have fluctuated violently. Most experts, observers and traders alike, agree that the ups and downs have greatly exceeded variations in rational estimates of fundamental values. The excess volatility reflects short-range speculations, distorting the signals the markets give for trade and long-range investment.

The financial authorities of the economic summit countries evidently subscribe to this diagnosis. Since 1985 they have reduced the volatility of dollar

*First published in Steinherr and Weiserbs (eds), *Evolution of the International and Regional Monetary Systems: Essays in Honour of Robert Triffin*, Basingstoke: Macmillan, 1991. (Professor Triffin died in 1993.)

exchange rates. They have reached and announced informal *ad hoc* agreements on desired trading ranges, at the Plaza Hotel in 1985, at the Louvre in 1987 and, after the Louvre agreement fell apart in the October 1987 financial crisis, once again last winter. Their central banks have bought and sold dollars as necessary to keep markets within the agreed target ranges.

Is a more fundamental and formal reconstitution of an international monetary system necessary? Desirable? Possible? The grass always looks greener on the other side of the fence. The travails of the world economy since 1973 inspire nostalgic longings for Bretton Woods and even for an older and purer gold standard. (The G7 Finance Ministers made a gesture in this direction by announcing that a commodity price index they will jointly monitor for early warnings of inflation will give some weight to gold.) Other systemic proposals would keep the floating rate régime while codifying limits on fluctuations and formalizing the responsibilities of the several nations to keep exchange rates on track.

Here I shall argue for quite a different proposal, which I first advanced in 1978.[1] An international uniform tax would be levied on spot transactions in foreign exchange (including, of course, deliveries pursuant to futures contracts and options). The proposal has two major motivations. One purpose is to increase the weight market participants given to long-range fundamentals relative to immediate speculative opportunities. The second is to allow greater autonomy to national monetary policies, by creating a larger wedge between short interest rates in different currencies.

I anticipated superimposing the proposed tax on a régime of market-determined exchange rates with minimal official interventions. However, the tax could also be helpful to systems involving greater interventions, from the present *ad hoc* agreements on target ranges to a restoration of Bretton Woods itself.

The proposal is directed at the major macroeconomic powers and their currencies, the Group of Seven, for example. Currency transactions within the European Monetary System might be exempt from tax, and similar exemptions might be allowed within other currency areas or for small countries that choose to tie their currencies to a key currency. The International Monetary Fund could be entrusted with administering conditions for exemptions.

My proposal is a realistic 'second best'. I of course understand the advantages of free trade in goods and services and financial instruments with a common currency, because I live in the economy where their blessings are the most obvious and spectacular. It's a good thing that the Michigan dollar cannot be devalued relative to the California dollar, or the Texas dollar against the Massachusetts dollar. Given that such expedients are forsworn, other private and public institutions are in place to cope with economic imbalances among states and regions.

A common currency works to great advantage when sustained not only by a single central bank but by other central governmental institutions, among them free movements of goods and persons as well as of financial capital; common laws, courts, taxes, regulations and customs; and a common system of social security and other entitlements. Regional and sectoral fortunes inevitably wax and wane. When relative price adjustments are limited, people have to be free to move, and the society has to have sufficient sense of community to help the less fortunate.

If tomorrow similar institutions, similarly viable, could unite the economies of Japan, North America and Western Europe, I would enthusiastically prefer that solution to my 'sand in the wheels' proposal. Unfortunately a common currency is not a live alternative.

Fixed rates of exchange among national currencies, which central banks are committed to maintain by market interventions, are by no means an approximation to a common international currency. As long as distinct national currencies exist, the parities can be changed. Indeed they will inevitably be changed when countries run out of international reserves and credit lines. As long as parity changes are possible and even inevitable, private agents will be bound to speculate on such changes.

In this respect, a system of adjustable pegs of national currencies, for example pegs to dollars or to gold, differs very little from a floating rate régime. In both cases there will be speculation on depreciations and appreciations. The only difference is that adjustments of pegs occur in discrete jumps. Every jump is financially and politically traumatic, a crisis in which the government whose currency is under attack runs short of reserves and goes hat in hand to seek credit from more fortunate or 'prudent' nations. Anyone who thinks that the shocks to the world economy since 1973 would have been less disturbing under a régime of adjustable pegs has a short memory and a weak imagination.

In certain past periods, it is true, the gold exchange standard functioned successfully – most recently for the first 20 years after World War II. At least one of two conditions appears to have been necessary to such successes, and neither is met today. One is that the system is managed by a country which is not only financially and economically dominant but is prepared to take commensurate responsibilities for world developments – Britain before 1914, the United States after 1945. The second is that financial transactions across currencies are limited, either by intrinsic costs and risks or by national controls.

Beginning in the late 1960s, the US became just another big economy, an increasingly uncompetitive one at that. The emerging world economic powers, Japan and German-dominated Western Europe, were perhaps unable, certainly unwilling, to assume world responsibilities commensurate with their economic weight. At the same time, currency transactions were decontrolled and became technically easy and cheap. Bretton Woods was doomed.

When the US Federal Reserve System was established in 1913, Congress set up 12 district banks and anticipated that each bank could set a discount rate appropriate to the credit needs of its region. The rapid development of a nation-wide money market made such interest differentials impossible. The same would be true as between New York, Tokyo, London, Frankfurt and Zurich if their currencies were unalterably locked together.

Perhaps Europe in 1992 can establish strong enough community ties and institutions to make an ECU or *monnet* feasible. Certainly the European Monetary System as it has operated until now is far from a common currency (though not far enough to be attractive to the United Kingdom and to Scandinavia). It would be whistling in the dark to establish a common currency without assuring the prerequisites.

Whatever may be the case within Europe, the differences among Europe, North America and Japan are much too great to establish a common currency among them. One has only to observe the immense differences in macro economic institutions, policies and beliefs. I am going to speak bluntly. From an American perspective, it is bad enough to let the Bundesbank and the Federal Republic depress most of Europe and exert chronic drag on the world economy, without surrendering our own prosperity and growth, and that of the rest of the world, to West German macroeconomic doctrine.

A true world-wide common currency is decades premature. Yet vast private funds are prepared to arbitrage away differences in national interest rates and to speculate on movements of exchange rates. Here, as in so many other dimensions of human life on this globe, technologies have outrun political and social institutions. I propose to make distinct national currencies tolerable, and to make international money markets compatible with modest national autonomy in monetary and macroeconomic policy.

A 0.5 per cent tax on foreign exchange transactions in both directions is equivalent to a 4 per cent difference in annual interest rates on three-month bills, a considerable deterrent to persons contemplating a quick round trip to another currency. Yet the tax would be a negligible consideration in a long-term portfolio or direct investment in another economy. The intent is to slow down capital movements, not commodity trade. But even if it were not possible to exempt *bona fide* commodity transactions, the tax would be too small to be protectionist.

J.M. Keynes in 1936 pointed out that a transactions tax could strengthen the weight of long-range fundamentals in stock market prices, as against speculators' guesses of the short-range behaviours of other speculators. The same is true for the foreign exchange markets. Vast resources of intelligence and enterprise are wasted in financial speculation essentially in playing zero-sum games. Transactions taxes might reallocate some of these resources. To the extent that they do not, they will at least produce needed government revenues without bad side effects. It is estimated that more than $1000 billion gross foreign exchange transactions occur every business day.

In the case of currency transactions, it is obviously necessary to have international agreement on the tax. My suggestion is that most of the proceeds go to the World Bank, but other dispositions, including less altruistic ones, could be considered.

While the proposed tax would give national macroeconomic authorities greater autonomy, it would certainly not permit them to ignore the international repercussions of their policies. The summit governments would still need to coordinate policies, I emphasize, however, that temporary *ad hoc* agreements on exchange rates are not true coordinations of policies. Since the target rates do not follow consistently from agreed national monetary and fiscal policies, they put the cart before the horse.

The reason that policy coordination is necessary in a floating-exchange-rate world is that national monetary policies work, to a substantial degree, by inducing changes in inter-currency capital flows, in exchange rates, and correspondingly in current accounts. Usually, though not necessarily, the induced capital flows are responding to international interest rate differences associated with differences in monetary policies. In a world with fluid capital markets, monetary policies have a 'beggar-thy-neighbour' aspect. One country's expansionary policy gains employment at the expense of less employment among its trading partners, and at some domestic cost in price increases. One country's contractionary policy achieves some disinflation via lower prices of tradeable goods at the expense of some higher prices in the currencies of its trading partners, and at some domestic cost in employment and output.

The role of policy coordination is to prevent collectively counter-productive jockeying for macroeconomic advantage. When all central banks are focusing on interest rate differentials, the overall world average of interest rates will be nobody's business. It may end up too high for general prosperity, or too low to keep inflation at bay. The world interest rate level requires international coordination. Likewise, coordination is needed to define permissible national deviations from the agreed average. Two principles are relevant to the determination of these differentials.

The first relates to short-run stabilization. A country whose economy is underemployed can reasonably have relatively low interest and exchange rates, while those of a country with an overheated economy should be relatively high. The criteria of under- and over-employment and -production must necessarily be each country's own. But they must be declared in advance and consistently adhered to, used in the joint decisions both on average interest rates and on the national deviations.

The second is a longer-run criterion, relating to the pattern of current accounts. The desired future pattern should be estimated in the light of the various national domestic saving and investment balances. Currency values should be low but rising for countries with excessive current account deficits, high and falling for countries with excessive surpluses. To make these developments possible, fiscal policies should be tight in the former countries and easy in the latter countries.

Naturally, the appropriate directions of fiscal policies for long-run current account equilibrium will be taken into account in determining the target pattern of interest rates. For example, an economy like the United States of three years ago would need low interest rates both for short-run macroeconomic recovery and for an exchange depreciation to correct its balance of trade in concert with a gradual withdrawal of fiscal stimulus. An economy like the United States of today, however, could expect to have a relatively low interest rate only for the second reason, because without fiscal austerity there is no room in the economy for an improvement in net exports.

Policy coordination of this kind is not easy, either intellectually or politically. But it is worth a try. Agreed interventions in currency markets make sense only if they are implementing rational coordinated monetary and fiscal strategies of the kind described.

NOTE

1. 'A proposal for International Monetary Reform', *Eastern Economic Journal*, **4**, July–October 1978, pp. 153–9, reprinted in Tobin, *Essays in Economics, Volume 3: Theory and Policy*, Cambridge, Mass.: Massachusetts Institute of Technology Press, 1982, Chapter 20.

PART V

Social Policy

Part V Social policy

In the final Part are three essays on social problems and policies in the United States, each of which is related, as cause or effect or both, to the macroeconomic and fiscal issues of previous Parts. Chapter 24 concerns the alarming persistence of poverty, despite overall economic growth and prosperity. It appears that we can no longer count on macroeconomic performance to erode poverty. This fact is related to another disturbing trend recently documented, the growth of inequality of income and wealth since 1980.

Chapter 25 explores the difficulties facing federal old-age insurance, 'social security', because of adverse demographic and economic trends. While these do not add up to an imminent crisis, they do require action within the next decade. The social security system contributes to the nation's future fiscal problems and to the shortage of national saving and investment. I propose eventual replacement of the present pay-as-you-go system with a funded 'defined-contribution' plan.

Health care reform was supposed to be the major achievement of President Clinton's first term. In the end, he failed to get his plan through Congress, and no alternative plan commanded majorities either. The Clinton Administration had counted on health care reform to slow the growth of the costs of federal health programmes, Medicare for the aged and Medicaid for the poor. Without such help, these programmes are the principal obstacles to balancing the budget in 2002 or 2005. In retrospect the Administration's mistake was to spend most of a year designing a very complex and intricate plan by itself, then presenting it as a *fait accompli* to Congress, the numerous interest groups and the public. Better to have combined the design, the political negotiations and the inevitable compromises from the very start, under the aegis of a blue-ribbon commission involving Administration officials, members of Congress of both parties, industry representatives and experts. In Chapter 26 I set forth an alternative to the Clinton plan designed and advocated by Professor Michael Graetz of Yale Law School and myself.

24. Poverty in relation to macroeconomic trends, cycles and policies*

Robert Lampman of the University of Wisconsin is the intellectual father of the War on Poverty, at least to the extent any economist can claim paternity. He was the principal author of Chapter 2 of the 1964 *Economic Report of the President*, where the economic rationale and strategy of the War were laid out. As an alumnus of the President's Council of Economic Advisers, called to Washington in December 1963 to help shepherd the annual Report into print, I participated in editing the chapter. Walter Heller, the Council's Chairman, had proposed the anti-poverty initiative to President Kennedy, whose sympathetic interest had been whetted by reading Michael Harrington's *The Other America* and John Kenneth Galbraith's *The Affluent Society*. President Johnson enthusiastically adopted the War on Poverty as an integral part of his Great Society and a corollary of the Civil Rights revolution, a cause he had also embraced.

In June 1967 I published an article in *The New Republic* entitled 'It Can Be Done! Conquering Poverty in the US by 1976'. Sargent Shriver, the anti-poverty 'czar', had boldly, one could say recklessly, announced this ambitious Bicentennial goal. When I wrote the article, its title was not as outlandish as it sounds now. I was not relying solely or even principally on Shriver's direct programmes. These, in Lampman's spirit, were measures to improve the earning capacities of individuals and communities by education of infants, children, youth and adults; by improving public health and individual health in disadvantaged localities; by programmes offering vocational training and job experience; by comprehensive neighbourhood development initiatives. These programmes could not be expected to work miracles in one decade. Over that short horizon, I put greater weight on the market magic of general prosperity and growth. My primary argument was that the poverty remaining after those two forces had done their work was within the feasible reach of means-tested transfers like the negative income tax. Those transfer programmes were not enacted, of course, and in 1976 the economy was just recovering from a deep stagflationary recession. The promised land receded. We'll be lucky to reach it by 2026.

*First published in Danziger *et al.* (eds), *Confronting Poverty*, Cambridge MA: Harvard University Press, 1994, originally an address to a Conference on Poverty and Public Policy at the Institute for Poverty Research, University of Wisconsin, Madison, 28 May 1992.

I am afraid that it's a mistake to declare wars against social and economic conditions or national crusades for societal reforms. The goals are elusive, the troops unruly, the enemies amorphous. Wars on poverty, energy dependence and drugs have proved to be incapable of sustaining the degrees of commitment essential to their prosecution, even by the Presidents who declared them. William James longed for moral equivalents of war, but evidently Americans can't do better than football.

MACROECONOMIC PROGRESS AND POVERTY REDUCTION

'Rising tides lift all boats' is an overused cliché. For our purpose, the proposition is that good macroeconomic performance reduces poverty. The idea is sometimes caricatured as 'trickledown', but I think that label should be

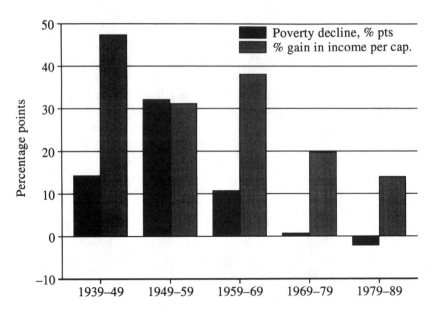

Note: *Ten year decline in percentage points national poverty rate of persons, compared to percentage gains in real income per person, 1939–89*. Poverty rates prior to 1959 estimated by Reynolds Farley from Decennial Census data for *A Common Destiny*, report of the National Academy of Sciences Committee on the Status of Black Americans, 1988; subsequent poverty rates, official Census data; personal income, US Department of Commerce, National Income and Product Accounts.

Figure 24.1 Progress against poverty, five decades

confined to proposals to better the lot of the poor by transfers or tax concessions to the rich. In any case the cliché sometimes serves as an excuse for
doing nothing specific about poverty. Today the tides don't seem to rise as
much, and leaks seem to consign some of the boats to the bottom.

Until about 1970, macroeconomic progress was an extremely powerful
engine of poverty reduction. In the 1930s Franklin Roosevelt saw one-third
of the nation ill-fed, ill-clothed, ill-housed. Backward application of Molly
Orshansky's absolute poverty income thresholds puts the figure closer to two-
thirds.

The war against Germany and Japan was the most effective war against
poverty in America's recorded experience; some of the war's achievements
showed up in the subsequent decade. In the 1940s military and economic
mobilization truly generated jobs for all. In 1944, when defence purchases
accounted for two-fifths of GNP, the remainder available for civilian use was
greater in real terms than the entire GNP of 1939.

During the 1940s and 1950s, shifts of labour from subsistence and other
labour-intensive agriculture into jobs of higher value added in urban industry,

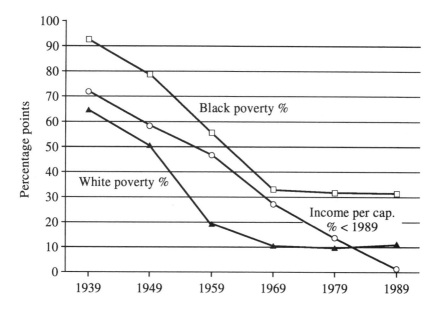

Note: Black and white poverty at ends of six decades compared to personal income shortfall.
Poverty: percentage of persons living in poor households. Personal income shortfall: percentage
shortfall of national personal income (per capita in 1990 dollars) below 1989. (For data sources,
see Figure 24.1).

Figure 24.2   Poverty by race and aggregate income, 1939–89

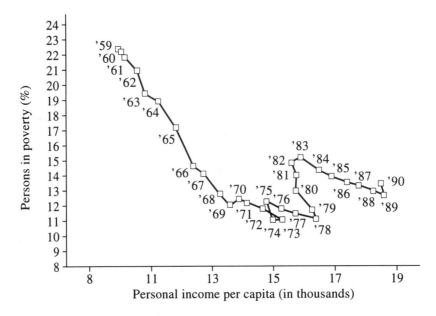

Note: National poverty percentage plotted against personal income per capita (1990), yearly, 1959–90. (For data sources, see Figure 24.1).

Figure 24.3   Poverty and income per person

often involving migration from South to North, were an important source of overall economic growth. Edward Denison (1974) credits such shifts with 19 per cent of the growth in net national product per person employed in 1941– 48 and 14 per cent in 1948–54. This growth was especially important for reduction of poverty among migrants, both blacks and whites. Today the urban industries that gave them jobs have been moving away from big cities – to suburbs, to the South, overseas. Many jobs have been lost to global competition and new technology, and many of the remaining ones have moved away. The few jobs that replace them are generally by location and specification inaccessible to the populations left behind, especially the minority populations. The obstacles to migration and occupational shift are formidable.

Figure 24.1 compares for five decades, 1940 to 1990, the reduction of poverty in percentage points and the percentage growth of per capita real GNP. Figure 24.2 shows the progress against poverty over the 50 years since 1939 for blacks and whites separately, and also plots the reduction in the percentage shortfall of real personal income per capita from its 1989 value. The latter is a graphically convenient measure of overall economic progress, to which the decline in poverty can be compared.

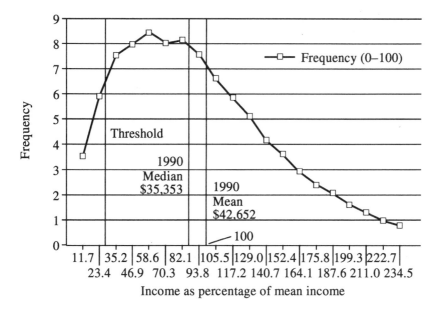

Source: US Bureau of the Census, Current Population Reports, series P-60, nos. 180, 181.

Figure 24.4   *Family money income, 1990: Frequency distribution, that is, percentage of families at indicated ratios of income to population mean income (Families in the income bracket corresponding to 11.7 per cent of mean family income are about 3.5 per cent of all families, for example)*

Figure 24.3 plots 1959–90 annual poverty rates against per capita real personal income. In Figure 24.3 can be seen the episodic setbacks to progress against poverty, relative to macro performance, in cyclical recessions. The setback in the 1980s was the most serious.

It was to be expected – and it was expected, certainly, by Lampman – that there would be diminishing returns in poverty reduction to overall gains in per capita income, just because the densities of the income distribution would diminish as the poverty rate declined. When the Orshansky thresholds were near the mode of the distribution, a small proportionate rightward shift in the distribution, resulting from macroeconomic growth, could take many people out of poverty. The numbers would be much fewer in the thinner left tails of the distribution. Figure 24.4 illustrates this effect by expressing the 1990 family income distribution in terms of the ratio of income to mean income and assuming that the distribution thus transformed applied also in the past. Trends of overall economic growth take the form of leftward treks of the ratio of thresholds to mean or median income. Diminishing returns from this source were important before 1970, when the poverty threshold occurred at the high frequencies of the distribution, but they have not been of much significance since.

DISAPPOINTING MACROECONOMIC PERFORMANCE SINCE 1973

Clearly macroeconomic performance has been less successful in reducing poverty since 1973 than before. Both of the two obvious possible explanations, the weakness of the tide and the leakiness of the boats, apparently hold. Macroeconomic performance itself has been disappointing, and so has been the response of poverty numbers to the macroeconomic performance that did occur.

The growth of per capita real GDP slowed down. The trend growth of productivity per person-hour in the business sector has been about two percentage points lower since 1973 (0.8 per cent per year) than in the previous quarter-century (2.9 per cent per year). Not only was the growth of potential output at full employment weaker, but potential was less frequently and fully realized. Cyclical recessions were more severe after 1973, and the unemployment rate averaged 2.2 points higher.

Figure 24.5 compares potential and actual GDP since 1973. Cyclical recessions and slowdowns generate increasing shortfalls of actual from potential, and it has taken long and slow recoveries to erase these gaps. Figure 24.6 shows how closely correlated these GDP gaps are with the unemployment rate. This correlation, known among economists as Okun's Law, is one of the most important and reliable regularities in macroeconomics. Arthur Okun also pointed out that, as is evident in Figure 24.6, changes in the GDP gap are a multiple of the changes in unemployment rates. The same cyclical macroeconomic forces that move employment up and down move labour force participation, hours of work and productivity in the same direction. The average 2.2 points of higher unemployment since 1973 translates into an average percentage GDP gap about six points higher.

Parts of the recent story of weaker macroeconomic performance are breaks in the relationships between broad measures – such as per capita real GDP, personal income per capita and overall unemployment rates – and measures closer to the determination of poverty status. In particular, both David Cutler and Lawrence Katz (1991) and Rebecca Blank (1991) have called attention to changes in the structure of wages disadvantageous to the poor.

Real hourly and weekly earnings have been declining for 20 years. The growth of worker productivity has slowed down. Moreover, earnings have

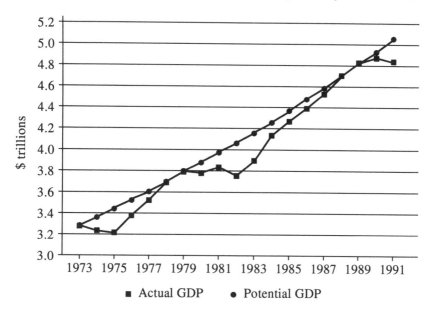

Sources: Actual GDP, US Department of Commerce, National Income and Product Accounts; potential, authors estimates.

Figure 24.5   Actual and potential gross domestic product (trillions of 1987 dollars yearly, 1973–91)

even fallen behind productivity, an unusual phenomenon. As Cutler and Katz point out, however, the share of labour in business value-added has stayed fairly constant. Compensation inclusive of fringe benefits has risen roughly in step with productivity. This is the labour cost that matters to employers. But the explosion of employment-related fringe benefits, largely for health insurance, has been of value mainly to long-term employees with high wages and salaries. It has meant little to workers and families at risk of poverty, for whom the relentless decline of take-home pay has been the grim reality.

Cutler and Katz point out that the rise in the wages of unskilled and less educated workers relative to skilled and better educated workers, a stylized fact of past business cycle recoveries, did not take place in the 1980s. Blank finds, using Current Population Survey (CPS) data of the Census Bureau, that the jobs taken by the working poor pay relatively less well than in the past. Likewise, James Medoff (1992) has found from CPS data that since 1979 the job openings that can be found by job losers are, relative to the universe of jobs, lower in pay and more frequently without pensions and health insurance.

Sources: Output gap and percentage shortfall of actual GDP from potential GDP shown in Figure 25.5; unemployment rate, US Bureau of Labor Statistics.

Figure 24.6   *Output gap and unemployment rate. Gap between actual and potential GDP, as percentage of actual GDP, compared with yearly average national unemployment rate, 1973–91*

ESTIMATING MACROECONOMIC EFFECTS ON POVERTY

Two macroeconomic outcomes of crucial importance for the prevalence of poverty are real wages and unemployment. As real wages rise throughout the economy, more and more workers are able to earn enough for themselves and their families to escape poverty. Decade to decade, it is the trend in real wages that matters. But the trend has not been constant; wage growth has slowed since about 1973.

The overall unemployment rate is a barometer indicative of opportunities to work. It would be expected to be an important determinant of poverty, even though most unemployed are not poor and most poor are not unemployed (according to the Census definition, which requires an individual to be both entirely jobless and looking for work).

Changes in poverty rates from year to year can, I have found, be fairly well explained by these two macroeconomic variables, specifically by regressions

Table 24.1 *Time series regressions of annual changes in poverty rates*

Sample years	Dependent variable	Constant	Independent variables			Adjusted R^2
			DE (1982$)	T/M (−1) (%)	DUWM (%)	
1. 1961–83	DPP (% points)	0				0.59
Coefficients			−0.04	−0.0089	0.465	
(Standard errors)			(0.024)	(0.0033)	(0.168)	
Variable mean	−0.3		0.46	42.78	0.16	
Variable s.d.	0.92		7.01	5.08	1.00	
2. 1961–90	DPP (% points)	0				0.58
Coefficients			−0.053	−0.0075	0.386	
(Standard errors)			(0.020)	(0.0026)	(0.125)	
Variable mean	−0.25		−0.07	41.3	0	
Variable s.d.	0.71		6.31	4.33	0.99	
3. 1961–90	DFP (% points)	0				0.61
Coefficients			−0.038	−0.0073	0.382	
(Standard errors)			(0.018)	(0.0024)	(0.115)	
Variable mean	−0.25		−0.07	41.3	0	
Variable s.d.	0.71		6.31	4.33	0.99	

Table 24.1   continued

| Sample years | Dependent variable | Constant | Independent variables | | | Adjusted R^2 |
			DE (1982$)	T/M (−1) (%)	DUWM (%)	
4. 1968–83	DPPP (% points)					0.78
Coefficients		0	−0.039	0.001	0.555	
(Standard errors)			(0.019)	(0.003)	(0.132)	
Variable mean	0.3		−1.31	39.77	0.36	
Variable s.d.	0.9		7.52	1.53	1.07	
5. 1968–83	DPPP < 65 (% points)					0.79
Coefficients		0	−0.038	0	0.633	
(Standard errors)			(0.019)	(0.003)	(0.137)	
Variable mean	0.29		−1.31	39.77	0.36	
Variable s.d.	0.97		7.52	1.53	1.07	

Notations of variables:

DPP   First difference, poverty rate (%) of all persons.
DFP   First difference, poverty rate (%) of families.
DPPP   First difference, pre-transfer persons' poverty.
DPPP < 65 First difference, pre-transfer poverty, persons aged less than 65.
DE   First difference, average weekly earnings in 1982 dollars.
T/M (−1)   Previous year's value, poverty threshold income for four-person family as per cent of median family income.
DUWM   First difference, unemployment rate, white males aged 20 and older.

on changes in average real weekly earnings and in an unemployment rate. First differences of the dependent variable and these two explanatory variables are used to avoid spurious correlations and biased estimates due to serial persistence. A third independent variable is also both logical and empirically successful. It is the *level* of the ratio of the poverty threshold for four-person families (constant in real terms) to the previous year's median family income.

Several such regressions are reported in Table 24.1 for post-transfer poverty from 1961 to 1990 and pre-transfer poverty from 1967 to 1988. In them the constant is constrained to be zero, so that no time trend in poverty is built in. Trends may improve fits, but when they have no convincing rationale they are statistical artifacts of little help in understanding, forecasting and policy-making. The earnings variable is in constant 1982 dollars, because poverty thresholds are defined in real dollars. The unemployment variable is the rate for white male adults, chosen for its quality as a macroeconomic cyclical barometer rather than its direct relevance to persons at risk of poverty. The third variable serves as a proxy for the density of the income distribution in

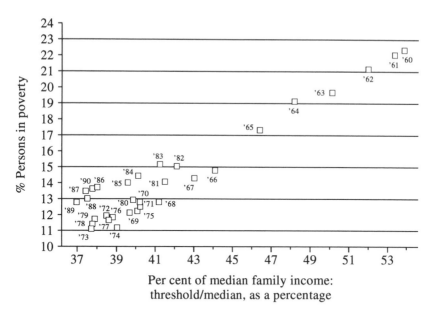

Source: See Figure 24.4.

Figure 24.7 Poverty and median income. National percentage of persons in poverty, plotted against the ratio of family poverty threshold to median family income, yearly, 1960–90

Table 24.2   Cross-section regressions of state poverty rates (50 states and the District of Columbia)

Sample years	Dependent variable	Independent variables				Adjusted R^2
		Constant	DHE	DUR	PP 1979	
Changes between Two years						
1A. 1979–87	DPP (% points)					0.56
Coefficients		−0.069	−0.766	0.709		
(Standard errors)			(0.476)	(0.098)		
Variable mean	−0.71		0.238	−0.639		
Variable s.d.	2.23		0.455	2.217		
1B. 1979–87	DPP (% points)					0.57
Coefficients		−0.087	−0.683	0.744	0.064	
(Standard errors)			(0.484)	(0.104)	(0.065)	
Variable mean	−0.71		0.238	−0.639	11.23	
Variable s.d.	2.23		0.455	2.217	3.5	

Levels One Year

	PP (% points)	HE	UR	
2. 1986				
Coefficients	17.93	-1.737	1.806	0.77
(Standard errors)		(0.279)	(0.145)	
Variable mean	13.82	9.6	6.96	
Variable s.d.	4.44	1.15	2.21	
	PPP (% points)	HE	UR	
3. 1985–86				
Coefficients	19.76	-1.725	1.673	0.74
(Standard errors)		(0.281)	(0.146)	
Variable mean	14.85	9.6	6.96	
Variable s.d.	4.23	1.15	2.21	

Notations of variables:

PP   Poverty rate (%) of all persons.
DPP   Change in PP from 1979 to 1988, in percentage points.
PPP   Pre-transfer poverty rate of all persons.
HE   Hourly earnings in current dollars.
DHE   Change in hourly earnings from 1979 to 1987, in 1979 dollars.
UR   Unemployment rate, all workers.
DUR   Change in UR from 1979 to 1987.

the neighbourhood of the poverty line. As illustrated earlier in Figure 24.4 and now again in Figure 24.7, macroeconomic progress against poverty can be described as a downward trend in this ratio. Using its level in the year before as a regressor for the change in poverty is like using a non-linear function of the previous level of the poverty rate itself, recognizing that the potential for reductions in poverty declines with the actual poverty rate.

The specifications of these equations are simple, straightforward and parsimonious. They implement *a priori* hypotheses, without trial-and-error 'data mining'. The results confirm expectations of the signs of the coefficients. Over half of the variance in year-to-year changes in poverty is explained. It is not surprising that other systematic and stochastic determinants are also at work.

Welfare benefits and other transfers would affect post-transfer poverty rates more than pre-poverty rates; the better fits shown for the latter equations (Table 24.1, regressions 4 and 5) were to be expected. Likewise it is logical that unemployment has a bigger effect on pre-transfer poverty. Regressions 1 and 2 in Table 24.1 provide some evidence that in the 1980s unemployment effects became smaller and wage effects larger than before. The slowdown in progress against poverty in the 1980s is evident in Figure 24.7; the poverty rate was higher in that decade relative to the ratio of the poverty threshold to median income.

Earnings and unemployment also explain variations in poverty rates among states. Table 24.2 reports results for single-year cross-section, for both official poverty rates and pre-transfer rates. It also shows a regression for cross-sections of changes in official poverty by state between two years, 1979 and 1987. The fit of this regression is not significantly improved by adding the 1979 poverty rate as a third explanatory variable.

It is reassuring that all the cross-section regression coefficients on earnings and unemployment variables have the same signs as in the national time series regressions. In Table 24.2 equations 1A and 1B are similar to the time series regressions of Table 24.1, in that the change in the poverty rate is the dependent variable. In the state cross-sections, however, 'change' is for each state the difference between two years that are nine years apart, 1978 and 1987. Only the unemployment rate is significant by usual standards. The earnings coefficient passes the test only marginally, at a 10 per cent significance level. That those coefficients are larger in absolute magnitude than their counterparts in Table 24.1 is to be expected. They reflect the associations of poverty with these two explanatory variables not only in economy-wide trends and cycles, but also in the sharper swings in the fortunes of particular states and regions.

In the state cross-section regressions, 2 and 3, the dependent variable and the two basic explanatory variables are levels in a single year. The coefficients are larger than in the change regressions. They reflect persistent inter-state differences in prosperity and affluence, in all their dimensions. A state with a chronically high unemployment rate or a chronically low wage rate is likely to suffer a high poverty rate. But gains in earnings and employment over one year or even nine years will not reduce a poor state's poverty to the level of states that have long been prosperous. Lasting differences among states in affluence will be reflected in the generosity of welfare benefits and other transfers. This may be the reason why here, unlike the national time series regressions of Table 24.1, the macroeconomic variables explain post- and pre-transfer poverty about equally well.

There is some evidence that year-to-year poverty changes in recent years have been algebraically greater than equations fitted to observations through 1983 would predict. This is illustrated by Figure 24.8, for changes in official poverty for all persons, which exceeded such forecasts in every year from 1984 to 1990. (This was not a wholly new phenomenon; within the sample

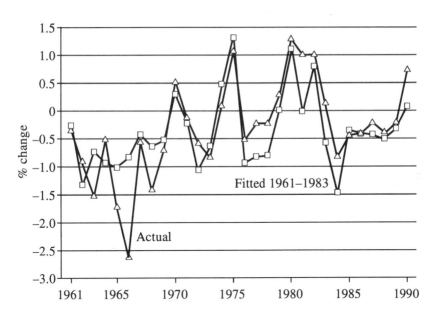

Note: Changes in national percentage of persons in poverty, actual and as estimated from 1961–83 regression on three macro variables: first difference of average real weekly earnings; first difference of an unemployment rate; the *level* of the ratio of the poverty threshold for four-person families (constant in real terms) to the previous year's median family income. (Earnings and unemployment data. Bureau of Labor Statistics; income and poverty data, see Figure 24.4; regression, see Table 24.1, no. 1).

Figure 24.8   Yearly changes in poverty, 1961–90

period most of the unexplained residuals were positive after 1976.) The errors of forecasts averaged 0.26 percentage points over 1984–90 and reached 0.64 in 1990. Similar consistent overoptimism shows up in forecasts from 1984–88 from 1967–83 regressions for pre-transfer poverty rates for all persons and for persons aged less than 65 years.

These underpredictions of poverty since the mid 1980s are consistent with the findings of Cutler and Katz, Blank and Medoff cited earlier. I can report two additional possibilities, related to each other. One concerns the relationship to the overall civilian unemployment rate of unemployment rates specific to age–sex–race populations vulnerable to poverty, as estimated by simple regression without trend or other explanatory variables. For black males, both teens and adults, unemployment rates since 1983 are higher than would be expected from equations fit through 1983. For black adults these errors of forecast are as high as 2.3 percentage points and average 1.6 over 1983–91; for black teens, they are as high as 5.2 points and average 3.6. In both cases 1959–91 regressions with a multiplicative dummy variable, which turns out to increase the sensitivity of specific unemployment to general unemployment after 1982 by about 15 per cent for black adults and 17 per cent for black teens, fit well.

These effects do not apply to black females. Indeed the reverse appears to be true: their recent unemployment rates are lower in relation to the economy-wide rate than past relationships would predict.

The second findings reinforce the first. They concern the relationship of the labour force participation rate of a demographic group to its own unemployment rate and/or the general employment rate. Broadly speaking, regressions of this kind support the familiar 'discouraged worker' effect: higher unemployment rates lead to withdrawal from the labour force. This effect appears to be stronger since 1983 for black males, especially teens and young adults. Their labour force participation has been less since 1983 than regressions on pre-1983 unemployment observations predicted. No such behavioural change has been evident for whites or for black females.

Together these results add up to disturbing declines in the employment/population ratios of potential workers and breadwinners in demographic groups vulnerable to poverty. Such declines are not easy to overcome by strong macroeconomic performance.

Some clues to these adverse developments are provided by Medoff (1992). He finds that aggregate job vacancies, as measured by the Help Wanted Index compiled by the Conference Board, a New York non-profit business research institution, have been abnormally low in recent years relative to contemporaneous unemployment rates. Vacancies are what pull people from the category NILF (not in labour force) into LFP (labour force participation, employed or looking for work). As already noted, Medoff also finds that meaningful vacancies are for jobs inferior in pay and other terms.

All these findings are consistent with the view that, independent of overall macroeconomic performance, changes in the nature and location of jobs are adverse to persons and families at risk of poverty.

I confess I come to conclusions of this kind reluctantly. In the past I have been sceptical of periodic structural explanations of higher unemployment rates and higher poverty rates. I have thought that the American people are very mobile and adaptable and that the US economy adjusts quickly to sectoral shocks, provided an overall macroeconomic climate of prosperity is maintained. Think of the country's smooth economic demobilization after World War II, which confounded the pessimists. Think of the fashionable structural explanations of high unemployment in 1960–61 and 1979–82, both followed by recoveries that brought unemployment rates below what they had been at previous cyclical peaks. In my experience, structural hypotheses have usually been excuses for policy-makers to do nothing to stimulate the economy.

This may be the case today too, although the current structural problems should lead to the opposite conclusion, namely that more macroeconomic stimulus is needed and is safe. Because labour shortages are the sources of wage inflation, the scarcity of vacancies, even while unemployment rates are below rates at the troughs of previous business cycles, suggests that expansionary monetary and fiscal policies will be helpful and not inflationary.

Expansionary monetary policy, the province of the Federal Reserve, would consist mainly in further reduction in the discount rate at which the Fed lends to banks and in the money market rates the Fed controls by its open-market operations. In addition the Fed, in cooperation with the Treasury, could enter government bond markets with a view to lowering long-term rates. Besides stimulating business investment and home-building, these measures would have as a by-product a lower foreign exchange value of the dollar, making American goods more competitive in world markets and trimming the nation's trade deficit.

Expansionary fiscal policy would also be desirable, probably essential. This business cycle is the first in 40 years in which no fiscal stimulus has been given to help recovery, by new expenditures or tax cuts or both. Fiscal stimulus to aggregate demand for goods and services and labour is necessarily deficit-increasing, at least in the short run. At present, fiscal policy is paralysed by the political fear of adding to the mammoth deficits inherited from the 12 years of the Reagan and Bush Administrations.

Whether recovery comes about by deliberate policy or by good fortune, even when prosperity is restored, the prospects for poverty-vulnerable workers are not promising. More of them are likely to be unemployed or not in labour force than was true before 1980s.

THE UNEMPLOYMENT–INFLATION TRADE-OFF

An overall unemployment rate between 5 and 5.5 per cent is very likely to be as low as we can hope and expect. The Federal Reserve, whose monetary and interest rate policies are the major macroeconomic controls on the economy, will probably not want to allow lower unemployment without convincing evidence that it would not trigger ever higher wage and price inflation. At present estimates of the inflation-safe national unemployment rate, unfortunately, the unemployment rates of black male teens and adults will be extremely high and, evidently, even higher than in the past. And many potential workers vulnerable to poverty, again more than in the past, will not even be in the labour force. Joblessness in these disadvantaged groups does virtually nothing to mitigate the wage and price inflation rates that concern the Federal Reserve.

Could the unemployment target of federal monetary and fiscal policy be moved below 5 per cent? Policy-makers may often exaggerate the social costs of inflation, but they will probably be unwilling to accept more inflation risk as long as the public also exaggerates those costs. But policy-makers could respond to evidence that inflation is a lesser risk than in the past. In 1979–80 the Federal Reserve and most economists thought the inflation-safe unemployment rate was 6 per cent or higher. Thanks to good wage and price behaviour in the 1980s, the Fed kept the recovery going until unemployment fell below 5.5 per cent.

Are there reasons to expect further improvement in the inflation–unemployment trade-off? The scarcity of job vacancies is one reason. Moreover, both employers and employees, union and non-union alike, are more sensitive than they formerly were to competitive threats to their markets and jobs. There is renewed interest in public and private programmes to train and retrain workers and to assist conversions and adjustments of firms, industries and localities.

These developments might somewhat enhance future contributions of macroeconomic performance to poverty reduction. But not by much. It would be wishful thinking to count on significant help from this source, especially over the short and medium run.

MACROECONOMICS AND THE POLITICS OF ANTI-POVERTY POLICY

Another avenue of transmission of macroeconomic performance to poverty is its effect on the adequacy and efficacy of anti-poverty programmes and transfers. As we know, the political climate of the 1970s and especially the

1980s was inclement. War on Poverty programmes on which Robert Lampman, Sargent Shriver and Lyndon Johnson pinned their hopes were stingily financed, even discontinued. Means-tested cash assistance fell sharply in purchasing power. Differences between pre-welfare and post-transfer poverty percentages and poverty deficits narrowed during the 1980s. (I realize that causation cannot be surely inferred from these comparisons. Disciples of Charles Murray could doubtless contrive explanations based on extreme endogenous welfare dependency.) At the same time, government outlays for open-ended in-kind programmes of benefit to the poor have greatly increased. One such programme is Food Stamps, which has the political protection of agricultural interests. The most important, the most expensive and the fastest growing is Medicaid, though not because poor patients are getting care of noticeably higher quality. Faced with exploding health care costs, federal and state politicians and voters feel they are doing their bit, or more, for the poor, and their hearts harden against cash assistance.

The general macroeconomic disappointments of the 1970s and 1980s have a great deal to do with the political unpopularity of means-tested cash assistance. Lyndon Johnson's instinct was that cutting pieces of the pie for the poor was easier when the pie was rapidly growing. The declining trend of real wages made the great middle class cynical of government, fed up with taxes and sceptical that welfare beneficiaries deserved help.

FUTURE PROSPECTS

What can we expect in the future? According to the regressions of Table 25.1, return to an overall unemployment rate of 5 per cent, with a corresponding adult white male rate of 3.6 per cent, 0.7 points below the 1990 rate, could by itself lower poverty rates for persons, pre- and post-transfer, by 0.3 to 0.4 points. These reductions would be a one-time contribution of successful countercyclical macroeconomic policy. Yet the present disposition of our monetary and fiscal policy-makers evidently means that so low an unemployment target is unrealistically ambitious.

Full recovery, to whatever target will appear inflation-safe to the Federal Reserve, seems likely to take several years. One reason, of which the weak Help Wanted numbers cited above are symptomatic, is the irreversible nature of many recent and prospective lay-offs. Some of these eliminations of jobs are belated adaptations by American companies to the global competition assailing them ever since 1980. Others are permanent cutbacks of the armed services and of defence-related jobs all over the country, the clouds of which peace dividends are silver linings. Because the armed services have provided important opportunities for minority youth, their force reductions are particularly bad omens for progress against poverty. This cyclical recovery will depend in unusual degree on the creation of new jobs rather than the restoration of old ones. Permanent new jobs will require policies that generate and are expected to sustain adequate aggregate demand. Commitment to a sustained long-run programme of public investment in infrastructure, education and training, and environmental protection would be a good way to promote recovery in the short run while meeting long-term social needs.

I am more optimistic about the trend of real wages. Productivity growth in manufacturing was a bright spot in the 1980s recovery. Companies whose structural adjustments are eliminating jobs are also becoming more efficient, leaner as well as meaner. Modest improvements in productivity growth should now show up in earnings as well as, indeed even more than, in compensation. In the years ahead fringe benefits are likely to fall relative to take-home pay. But the yields in poverty reduction will be small and slow. An increase in the real wage by 1 per cent a year will reduce poverty by only about 0.13 points a year.

These unemployment and earnings effects together would lower poverty by a bit less than two points in one decade – nothing to write home about. We will need specific war-on-poverty measures – though not a new declaration of war – and more adequate and effective transfers to achieve speedier progress. As to the possibility that improved macroeconomic performance will soften the hearts of taxpayers and of politicians seeking their votes, it is hard to imagine conversions that will make additional budgetary resources available for new battles against poverty or for more adequate transfers.

The federal budgetary outlook is grim. After the defence share of GDP hit its 1980s peak in 1986 at 6.5 per cent of GDP, the share fell to 5.4 per cent of potential output in 1991. The Clinton budget will reduce it further to 3.2 per cent or less in 1997, a decline in annual expenditures of more than $100 billion in 1991 dollars. But increases in other outlays are eating up these peace dividends. The principal villains are interest on the debt, the legacy of the profligate tax cuts and defence spending of the Reagan–Bush years, and health care, especially Medicare and Medicaid.

Although the Clinton economic and fiscal programme for the five years 1993–97 contemplates using a third of the gross budgetary resources resulting from tax increases and expenditure cuts, mainly defence savings, for new non-defence initiatives, these initiatives are largely for public investments in infrastructure and education. Little is budgeted for anti-poverty programmes beyond further liberalization of the refundable Earned Income Tax Credit against personal income taxes. Welfare reform is geared to reducing dependency more than to reducing poverty.

Whatever is done to reform health care will have major fiscal consequences. Without reform, Medicare and Medicaid will add 2 per cent of GDP to the federal deficit between 1996 and 2002. The reforms are likely to help the poor, especially those uninsured or dependent on Medicaid. But they will reinforce the squeeze on other government programmes.

Entitlements to non-needs-tested transfers, especially social security, are often the targets of deficit hawks who do not have to run for office. But the Social Security Trust Fund is running ever growing annual surpluses, now about $70 billion. The Clinton tax plan would raise from 50 to 85 per cent the fraction of benefits taxable to the affluent elderly. If social security benefits of future retirees are to be reduced, the natural corollary would be to reduce the social security taxes they contribute while active workers. If so, no deficit reduction would be achieved. Otherwise payroll contributions would become ordinary taxes, regressive ones at that, blatantly used for general federal purposes. Although it would be possible and defensible to reduce equally social security benefits and contributions and then to increase ordinary income taxes in order to reduce the deficit, this triple play would be politically dubious.

Unfortunately, the Reagan Administration succeeded all too well and all too permanently in its objective of crippling civilian government by giving away tax revenues, creating a political taboo against raising taxes, and generating a deficit and debt to brandish against civilian expenditures. The victory may yet be sealed by a Constitutional amendment requiring super-majorities in both houses of Congress either to adopt a deficit budget or to raise taxes.

Although chronic budget deficits of the magnitudes of the Reagan and Bush years are harmful, cures for them can easily turn out to be worse than the disease. The point of deficit reduction is to free savings absorbed by the deficit for the financing of productive investments by the private sector. This process, the reverse of 'crowding out', requires reductions in interest rates to entice businesses and households to borrow money and built plants, buy equipment, introduce new technology, engage in research and development, and construct houses. The theory is that these capital investments will benefit future Americans, raising their productivity, wages and living standards.

The process requires the active cooperation of the Federal Reserve to bring interest rates down and to overcome the immediate adverse effects of deficit reduction on business activity and jobs. Without the Fed's aggressive help, deficit reduction could arrest or reverse cyclical recovery and actually diminish private investment and other future-oriented uses of resources. Even in prosperous times, the effects of deficit reduction on the future well-being of the society depend on how it is done. If it occurs at the expense of consumption by present-day affluent taxpayers or of unnecessary and unproductive defence or non-defence expenditures, future generations come out ahead. If it comes at the expense of public investments in education, infrastructure, housing, inner city development, improved health care, jobs programmes and welfare reform, the verdict is not so clear. Given the patent economic and social deficiencies of America today, my judgement is that those public investments, neglected as they have been since 1980, will serve future generations better than holding down the federal debt in order to channel more funds to private borrowers.

A FINAL REMARK

Looking back to the optimistic expectations I had in the 1960s, I do not think I can account for the extent of their disappointment by macroeconomic factors or by any economic factors. My own city of New Haven is a miniature version of the web of urban pathologies of New York, Washington DC, Detroit and Milwaukee, possibly also of Los Angeles. Manufacturing jobs have moved to the suburbs or more distant locations. Middle- and upper-class households, predominantly white, have moved out as well. Minority populations and poverty are concentrated in city neighbourhoods. According to the 1990 Census, only 21 per cent of the 49,000 New Haven households but 39 per cent of the 255,000 suburban households (in New Haven County outside the city itself) have incomes over $50,000 a year. The median city household income is $22,000, the suburban median is $40,000. In the city are the major problems of poverty, troubled public schools, welfare, joblessness, homelessness, ill health, crime, drug trade, family instability and fiscal crisis. Outside the city is the tax base, and there is no way to tap it to help the city. These urban problems reinforce each other. Together they constitute a socio-economic system dynamically unstable downward – a vicious circle.

What unforeseen developments are the most obvious negative 'shocks' – to use economists' jargon – to which the demoralizations of inner city neighbourhoods can be attributed? They are drugs, guns and AIDS, all obviously interrelated. Although they are outside my assigned topic, it is clear that understanding them and prescribing remedies are crucial if improving macroeconomic trends and policies are to have good effects inside, as well as outside, these neighbourhoods.

REFERENCES

Blank, Rebecca (1991), 'Why Were Poverty Rates So High in the 1980s?' NBER Working Paper 3878, October.

Cutler, David M. and Lawrence F. Katz (1991), 'Macroeconomic Performance and the Disadvantaged', *Brookings Papers on Economic Activity*, no. 2, pp. 1–61.

Denison, Edward (1974), *Accounting for U.S. Economic Growth 1929–1964*, Washington: Brookings Institution, p. 147.

Medoff, James L. (1992), 'The New Unemployment', prepared for the Subcommittee on Economic Growth, Trade, and Taxes of the Joint Economic Committee, US Congress, mimeo, April.

25. Social security, public debt and economic growth*

Social security has once again come to the forefront of debate in Congress and in the wider public arena. The immediate occasion is the current act of the seemingly endless fiscal drama – a new subject is welcome relief from the repetitive boredom of the annual budget-making rituals. Once its finances have taken centre stage, all aspects of social security are on the agenda.

I am referring to 'social security' in its original sense, benefits to the elderly retired and their dependents, specifically Old Age and Survivors Insurance (OASI). Disability insurance was grafted onto this programme. Their finances are intertwined as OASDI. I shall not be discussing Medicare, which chronically raises serious fiscal and social issues of its own.

I shall discuss several interrelated issues. What should be the target for the federal budget deficit over the next few years and in the longer run? What are our priorities as between deficit reduction and public investment expenditures? Should social security finances be segregated? Should OASDI be financed on a pay-as-you-go basis, or should it be at least partially funded, like private retirement insurance? How will old-age benefits for the baby-boom generation be paid for? What issues of intergenerational equity are involved? How tight should be the link, if any, between the payroll taxes (officially known as federal insurance contributions) paid by an individual and his or her ultimate benefits? Are payroll taxes regressive?

THE 1983 AMENDMENTS TO THE SOCIAL SECURITY ACT

Social security was the subject of important legislation in 1983. The OASDI trust funds were running out of cash. The crisis was widely believed to put the continuation of monthly benefit payments at risk. The trust funds for OASI and DI are accounts to which active workers' federal insurance contributions are credited and cheques for beneficiaries are debited. Normally the

*First published as 1990 Frank M. Engle Lecture of The American College, Bryn Mawr, Pennsylvania, 1990, delivered at the College 19 April 1990.

account balances are positive, mostly evidenced by holdings of interest-bearing US Treasury bonds. There's no reason, of course, why the account cannot borrow if necessary. Retirees' benefits were not in danger, but consternation over social security's insolvency focused attention at the highest political levels on its long-run problems.

In December 1981 Congress and the President assembled a bipartisan blue-ribbon Commission chaired by Alan Greenspan. The 15 members, drawn from both Congress and the public, spanned the spectrum of opinions and interests. The Commission's January 1983 report was the catalyst for a compromise between Speaker O'Neill and President Reagan, probably the only example of statesmanship our recent political history exhibits.[1]

The legislation based on the report's recommendations was designed not only to resolve the immediate 'crisis' but to ensure the solvency of the trust funds for 75 years. Among the measures included were increases in payroll tax rates sooner than previously scheduled, partial inclusion of social security benefits in taxable incomes of more affluent retirees, and eventual increase in the normal retirement age from 65 to 67. So well did the Commission do its work that it is the trust fund's floods of black ink, not its possible red ink, that now bring the system back to the spotlight.[2]

The Prospective Buildup of OASDI Trust Funds

The 1983 amendments of the Society Security Act represent a radical change in the theory and practice of financing OASDI. The trust funds are realizing huge surpluses – $65 billion in the current fiscal year, 1.2 per cent of GNP; $98 billion, 1.7 per cent is expected in fiscal year 1993 and $130 billion, 1.7 per cent, in fiscal year 1995. Around 2015 the fund (by which I mean the combined OASI and DI funds) will have risen to five and a half times its annual benefit outlays, nearly 30 per cent of GNP. For comparison I remind you that the federal government's debt to the public is currently about 43 per cent of GNP. These estimates depend, of course, on economic and demographic projections necessarily quite uncertain. The same projections contemplate that the fund will be used up by 2060, triggering, in the improbable absence of other commissions and amendments, a new red-ink crisis (Figure 25.1).

Prior to 1983 social security followed pay-as-you-go financial policies. The trust fund was meant to be a working balance of a few months' outgo, a buffer against contingencies. A larger fund balance, actual or prospective, was an opportunity for Congress to improve benefits or enlarge coverage. A vanishing balance, such as occurred in the early 1980s, was a signal to raise payroll tax rates.

The opposite of pay-as-you-go financing is funding. The founders of social security in 1935 initially contemplated funding of obligations to future ben-

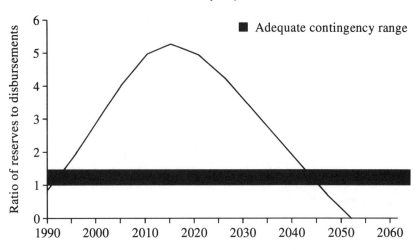

Source: OASDI, *The 1988 Annual Report of the Board of Trustees*, p. 83.

Figure 25.1   Projected OASDI trust fund reserves

eficiaries, like a private insurance company. But this policy was soon reversed, partly because of the unwelcome macroeconomic effects of budget
surpluses on the still depressed economy in 1937–38, partly because President Roosevelt feared that Congress would find the accumulating funds too
tempting.

The 1983 amendments deliberately enacted a funding policy. But the funding will be far from complete. Moreover the system would be back to a pay-
as-you-go basis in mid century if nothing further were done. The purpose of
the partial funding is to handle the coming demographic transition. The
numerous baby-boom generation, when retired, will coexist with sparse generations of younger workers paying federal insurance contributions.

Moynihan, Bush and Rostenkowski

Senator Daniel Patrick Moynihan, the foremost intellectual in Congress and
perhaps the foremost intellect too, was an important member of the Greenspan
Commission. He accepts with pride credit for the 1983 legislation. Yet at
Christmastime 1989 he woke Washington up by proposing to abandon the
scheduled increases of payroll taxes responsible for the growing trust fund
surpluses. He said, in effect, let's go back to 'pay-as-you-go'. Why? Because,
he said, the President is using the social security surpluses to 'mask' continuing large deficits in the rest of the federal budget, to meet the requirements of
the Gramm–Rudman–Hollings law (GRH), and above all to avoid the politi-

cal costs of raising regular taxes. Indeed the President is proposing to *cut* taxes! Congressional Democrats not only acquiesce in the deceitful masking but propose tax cuts of their own. Moynihan notes that all these proposals would cut taxes for the affluent at the expense of ordinary and even poor workers paying higher payroll taxes. The 'regressive' payroll tax has replaced the personal income tax as the largest source of federal revenue.

Moynihan's bombshell shook things up and put social security in the headlines and on op-ed pages once again. But his proposal has not picked up many likely votes in Congress. Some Democratic strategists do see it as a way of stealing the low-taxes issue from the Republicans and regaining the support of rank-and-file workers. But the Congressional leadership shies away from any responsibility for increasing the federal deficit.

At this point I should pause to remind you of the Orwellian language used in discussing the federal budget. Politicians, media and general public do not seem capable of focusing on more than one concept of the budget *deficit*. Before 1969 the focus was the deficit in the 'administrative' budget, from which the social security accounts were excluded. (I recall that in the early 1960s I and my colleagues in the Kennedy Administration took advantage of this exclusion to get some fiscal stimulus without the public relations taint of deficit spending.) Anyway, trust fund income and outlay were so close to balance that the definition of the deficit mattered little in practice. In 1968 a Commission of wise and conscientious economists persuaded President and Congress to focus on the 'unified' budget and its deficit. Their impeccable reasoning was that the deficit should be a complete measure of federal saving or dissaving.

The Greenspan Commission foresaw that preoccupation with the unified deficit would have the result of which Pat Moynihan now complains: trust fund surpluses would mask the deficit in the remainder of the budget. For that reason the 1983 legislation directed that trust fund revenues, payments and deficit be labelled 'off-budget'. GRH postponed and undermined this require-ment by expressing its mandates for deficit reduction in the old terms of the unified budget deficit. The annual budget documents keep a straight face while presenting both 'on-budget' and 'off-budget' accounts and their alge-braic sums, the 'total budget', formerly 'unified'. After fiscal year 1993, when GRH requires balance in the total budget and then expires, attention is supposed to shift at long last to the 'on-budget' budget.

Senator Moynihan had warned that he would not quietly acquiesce in counting the social security surplus to cover the deficit consequences of the irresponsible tax and spending policies so shamelessly but successfully ex-ploited in recent elections. He wrote the warning into the 1989 report of another bipartisan blue-ribbon group, the National Economic Commission (NEC).[3] The purpose of this Commission was to provide the new President elected in 1988 with a protective shield behind which he and Congress could agree on a grand fiscal compromise, just as the Greenspan Commission had engineered a social security compromise. It was not to be. George Bush thumbed his nose at the NEC during the campaign and again after he won the election. Instead of looking for a way to modify his 'No new taxes, read my lips' pledge, he has repeatedly reaffirmed it. So Moynihan, in turn, is sticking by *his* words.

The contours of the architecture of a 'grand compromise' have been pretty clear for a long time. Democrats, at least liberal Democrats, would concede some social security benefits – probably making a larger fraction subject to income tax and freezing for one year their indexed cost-of-living increases. Perhaps some other civilian programme would be cut too. Republicans would eat crow on tax increases – maybe agreeing to higher excises on gasoline, tobacco and alcohol and probably a 33 per cent marginal tax rate for top personal incomes. The Administration would agree to deeper cuts in defence spending. President Bush blocked the NEC from coming up with this sort of package. He and his Management and Budget Director, Richard Darman, have cultivated an image of affability in relations with Congress, but they have been no less adamant on the central issue of taxes than their predecessors.

One man only, Congressman Dan Rostenkowski, Chairman of the Ways and Means Committee, has had the courage actually to propose the grand compromise. He gets compliments from the President and Darman and from the Democratic leadership in Congress, but nothing more. However, he and Moynihan between them may have derailed the tax *cuts* proposed by the Administration and by their Congressional colleagues.

BOOSTING NATIONAL SAVINGS

What is the reason for segregating the social security budget and redirecting the political force of the balanced-budget ethic on the 'on-budget'? Weren't the economists on the 1968 Commission right that saving is saving and dissaving is dissaving, whatever the transactions that gave rise to them? Why insist on unified budget *surpluses*? Wouldn't it be enough to restore pre-Reagan fiscal prudence, under which unified deficits averaged about 1 per cent of GNP? Aren't we well on our way to that outcome? The ratio of publicly held debt to GNP, which rose from 25 per cent in 1980 to 43 per cent, has passed its peak (Figure 25.2). It will decline as long as the deficit is less than 3 per cent of GNP. The Congressional Budget Office projects the deficit to fall to 1.5 per cent of GNP in fiscal year 1995, even without peace dividends and other departures from current policies (Figure 25.3). Isn't that good enough?[4]

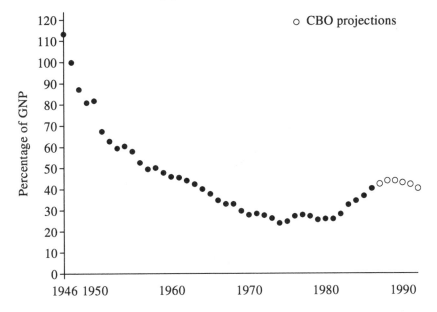

Note: ᵃPublic debt holdings include those of Federal Reserve banks but not those of social
security trust funds and other federal agencies.

Sources: *Economic Report of the President*, Jan. 1987, table B-3. Congressional Budget
Office, *The Economic and Budget Outlook: Fiscal Years* 1988–1992, Jan. 1987, table 11-8.

Figure 25.2   Ratio of federal debt to GNP, 1946–92ᵃ

The answer is that the United States as a nation needs not only to restore its
saving rate to pre-Reagan norms but to raise it significantly above them.[5] The
intended purpose of the trust fund buildup was not to finance the nation's
new-found profligacy, private and public. It was to provide the extra saving
needed to meet the social security commitments to the large cohorts eligible
for benefits from 2010 to 2050.

The decline of the national saving rate in the 1980s is an oft-told tale.
Table 25.1 tells it again, and I shall be brief in summarizing it in round
average numbers.

In earlier decades the non-federal sectors of the US economy supplied net
saving equal to 9 per cent of net national product (NNP). (The 'net' concepts
exclude replacement of obsolete and worn-out capital.) The federal deficit
took less than 1 per cent of NNP, and another small amount was invested
abroad, thanks to surpluses in international trade and property incomes. Domestic net private investment was about 8 per cent of NNP. This was enough
gradually to raise the stock of capital relative to hours of labour employed

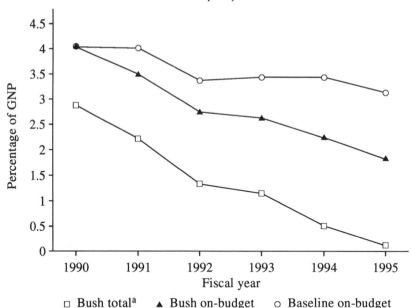

Bush total[a]   ▲ Bush on-budget   ○ Baseline on-budget

Note: [a]'Bush total' is the Congressional Budget Office (CBO) estimate of total deficits under President Bush's budget proposals of January 1990. 'Bush on-budget' is the CBO estimate of on-budget deficits under those proposals. The difference is the social security trust funds surplus. 'Baseline on-budget' is the CBO's estimate of the on-budget deficits, assuming continuation of programmes and policies prior to 1990.

Source: Congressional Budget Office, *An Analysis of the President's Budgetary Proposals for Fiscal Year 1991*, March 1990.

Figure 25.3   Federal budget outlook

and relative to national output, with beneficial results in productivity growth and real wages, at least until 1973. In the 1980s non-federal saving fell to 6 per cent of NNP. Despite cuts in tax rates and other supply-side inducements, households and businesses saved less. Meanwhile the federal government was dissaving like mad, 4 per cent of NNP, now down to 3 per cent. Domestic investment, down to 6 per cent of NNP, could not be financed from domestic saving, but required 4 per cent, now 3 per cent, in imported capital, the counterpart of our trade deficit. It is not quite true that the trade deficit is a measure of the degree to which we are living beyond our means, but it is a measure of the degree to which we are saving less than we are investing.

The above calculations have been challenged on several grounds. My good friend Professor Robert Eisner of Northwestern points out that they ignore many uses of resources that should be counted as saving and investment.[6] The

Table 25.1   Sources and uses of net national saving as percentage of net national product (selected years, 1956–87)

	1956	1965	1978	1986	1989
Sources					
Personal	4.3	5.2	5.5	3.1	4.4
Business	4.0	4.8	3.4	2.9	1.0
State and local	−0.3	0.0	1.4	1.6	1.0
Federal	1.2	0.1	−1.5	−5.4	−3.4
Total national saving[a]	9.2	10.1	8.8	2.2	3.0
Uses					
Net domestic investment	9.5	9.1	9.3	6.2	5.1
Net foreign investment (Current account surplus)	0.1	1.0	−0.5	−3.8	−2.3
Total investment	9.6	10.1	8.8	2.4	2.8

Note: [a]The sum of sources for each year should in principle be equal to the sum of uses. Differences are 'statistical discrepancies'.

Source: Department of Commerce, National Income and Product Accounts. See tables C-28 and C-22, *Economic Report of the President*, February 1990.

most important are public investments (roads, air transport facilities, environmental protection, sanitation, other infrastructure, science and technology, and educational facilities) and the building of human capital by education and training. He is right, but these investments too have been neglected in the 1980s. Their inclusion may make us feel better by raising the absolute saving and investment percentages, but they would make the 1980s look still worse relative to the past.

A second objection is that *gross* private fixed investment in plant and equipment has been, no less than in the past, 16 per cent of GNP. This is small consolation, for it reflects a shift to short-lived capital goods, equipment rather than plant.

A third point is related. Both net and gross investment look considerably better if calculated, not as dollar investment shares of dollar national products, but as 1982-dollar investment shares of 1982-dollar products. The reason is that the Department of Commerce estimates that the prices of investment goods have fallen sharply relative to the prices of other GNP goods and services – 8 per cent since 1979, largely because the Department counts improvements in the quality of computers as price reductions. Computers represent a significant share of equipment investments in the 1980s, but they

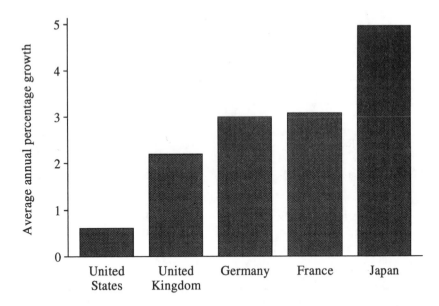

Note: ªBased on 1980 prices.

Source: Organization for Economic Cooperation and Development, Department of Economics and Statistics.

Figure 25.4   Productivity growth in five countries, 1966–85ª

rapidly become obsolete. Their contributions to economy-wide productivity have yet to show up. We cannot be complacent about the adequacy of capital investment in this country.

In any case we are saving and investing less than other major democratic capitalist countries, notably Japan, Germany, Italy and France. It is not accidental that they all surpass us in rates of productivity growth (Figures 25.4, 25.5 and 25.6). Moreover, to the extent that we lag in productivity in internationally traded goods, we can balance our trade only by depreciating the dollar and our terms of trade at the expense of our living standards. That is, it will cost us more both of our labour and of American products to import Sonys, BMWs and Burgundy wines.

Some economists take a relaxed view of federal deficits and national saving for quite different reasons from those of Eisner *et al*. Professor Robert Barro of Harvard has made a big splash in the profession by reviving an argument first advanced by David Ricardo in the early 19th century. According to what is known as the Barro–Ricardo equivalence theorem, taxpayers

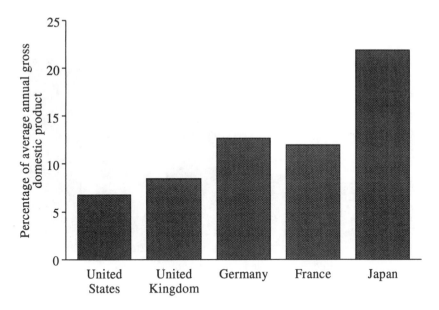

Note: ᵃRates are based on the average annual gross domestic product.

Source: Organization for Economic Cooperation and Development, Department of Economics and Statistics.

Figure 25.5   Net saving rates for five countries, 1960–85ᵃ

will 'internalize' the borrowing of their government, regard it as their own dissaving, and save extra to enable themselves and their heirs to pay the future taxes the deficit spending will ultimately entail.[7] The drastic change in United States fiscal policy in the 1980s would seem to provide a rare opportunity to test hypotheses like that. Since private saving fell rather than rose as federal deficits and debt skyrocketed, the *prima facie* case for rejecting the equivalence theorem is strong. Perhaps the public believed the leaders who assured them that despite the deficit spending taxes would never have to be raised again. Another aspect of the strong evidence that the deficit spending was not neutral is that real (inflation-corrected) interest rates were four points higher in the 1980s recovery than in previous post-war recoveries (Figure 25.7). Perhaps the private sector, having enjoyed a consumption binge in the 1980s, can be expected to save correspondingly more in this decade and later. So far there is no evidence of such a dramatic correction.

Eisner is right to remind us of the importance of public investment. Federal deficit reduction is not a desideratum *per se*. It is desirable as a means of

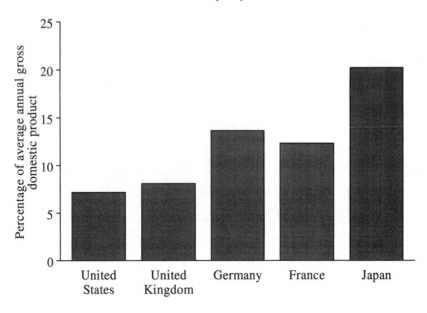

Note: ᵃRates are based on the average annual gross domestic product.

Source: Organization for Economic Cooperation and Development, Department of Economics and Statistics.

Figure 25.6   Net investment rates for five countries, 1960–85ᵃ

enhancing the nation's accumulation of socially productive wealth and thus increasing the standards of life attainable by future Americans. It would be foolish and futile to reduce government deficits by cutting back on public investments. Schools, streets and sewers surely deserve no lower priority than motels, casinos and shopping centres. Indeed recent economic research suggests that neglect of public investment bears a considerable share of the blame for the slowdown in productivity growth in this country.[8]

The moral is clear. The way to set straight our fiscal affairs is to raise taxes that bear on consumption, especially the consumption of the affluent, to reduce defence spending as fast as world conditions permit, and to cut back on government consumption outlays other than those that benefit the poor.

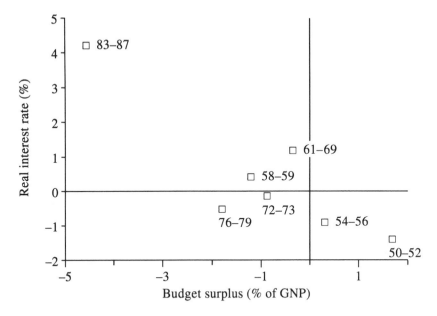

Note: ᵃFederal surplus is defined on a National Income and Product Accounts basis, average of calendar-year figures. Real interest rate equals the three-month T-bill rate minus the annual percentage change in the GNP deflator, the average of annual averages.

Source: *Economic Report of the President*, Jan. 1987, tables B-3, B-68, B-77.

Figure 25.7   Budget surplus and real interest: seven recoveries, 1950–87ᵃ

FINANCING BABY-BOOMERS IN THEIR OLD AGE

The special problem the demographic transition poses for social security finance is quite easy to see in Table 25.2. Let me give you a fairly realistic numerical example. For 100 active covered workers there are today 30 OASDI beneficiaries, including both retired covered workers and their dependents or survivors. In 50 years there will be 50 (Figure 25.8). Suppose that then, as now, the average payment per beneficiary will be 33 per cent of the contemporaneous average covered (that is, subject to tax) wage. Under pay-as-you-go today it would take a payroll tax rate of 10 per cent (0.30 multiplied by 0.33) to finance the benefits. In 2040 it would take a tax of 16.5 per cent, as shown in the 2040a column of Table 25.2 (I refer to the employer and employee contributions combined. The actual 1990 tax is 12.4 per cent; this is more than pay-as-you go would require and is producing the surplus already described. I do not count the Medicare health insurance contribution,

Table 25.2 *Financing baby-boomers in their old age (some approximate pay-as-you-go arithmetic)*

	1990	2040a	2040b
Active covered workers (a)	100	100	100
Beneficiaries (b)	30	50	50
Benefit/wage ratio (r)	.33	.33	.20
PAYG tax rate (rb/a)	.10	.165	.10
Real wage (2% annual growth)	1	2.69	2.69
Real benefit	.33	0.89	0.54
Benefit/1990 benefit	1	2.69	1.63
Real wage (1.5% growth)	1	2.10	2.10
Real benefit	.33	0.69	0.42
Benefit/1990 benefit	1	2.10	1.27

Making up the 0.65 deficiency in the pay-as-you-go tax rate by partial funding:

Higher tax rate	.024	37%
Benefit reduction	.013	20%
Interest on bonds	.013	20%
Depletion of trust fund	.015	23%

which is 2.90 per cent on covered earnings now and is expected to need an increase of at least four points over the next half-century.)

This rough calculation says that the tax rate required to collect enough payroll taxes to meet benefit payments would be 6.5 points higher in 2040 than in 1990. The 1983 amendments increased the tax rate to 12.4 per cent, still four points short of the requirement. How is that difference to be made up? Partly – about one point – at the expense of benefits: by taxing as personal income up to half of the benefits of higher-income recipients and by raising the normal retirement age used in benefit calculations from 65 to 67. The remainder is to come from the advance funding now in progress, in two ways. The Treasury will pay the trust fund interest on its holdings of bonds, the equivalent of another 1.3 points. The fund will be depleted by about 9 per cent to cover the rest (Figure 25.9).

As I pointed out earlier, the 1983 amendments do not pretend to be a permanent solution for OASI financing. According to present projections the fund will peak around 2030 and will be exhausted by 2050 or 2060. The

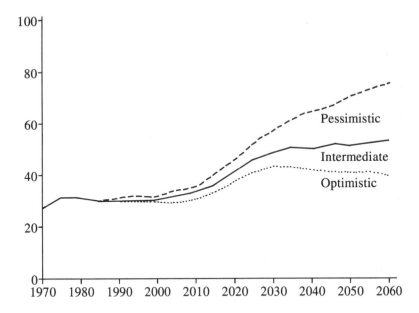

Notes:
[a]Ratio under three demographic assumptions.
[b]Beneficiaries include retired and disabled workers, spouses, children and survivors.

Sources: *1988 Annual Report of the Board of Trustees of the Old-Age and Survivors Insurance and Disability Insurance Trust Funds*, (Baltimore, Md.: Social Security Administration, 1988, table 30, pp. 79–80.
From Henry J. Aaron, Barry P. Bosworth and Gary Burtless, *Can America Afford to Grow Old?: Paying for Social Security*, Washington, DC, Brookings Institution, 1989. Used with permission.

Figure 25.8 Dependency ratio[a] (beneficiaries per 100 covered workers)[b]

traditional replacement ratio cannot be sustained without raising the tax rate sooner or later. If later, when the fund is virtually exhausted, the tax rate will have to be the pay-as-you-go rate, more than 15 per cent. If sooner, a significant trust fund could be maintained and earn interest.

Should the Replacement Ratio Be Lowered?

Payroll taxes can be lower if benefits are lowered further. Future generations will have to confront this basic issue in the next century.

Referring again to the rough but realistic numerical example, an alternative would be to stick to a pay-as-you-go system, hold the 10 per cent tax rate, and let the benefit/wage ratio fall from 33 per cent to 20 per cent (shown in column 2040b in table 25.2). If real covered wages grow an average of 2 per

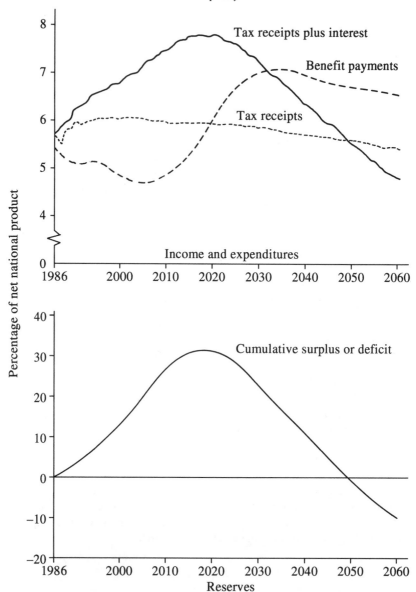

Sources: *Economic Projections for OASDHI Cost and Income Estimates, 1986.* Actuarial Study 98, Baltimore, Md.: Social Security Administration, 1987: SSA, Office of Actuary, unpublished data; and Aaron *et al.* Used with permission.

Figure 25.9   Trust funds' income, expenditure and surplus (includes
Medicare fund)

cent per year, in 2040 they will be 2.69 times what they are today. The same will be true of the real benefit, if the benefit/wage ratio is maintained at 33 per cent. A 20 per cent ratio would give the retirees of 2040 benefits 1.63 times those received by today's elderly. Even if real wages should grow more slowly, say at 1.5 per cent, both alternatives would yield benefits higher than those paid today – by 2.10 and 1.27 times, respectively.

This ratio, of per capita benefits to covered wages, is not the same as the *replacement ratio* usually cited in these discussions. The replacement ratio is the benefit for the average single worker relative to his or her wage the year before retirement. The benefit/wage ratio above is smaller because spouses and other dependents of retirees are counted among beneficiaries. But the two are closely related. The 33 per cent benefit/wage ratio corresponds roughly to a 40 per cent replacement ratio.

Of course, the old folks of the future, the baby-boom generation grown old, will be interested in how their OASI benefits compare with their accustomed standards of living, their pre-retirement wages, and the income of their younger contemporaries. It will be little consolation to them to be told that they are doing better than their parents and grandparents did when they were old.

The public believes that social security benefits are entitlements we all earn by the insurance contributions paid by and for us all the years we work. Certainly political discussions of the system give us every reason to believe that these entitlements are among the most solemn obligations of the republic. What exactly are the obligations? They are not precise at all. They are not like US Treasury bonds or Federal Deposit Insurance. Every contributor has the right to have the payments to which he or she is eligible under current law, but Congress can change the legislation at will. If there is any expectation of benefits that has moral force and political legitimacy, it is maintenance of the replacement ratio, which has averaged around 40 per cent since the inception of the programme. It is sanctioned by precedent, and it is built into the formulas used to convert earnings histories into benefits. When Congress has faced actuarial shortfalls, the presumption has been, as in 1983, that the balance will be restored mainly by tax increases. Replacement ratios have been maintained cohort after cohort, despite the fact that under pay-as-you-go the implicit rates of return on federal insurance contributions differ widely as between generations.

The size of the replacement ratio is related to a basic issue of public policy, the compulsory nature of OASI. Should the state force people to contribute to their own income in old age? Libertarians find such compulsion objectionable. Others may not deem paternalism so distasteful. Anyway, a society that helps citizens even when destitution is the result of their own imprudence has a right to require them to contribute in advance to such social insurance.

Universal participation has some important advantages: economies of scale and other positive 'externalities', in economists' jargon. It avoids adverse selection; permitting people to opt out could leave the government with the worst risks. Moreover, social security is the same all over the country, a completely portable pension plan.

It could be argued that the case for compulsory participation is weakened as benefits more and more exceed subsistence or poverty thresholds. Conceivably participation could be voluntary above certain levels of contributions and benefits. However, the system we have has worked well and enjoys the support of the overwhelming majority of the American people. In this support it differs sharply from needs-tested transfer programmes, just because it is universal and its contributors perceive that they are earning their pensions as a matter of right. OASI deserves the credit for the dramatic reduction in poverty among persons aged 65 and older.

The Economic Substance and Fiscal Requisites of Funding

My discussion of the future funding of OASI benefits has concentrated so far just on fiscal accounting, on the paper arrangements between the Treasury and the social security system. The more important question is the economic one. Does the advance funding mitigate the burden of 21st century non-working elderly populations on the economy – and in particular on their younger contemporaries?

Let's dispose quickly of a wrong answer to this question, one too often glibly repeated by pundits and even by economists who should know better. They allege that no financial arrangements can change the burden of providing goods and services for elderly non-workers. Those goods and services have to be produced at the time they are going to be consumed; the more of them go to OASI beneficiaries, the less there will be for the rest of the society.

It's true that we cannot put aside now the things the elderly will need and want in 2040. We wouldn't want to do that even if we could. We can, however, enhance the capacity of the economy to produce goods and services in 2040. We can use our present resources to build houses, factories, roads, hospitals, telecommunication networks and schools, to produce machines, computers, airplanes and appliances, to educate future workers, to develop new processes and products, and to acquire productive assets of future value in the rest of the world. The trust fund surpluses are savings that can be used to divert resources to these future-oriented uses.

Accumulation of extra capital of any and all of these kinds could raise national productivity and national product and thus augment the pool of resources available for future consumption by old and young alike. The gains would show up both in real wages and in the profits, interests and rents yielded directly or indirectly by the capital. How would those gains alleviate the burdens of social security finance?

The extra real wages would generate additional revenues from any given payroll taxes, but if the customary replacement ratio were maintained, OASDI benefits would rise by roughly the same amount. Higher real incomes would make it easier for workers to pay higher payroll taxes and for retirees to accept lower replacement ratios.

If the trust fund had invested its surpluses directly in income-earning capital, it would receive the yields of the extra capital and channel them directly to the beneficiaries. In practice the fund receives earnings on its savings indirectly, in the form of interest on Treasury bonds. The outcome is essentially the same. Having placed some bonds with the trust fund, the Treasury has a smaller burden of interest payments to the general public. The same 'on-budget' revenues would suffice, but the revenue yields of given income tax rates and excises would actually be higher.

The story makes clear why the funding strategy of the 1983 legislation can succeed in an economic sense if, and only if, the savings of the trust fund are not offset by extra dissaving by the rest of the federal government over the next 40 or 50 years.[9] The total debt of the federal government, trust fund holdings plus public holdings, must be the same as it would have been in the absence of OASDI funding. Then less of the public's saving will be absorbed by federal debt issues and correspondingly more will be available for financing capital investments, domestic and foreign, private and public.

If, on the other hand, the President and Congress treat the social security surpluses as fortuitous windfalls that permit the continuation of post-1980 tax and expenditure policies, the federal debt outstanding in the hands of the general public will grow as much during the next decades as if social security were still on a pay-as-you-go basis. No private saving will be freed to finance additional accumulation of capital; GNP, wage incomes and property incomes will be no higher than under pay-as-you-go. The trust funds will have their Treasury bonds all right, but to pay the interest on them the Treasury will need revenues from new taxes. An alternative scenario with essentially the same results would be for the federal government ultimately to try to inflate its way out of its double accumulation of debt: to the public and to the trust fund.

I have sketched for you the rationale for segregating the social security trust funds from the federal budget, essentially for adopting as fiscal policies the deficit goals that prevailed before 1980, before there was any significant difference in deficits or surpluses between the administrative and unified budgets. The segregation might be facilitated by officially focusing attention on the 'on-budget' deficit in whatever procedural legislation Congress imposes on itself in the wake of GRH. Or in principle the same substantive results could be attained by following a path of unified surpluses paralleling the trust fund surpluses.

But what about extra public investments, undertaken directly by the federal government or indirectly by loans or grants to state and local governments? The total debt that should 'remain the same' ought to exclude debt that finances those investments. To make sure public investments are not shortchanged in an undiscriminating rush to reduce federal deficits, I would dedicate half the trust fund surpluses to the purchase of federal, state and local bonds earmarked for financing incremental public capital.

Civilian public investments are mostly the direct responsibilities of state and local governments. But throughout the history of the republic the federal government has recognized the national importance of public improvements and has participated in promoting, planning and financing them. In the 1960s and 1970s under federal Administrations of both parties 'new federalism' meant revenue-sharing and generous grants-in-aid. In the 1980s it meant turning responsibilities over to the states and localities and withdrawing federal financing. Recently the Bush Administration unveiled a transportation programme of this type and explicitly urged states to raise gasoline taxes to pay for their increased expenses – this from an Administration that will not consider raising the federal gasoline tax and, like its predecessor, runs surpluses in highway and aviation trust funds to hold down its deficits. Unfortunately the anti-government and anti-tax ideology of Presidents Reagan and Bush is contagious. State and local governments have striven valiantly to pick up the budgetary responsibilities Washington has devolved upon them. The 1983–88 recovery made it possible, but now those governments face both the economic slowdowns that cut their revenues and the political perils of asking for higher taxes. They are not allowed the luxury of borrowing to meet current expenditures.

The budget is not the only federal policy instrument that has to cooperate in order to make economically meaningful the OASDI funding strategy now underway. Monetary policy also must cooperate, as it would have to with any tightening of fiscal policy. Cuts in public consumption by way of 'peace dividends' or other government economies and cuts in private consumption resulting from tax increases make room in the economy for investment. It takes easier monetary policy, lower interest rates, to ensure that investment expands to fill the room. Otherwise there will be a recession and higher unemployment, as there were when social security payroll taxes were first levied in 1937. If the Federal Reserve continues to gear its policy to macroeconomic performance, as it has done since 1982, we can expect the appropriate monetary responses to tighter fiscal policy. One of the differences between me and Eisner is that he does not believe the Federal Reserve either would or could offset the withdrawal of fiscal demand stimulus from the economy.

INSURANCE OR JUST ANOTHER TAX-AND-TRANSFER PROGRAMME?

Throughout its history the nature of social security, in theory and in practice and in the public mind, has wavered between two polar views of the connection between payroll taxes and benefits: the insurance view and the redistributive tax-transfer view.[10] The latter view is that there is and should be no more link between them than between any other taxes and any other particular federal outlays. Payroll taxes are one way among others that the government raises revenues, and retirement benefits are one kind of transfer payments among many other federal outlays. The insurance view is that individuals are earning entitlements to pensions by making those insurance contributions. Actual practice has been, and continues to be, a compromise mixture.

On an aggregative level, as I have explained, both pay-as-you-go and the 1983 amendments assume a link between payroll taxes and benefits, a link that requires the system to be both liquid and actuarially solvent. At an individual level the link between contributions and benefits is a mixture of insurance and redistribution.

Senator Moynihan's proposal is in the tax-transfer spirit (although the Senator, as an alumnus of the Greenspan Commission, has evidently come to that side reluctantly, believing that the President and Congress cannot be trusted to follow the insurance model). That is why he and many other commentators seize on the allegation that the payroll taxes are regressive. And so they are if they are just taxes. Is it fair to transfer dollars from a struggling young minimum-wage worker to a comfortable senior citizen? If, however, payroll taxes are contributions that earn benefits in return, they are not regressive.

In fact, considerable *progressivity* is built into the formula that converts earning histories into benefits. For an average worker in 1990 the replacement ratio is 42.3 per cent. For a worker with an earnings history only half the average, it is 69.7 per cent. For a worker who has always earned at least the top annual wages to which the taxes apply, it is 24.7 per cent.[11] (Naturally it is workers who are and expect to be in this high-wage category who are agitating to be allowed to invest their contributions in their own tax-deferred Individual Retirement Accounts (IRAs).) I think that the complaint about the regressivity of the payroll tax is irrelevant and misleading. Neither Moynihan nor anyone else is proposing an alternative tax source.

The progressivity built into the conversion formulas is progressivity within a cohort. In this case it has been generally accepted, but the recent revolt of the more affluent senior citizens against the plan to add coverage of catastrophic illness to Medicare suggests that redistributions among the already retired will not fly politically. Many protesters felt that medical assistance to low-income old people is a responsibility of the whole society, not just of other old people. Senior citizens don't mind voluntary payments for Medicare part B, which are the same for everybody.

I think it would be desirable to reinforce the personal link between contributions and benefits and to move the system further in the 'insurance' direction. Ultimately it would resemble an actuarial defined-contribution plan. Each participant would be informed annually how much a claim on the trust fund he or she had accumulated to date. As each cohort approached the designated normal retirement age – now 65 but to become 67 and perhaps raised further with improvements in health and longevity – the government would declare the rate of conversion of the claims of its members into pensions for participants and spouses and into ancillary benefits. The terms of these conversions would depend on legislation. A minimum – say, keeping pace with cost of living – could be guaranteed, charged to general 'on-budget' revenues if necessary. The amount of larger payouts would depend on economic and demographic circumstances and trends. The actuarial value of benefits would be strictly proportional to participants' claims. But the system could still be progressive. Progressivity would be introduced, not, as now, when covered earnings histories are converted into benefits but during the workers' active years. During years of low earnings due to unemployment, disability or other adversities, the government would make contributions from general revenues to the worker's OASI account.[12]

So fundamental a reform is not going to happen soon. In the meantime an important reason to oppose the Bush, Moynihan and Rostenkowski proposals (all three) is that they adopt, or at least give aid and comfort to, the tax-transfer view of social security. President Bush does so by counting on the OASDI surpluses to put his budgets into apparent balance without acknowledging the country's need for higher federal taxes. Senator Moynihan does so by abandoning his own earlier strategy for ensuring the long-run solvency of the system and by proposing to make the nation's savings deficiency worse. Congressman Rostenkowski does so by acquiescing in conservatives' long-held insistence that social security beneficiaries contribute to a grand budget compromise. The specific proposal would violate commitments to maintain the purchasing power of current retirees' benefits. Holding the indexation of benefits to 2 per cent when the actual inflation rate is 5 per cent 'for just one year' may seem a minor sacrifice, but it is actually a *permanent* benefit reduction of 3 per cent. No one would have the nerve to propose it or vote for it if it were framed in those words.

INTERGENERATIONAL EQUITIES AND CONFLICTS

There's no such thing as a free lunch, as economists tiresomely say. If the nation is to save more for the future, somebody has to consume less in the present. Of course, private decisions to consume less and save more are mostly voluntary. But if the federal government is to dissave less and save more, some of its taxpayers and transferees will be involuntarily consuming less, in order that they or others will be able to consume more in the future. Inevitably the financing of OASDI benefits over the next 50 to 75 years raises issues of intergenerational equity. Sometimes those issues give a nastily sharp edge to the debate.

Who will pay for the OASDI benefits of the baby-boomers? Under pay-as-you-go, the cohorts who come after them, including their children and grand-children plus immigrants, will bear the burden in the form of higher payroll taxes. Under the 1983 amendments much of the burden is shifted to the baby-boomers themselves. The partial funding – provided it has real economic substance – means that they pay for some of their benefits in advance by payroll taxes higher than are needed to support their own elders. Otherwise their replacement ratios would be lower. On their advance contributions baby-boomers will earn something like the rate of interest on government bonds.

The 1983 amendments also place some of the burden on present benefici-aries and other older cohorts. They also pay higher payroll taxes – many younger people may be surprised to know that if you work for an employer or for yourself after you start drawing benefits you not only suffer cuts in benefits until you are 70 but have to pay payroll taxes regardless of age. The legislation also cuts and taxes the benefits of pre-baby-boom cohorts. Some baby-boomers are nonetheless resentful that their predecessors got better deals from social security than they will get. That's the bounce of the ball. The slowdown in productivity growth and real wages from 1973 on is a misfortune, but it is virtually impossible to spread its effects evenly over the generations. As for the demographics that thinned the ranks of those who will be paying payroll taxes when the baby-boomers are old, we present oldsters could say that we always thought our kids should have more kids. They preferred the absence of younger dependents when they were young, and they couldn't expect that to be a free lunch either. The only way to avoid these problems is to have a completely funded system, but as we have seen that, too, would involve inequities during the transition from pay-as-you-go.

You see what I meant when I said these intergenerational issues can become nasty.

NOTES

1. *Report of the National Commission on Social Security Reform*, Washington, DC: GPO, 1983.
2. A thorough review of the present status and outlook of social security is given in Henry J. Aaron, Barry P. Bosworth and Gary Burtless, *Can America Afford to Grow Old?: Paying for Social Security*, Washington, DC: Brookings Institution, 1989.
3. *Report of the National Economic Commission*, Washington, DC: GPO, 1989. Part I is the report of the eight majority members, Part II that of the six minority members. On pp. 56–7 of Part II the following words appear:

    > Let no one suppose that a Democratic Congress will much longer allow a *payroll* tax to be used to serve a \$2 to \$3 trillion debt owned in vastly disproportionate amounts by wealthy individuals and institutions. It already requires nearly one-half the revenues of the *income* tax to pay the interest. This surely is the largest transfer of wealth from labor to capital in the history of our 'political arithmetic'. But at least this is a graduated tax. ... If, in the next five years, no arrangements are made to save the future incomes to the funds, Congress – you may depend on it – will return to 'pay-as-you-go' financing.
    >   This is not a threat. It is a political reality and, indeed, an ethical imperative. The nation struggled for a generation to ratify the XVIth Amendment to the Constitution. We are not about to see it effectively repealed by a reform in the financing of Social Security.

    Senator Moynihan acknowledges that he wrote these words.
4. Congressional Budget Office, *An Analysis of the President's Budgetary Proposals for Fiscal Year 1991*, March 1990.
5. This case is made and explained at length in Aaron *et al.* and in Charles Schultze, 'Setting Long-Run Deficit Reduction Targets: The Economics and Politics of Budget Design', in Henry J. Aaron (ed.), *Social Security and the Budget*, Proceedings of the First Conference of the National Academy of Social Insurance, New York: University Press of America, 1990.
6. Among Robert Eisner's many expositions of this thesis are his *How Real Is the Federal Deficit?*, New York: Free Press, 1986, and his Presidential address to the American Economic Association, 'Divergences of Measurement and Theory and Some Implications for Economic Policy', *American Economic Review*, **79**, March, 1989, 1–13.
7. Robert J. Barro, 'Are Government Bonds Net Wealth?', *Journal of Political Economy*, **22**, November–December 1974, 1095–1117. On the state of the controversy, see Aaron *et al.*, pp. 68–71, and the articles cited there.
8. David Alan Aschauer, 'Is Public Expenditure Productive?', *Journal of Monetary Economics*, **23**, March 1989, 177–200. Alicia H. Munnell, 'Why Has Productivity Growth Declined? Productivity and Public Investment', *New England Economic Review*, Federal Reserve Bank of Boston, January–February 1990.
9. Technical demonstrations using models of economic growth are given in Aaron *et al.* and Schultze. Aaron *et al.* compute tax schedule adjustments to keep the OASDI trust fund actuarially solvent into the 22nd century.
10. For the tax-transfer view, see Joseph A. Pechman, Henry J. Aaron and Michael K. Taussig, *Social Security: Perspectives for Reform*, Washington, DC: Brookings Institution, 1968. In the economics profession the pendulum has swung the other way. See Aaron *et al.*, *Can America Afford to Grow Old?*, pp. 8–9 and references cited here.

11. Aaron *et al.*, *Can America Afford to Grow Old?*, table 2–4, p. 28.
12. This plan is described in my earlier essay on social security, 'The Future of Social Security: One Economist's Assessment', Chapter 2 in Theodore R. Marmor and Jerry L. Mashaw (eds), *Social Security: Beyond the Rhetoric of Crisis*, Princeton, NJ: Princeton University Press, 1988, 41–68.

ENGLE LECTURE QUESTION AND ANSWER SESSION

Q. I frequently hear it said that 'the old are not poor'. I also hear that surpluses in social security are in the vicinity of $100 to $200 billion. Some people say that maybe we shouldn't have a social security system except for the very poor, that we should go to an insurance-type system driven by competition. And we do have a surplus now for the first time. We never had one before; the social security system was totally pay-as-you-go, and we really couldn't think about downsizing it. But now I wonder whether it makes any sense to take the surplus and to rebate part of that, perhaps by giving the taxpayer an opportunity to check off on the tax form some statement like: 'I will forego all my social security benefits if I can have my part of the surplus to invest as I see fit in some kind of super-IRA programme or an annuity contract'. That way over a period of 30 or 40 years we could downsize social security and make it into a means-tested programme.

A. The question was based on the observation that, first of all, since poverty has been greatly reduced among old people, the main problems of poverty in the country are not among old people anymore. That's true. And in fact that can be claimed as one of the achievements of the social security system. Of course there still are poor people among the aged, and there is a safety net for those who, for some reason, have no social security or insufficient social security – namely, Supplemental Security Income, paid for by general revenues, not by the social security system. The questioner went on to say that we are running surpluses now, but, since many of the old people are not that poor, maybe there is no reason to continue doing this. We could, in fact, rebate some of the taxes or give back to people the surplus – say 2.5 per cent of covered wages – and let them do what they want with it. The questioner would in fact, give them a tax holiday if they would invest what were tax funds in tax-free investments. That doesn't seem quite right – to compare what you can do with social security with what you could do if you didn't have to pay any taxes on your own investments.

In my talk I did say that the generations that are involved could consider whether they would rather keep the tax rate down and have a lower replacement ratio. The result I showed in Table 25.2: that if you kept the tax rate at 10 per cent, which is the pay-as-you-go tax rate necessary now, then the replacement ratios would not be 33 per cent for all beneficiaries relative to the wages of primary earners. It would be 20 per cent. With a good growth in real wages, that would still give higher benefits in absolute terms in the middle of the century than we are getting now – but not by much if the growth rate of wages went down. If the growth rate were only 1.5 per cent, it would be a close thing.

So the fundamental question in having a national old-age insurance system – and people have differences of opinion about it – is whether there is a reason for making people participate involuntarily. I agree that the logic of doing so is weaker the richer the country is and the richer the returns that system gives to its participants. The nation has assumed and will honour a social obligation, a moral obligation, to prevent old people – and other people for that matter – from starving or going without health care. We'll do that even if the reason they are in a bad position is that they were profligate and imprudent when they were younger and didn't save. So the argument for having a compulsory programme is this: since we know as a country and a government that we will bail such people out, we have a right to insist that they save at least the minimal amounts that would be necessary to prevent the government from having to intervene in that way.

There are other arguments for having a universal system; namely, you avoid the problems of adverse selection that would occur if the government permitted people to opt out. It's the people who would contribute to most to the programme, in an insurance sense, who would opt out. You also have the economies of scale and the assurance that private pensions cannot give in terms of cost-of-living indexing. (By the way, government guarantees of private pensions may cause us another problem like the savings and loan disaster.) And you have portability; no matter where you go you are still in the same programme. It's a very good thing that social security was enacted as a national programme rather than left to the states.

Whether it should always have as high a replacement ratio as it now has is an issue certainly worthy of political discussion and settlement. Maybe what we should have is a programme that has a lower compulsory amount and allows individuals or groups – employees of particular companies and so on – to participate on a voluntary basis for anything above the minimal amount.

Q.   Should we allow more working immigrants to raise our tax base?

A. The question is: 'How about allowing more younger working immigrants to raise the tax base?'. Yes, that's a possible way of doing it. Immigration at the currently expected rate is already assumed in the projections. To make much of a dent on the situation it would have to be substantially higher than it is now, which is something like 600,000 immigrants a year in a labour force of 120 million. That's not an awfully big number, and not all of the 600,000 are in the work force or of working age, and not all of them are going to be big contributors to the social security fund either. So there would have to be a lot more immigration to make a big difference.

Q. Is there any continuing economic justification for discrimination in benefit levels for those of us who were born between 1920 and 1924?

A. You have got it wrong, I think. This has to do with the notch question, and I believe the years are 1917 to 1921. I know very well because I am one of the notch babies, having been born in 1918. That's one of those things to which there's no solution that is going to be fair – or rather, that is going to be *regarded* as fair. It all depends on how you want to compare things. People born before 1917 got an unintended favourable deal. What happened was that in 1972, when indexation was put into the social security system, the law was poorly drafted and indexation was put in twice. The base social security benefit computed for a beneficiary at the beginning of retirement was essentially indexed twice instead of once. The result of that is that the people in a few birth year cohorts before 1917 got a deal that is exceptionally favourable. This was not intended by anyone and had to be corrected because the fund really would have been in trouble if it had continued that way.

To correct the problem you have to have some cut-off date beyond which you are not going to let that mistake continue. It happened to be the cohort of 1917. Congress didn't feel they could take it out on people who had already retired, so they 'took it out' on people who were about to retire. They legislated a stepdown or 'notch' in benefits for those people but not down to the normal level of benefits going to people born after 1921. Sure, the choice of dates is arbitrary, and people can feel offended by it, but I don't think they should. We notch babies have better social security benefits than we could have expected anyway, so rather than worrying about how the guys who were born a couple of years before are doing, we should just accept it. There are bigger problems in the nation than that one.

Q.   What are your thoughts on proposals to reduce the capital-gains taxes as a revenue-raising measure, and what are your thoughts on our present system of taxing savings as income?

A.   I don't think that reducing the tax on capital gains is going to raise revenue except in the immediate year in which it takes place, when there probably is a backlog of realizations that have been postponed in the hope that they will be realized with lower taxes. So you will get a bulge in tax receipts in the first year or so. After that it is the opinion and findings of most tax economists that receipts from a capital-gains tax will go down rather than up. I must say that I don't think that now, when we have the kinds of budget problems and the low savings problems that I've referred to, is a time for lowering any taxes. It's not tax cuts that should be on the agenda of the President and Congress, but tax *increases*. I'm very sorry to see a tax cut on the agenda. It's a kind of violation of the understandings in the Tax Reform Act of 1986, that we would get lower tax rates and in return we'd have a bigger income tax base with fewer exclusions. Let's remember that there's still a gaping loophole in the taxation of capital gains anyway, which is that you never need to pay the tax if you hold on to the assets until you give them to Yale University or The American College or until you leave them to your heirs. That way you can escape the capital-gains tax altogether.

Q.   You wouldn't go back to carryover basis?

A.   I would, I certainly would require that, and if that were done I think you could do some other things with the capital-gains tax that would make it better than it is now. The problem with most of the tax changes that are proposed in the name of increasing private saving is that they decrease public saving more than they increase private saving. You give a personal taxpayer a tax reduction of, say, $100, that goes along with a tax concession such as an IRA, a cut in tax rates or a new Bush family savings plan. You give them $100, and that's $100 more deficit in the federal budget if no other tax is increased to compensate for it. That is $100 loss from federal savings. So if there is going to be a net increase in national saving, the response from the taxpayer has to be to save an additional amount more than $100. If he or she saves only $90, there is a $10 increase in consumption and a $10 loss in national saving as a result of the transaction.

     That is what most people forget. They say: 'Let's encourage private saving', but the proposals to do so almost always have the defect that they reduce public saving, reduce tax revenues by more than they increase private saving. Now, the one thing these proposals usually neglect is that if you want to give people an incentive to do something, in this case to save more, you do not want them to take advantage of that by cashing in on things that they have already done years before or things that they were going to do anyway. I don't know about you, but when there were IRAs around that offered a $2,000 reduction from taxable income for putting the funds into IRAs, I shifted the $2,000 from investments I already had. So I qualified for the $2,000 cut in my taxable income and the corresponding later reduction in the tax on the income from the IRA investment. But I didn't save any more; all I did was shuffle my portfolio around to take advantage of that particular tax cut. That's what most people usually do. And the Bush family savings plan will have the same defect.

How about the capital-gains tax cut? Well, there again, if you are giving lower capital-gains tax for realizations on savings and investments that took place a long time ago, that's not a direct incentive for doing more things now. People claim that it will encourage saving and investment now, but most of it, the revenue-losing part of it, is just paying for a lot of things that people have already done. In other words, this tax cut is an ineffective incentive because there's no change in behaviour – the behaviour has already occurred.

Now, if we really wanted to reform the tax system in a way that rewards saving without these two defects – one defect being that it rewards people for what they have already done or what they would be doing anyway instead of giving them an incentive to do something different, and the other defect being that it's a regressive change in the tax system – then we could go to the progressive consumption tax. The progressive consumption tax would allow people a deduction for the net saving they do on a comprehensive basis. You wouldn't qualify for a deduction or special tax treatment simply by shifting assets around. You would have to be prepared to show that you had done some net saving. You couldn't borrow money and then put it in a tax-free asset and say: 'That is my new saving. Only it happened that I didn't save to get the funds to do it, I borrowed it instead'.

No, that's not an effective way to do it. If you want to have people claim income tax deductions for saving, you want them to be prepared to justify their claim by a net accounting of their changes in their portfolio, borrowing and asset holdings during the tax year. That would be what you would want to reward. If real savings increase you want them to keep more of their taxes. Moreover, since higher-income people can be expected to do more saving anyway than low-income people, you might want to have a threshold that you would have to exceed in order to qualify for the deduction from taxable income of your savings. If you're a high-income taxpayer, you might compute your net saving, and to the extent that it exceeds 30 per cent of your income you can deduct it for income tax purposes. That gives the incentive to get up to the threshold and then the marginal incentive to go beyond it. And for low-income people who wouldn't be doing much saving otherwise, you can make the threshold much lower, even zero.

I can understand a serious proposal to encourage national saving by that kind of a scheme, which moves towards taxing consumption rather than income. But I can't go along with all these other giveaways, whose rationale is that they are pro-saving. They are not pro-saving. We have done this for ten years, and we have a lower saving rate than when we started. We have a lower personal saving rate, we have a lower private saving rate, and we have the government deficits, which came about by giving away taxes.

Q. I'm confused when you say that by paying a tax, you are creating saving in the government. I always thought that when you pay a tax, somebody else spends the money. You're saying that when you are giving money to the government, it's a form of saving?

A. Well, it's a form of saving if it's an increase in revenue, which is used to avoid borrowing more in the market. The government competes for savings by selling bonds, which every year are in the net amount equal to the deficit of its revenues from expenditures. So if you raise revenues, the government doesn't have to sell as many bonds. If it doesn't have to sell as many bonds, more private savings are available to meet the demands on savings by private corporations. That is the sense in which the deficit is a dissaving by the government, and, in the sense that lower revenues mean that the deficit is bigger, that means that the government has to go to the capital markets for larger amounts. If it goes to the capital markets for larger amounts, it's taking savings in the capital markets that otherwise would be looking for equities and corporate bonds and other ways of financing private investments or state and local projects.

That's the standard sense in which what I said is true. I think that is quite understandable for the deficit of any economic agent in the society, whether it be a business or a household or a local, state or the federal government. The deficit is the excess of its current expenditures, its consumption expenditures, over its revenues. That's the demand on saving; that's negative saving as opposed to the reverse – surpluses.

Q. What you said is true, but how do you answer Milton Friedman on that? He says that if you give the government an extra dollar, Congress will end up spending some of that extra dollar, and you are really not saving.

A. Well, I'll answer that by saying that it hasn't happened that way. It certainly hasn't happened in reverse. Once I heard President Reagan say that the way to keep your kids from overspending is to reduce their allowances. And he meant by that that the way to keep Congress from overspending was by reducing the tax revenues they have to play with. Well, he sure did reduce the tax revenues that they had to play with, but it didn't result in reducing expenditures, because, for one thing of course, the President had certain expenditures that he wanted to increase, namely, defence expenditures. And then he had interest on the debt, which became a major part of the budget deficit because of the growth of the public debt itself and because of the need, as I tried to explain in the lecture, for having high interest rates to control the economy and counteract the big stimulus that the budget was giving to demand. Going back before 1980, I think that the record of the budget in those years also refutes Friedman's claim, because the budget deficit had remained low relative to national product during that period of time.

I agree that if the occasion for increasing taxes is the perception of need for financing education, financing wars on drugs, financing the saving of the environment, financing aid to Panama, financing aid to Nicaragua, financing aid to Eastern Europe – if those are the perceived needs that give rise to an increase in taxes, that should happen. It doesn't look like it will, but if it does then you will see the taxes and the expenditures rising together. But that's because Congress and the public thought it was worthwhile to raise the taxes in order to finance those programmes and not the fact that the coins from higher taxes were jingling in the pockets of Congress and making them look under the bed for new ways to spend them.

Q. With your recommendation to increase taxes, how would you adjust the income tax?

A. The top marginal rate is 28 per cent, and the top average rate is even less than 28 per cent, maybe 26 or 27 per cent. I think that is too low – certainly lower than the rate in any other capitalist democracy, including capitalist democracies that are much more successful than we are in rates of productivity growth. So as a minimum I would keep the 33 per cent rate as the top marginal rate for all incomes above the point – well,

all incomes up to infinity. Eliminating the 'bulge' would be the adjustment in the rates.

That I would favour. If the political situation permitted, I would go
back to having a more progressive rate structure. But I know that the
political situation doesn't permit that now, so I wouldn't push it. But
there are other things that could be done with the personal income tax.
One loophole left in the tax law was big enough to drive a truck through,
and that was the home equity loan. I sure would get rid of that loophole.
I would also limit the deduction of mortgage interest from personal
income for tax purposes to just one house per taxpayer. There are things
like that that could be done that would increase the yield of the income
tax without changing the rates and be more equitable at the same time.

In areas other than income taxes, I think there is no excuse for the
United States to have such a low gasoline tax. In every advanced country
outside North America – in almost every country on other continents
excluding the oil-producing Persian Gulf states – a gallon of gas costs at
least twice as much as it does in this country. That's because of taxes,
not because of the international price of oil. That is partly a matter of
energy conservation, partly a matter of making people who drive cars
and trucks pay for the highways and for the 'externalities' of what they
are doing – the congestion, the pollution and all that. In the US every
penny of gasoline tax provides a billion dollars more of revenue, so 20
cents would bring in $20 billion. Maybe people don't realize it, but the
price of gasoline per gallon is now lower in real terms, deflated for the
general cost of living, and is more of a bargain than it was before the
first oil shock for American drivers. That would be a good tax to increase by a substantial amount; it would be beneficial not only in producing revenue but in its desirable by-products.

There is no reason, by the way, that gasoline taxes and excise taxes on
alcohol and tobacco should be enacted in pennies, because as prices in
general rise that means the same number of pennies represents a smaller
percentage of the wholesale and retail price. The taxes on those 'sins'
have actually declined in percentage terms. I don't see any excuse for
that. And I am paternalistic enough to believe that we should tax alcohol
and tobacco, as well as gasoline, much more heavily than we do now.

If I can say another shocking thing, I will point out that a number of
other countries manage to operate financial markets with modest transfer taxes that are big revenue gainers, and their financial markets still go
up and down and people buy stocks and bonds. I think we should do the
same. A 1 per cent transfer tax on financial markets would yield a lot of
revenue. Nobody would object to it if brokers said: 'Our costs are
greater; we have to put the broker's price up'. Let's get some of that for

the federal government, and if it has the effect of making people think beyond the next ten minutes or the next ten days in making investments and in reducing the churning of in-and-out speculators, that's so much the better also.

So there are a number of 'good' taxes that would actually raise revenue at the same time they would bring about improvements in the economy and society.

26. Health care reform as seen by a general economist*

UNIVERSAL COVERAGE, ENTITLEMENT AND REQUIREMENT

How did health care reform rise to its present high priority on the nation's agenda? There were evidently two main reasons. One was increasing consciousness among ordinary people – those favourites of Bill Clinton who work hard and play by the rules – of the insecurity of their entitlements to medical ser ices. Forty million Americans have no insurance at all, and most others are vulnerable to losing their insurance when they become unemployed or change jobs, retire or change family attachments or, worst of all, become seriously in need of care. The other was the inexorable rise in the costs, relative to gross domestic product, wages, family incomes, employers' revenues and government budgets. Overall outlays have reached 14 per cent of GDP, and this percentage has been rising about a point a year. This industry is America's prime growth industry and source of jobs, rivalled only by 'corrections'. The index of medical care prices has been rising three percentage points faster than overall inflation. In the absence of reforms, Medicare and Medicaid outlays are projected to add 2 to 3 per cent of GDP to the annual federal deficit in the six years after 1996.

A magic moment was September 1993 when President Clinton and Hillary Rodham Clinton seemed to have wrought a revolution in American attitudes concerning medical insurance. They had achieved a broad consensus for universal coverage, without regard for ability to pay or risk of poor health. No one is to be denied medical care because of inability to pay fees or premiums, actual or potential illness or disability, losing a job, moving or changing family status. This principle has some very important and inescapable implications, by no means transparent to many of the enthusiasts of fall 1993. Congress and the public were not prepared for many of the difficulties now arising in transforming the principle of universal coverage into practical legislation and find some of them distasteful.

*First published as George Seltzer Distinguished Lecture, Industrial Relations Center, University of Minnesota, 1994. The lecture was delivered on 29 April.

Universal coverage has to be a requirement, not an option; a mandate, not just access. One reason is paternalism. We don't want to allow a child or even an adult to behave in ways likely to do irrevocable self-damage. But generally protection of individuals from themselves is intertwined with protection of society. In the case of medical care, this society will not in the end deny some kind and degree of treatment, if only life-saving, to residents who have not paid for it in advance and cannot pay for it. They won't be turned away from all emergency rooms, hospital beds and physicians. We do have even now messy unsystematic last-resort informal insurance, private or public or some mixture. It's inefficient and expensive insurance, just because it comes so late.

Adverse selection is a serious problem. The poor, the improvident, the bad risks are not covered by the health insurance policies most Americans have, and so they wind up as responsibilities of the providers of last resort, paid for by the general public in taxes, fees and premiums, and lower incomes for physicians and other medical personnel. The only way to avoid adverse selection is to require everyone to be adequately insured and to make it financially feasible for all. For similar reasons, most states require auto owners to carry liability insurance.

A more germane precedent is social security. The risk being insured against is that an elderly person outlives his or her means of support. Society offers life annuities as an entitlement, but it also requires participation in Old Age Survivors and Disability Insurance (OASDI). The reason is to avoid adverse selection. If persons were allowed to opt out, many of them would in old age become charges on their fellow citizens, given that society will not in the last analysis let its unlucky and improvident old people starve or go homeless. (Or at least that used to be true.) If, as many conservatives advocate, individuals were allowed to invest their payroll contributions in personal tax-deferred Individual Retirement Accounts (IRAs), the social security system would be left with the least affluent and most dependent elderly. The system works because it is universal, in both senses.

LIMITING THE DOMAIN OF INEQUALITY

The national ethos on universal social security and universal health coverage is a manifestation of what I call 'specific egalitarianism' or 'limiting the domain or inequality'. Americans are quite tolerant of inequalities of incomes and consumption standards, much more so than most other advanced democratic capitalist societies. Only 17 per cent of Americans surveyed say they resent the egregious compensations of stars in business, finance, sports and entertainment. But Americans do want to see certain necessities of life distributed fairly equally. Those basics make up our 'safety net'. One of them, the principal one nowadays, is medical care. The instant implication is that medical care is a commodity, or rather a whole bundle of commodities, that cannot be left wholly to free markets.

Does this specific-egalitarian ethic dictate that individuals should not be allowed to buy more and higher-quality health care than what society guarantees to everyone regardless of ability to pay? I think the answer is 'yes' if an essential service, included in the standard package, is scarce and incapable of being increased in supply for a long time. The ethic says that life-saving procedures, for example organ transplants, should not be auctioned to highest bidders. But the situation is different if we are talking about services of which the supply is elastic in response to demands. It makes no sense to say that rich people may spend their wealth on yachts and diamonds but not on cosmetic surgery and orthodontics.

COMMUNITY RATING AND RISK EQUALIZATION

If everyone is to have and to be compelled to have insurance for a common basic package of services, independently of ability to pay and of state of health, then clearly the insurers cannot be allowed to select risks or charge risk premiums. 'Community rating' will be a revolutionary change in the conduct of this business. But what community? The whole nation? This is the practice of OASDI and Medicare, precedents suggesting a 'single-payer' system for universal health care.

Is a decentralized system, to which most customers and providers are attached, consistent with community rating? It seems improbable, really impossible, that every insurer, every Health Maintenance Organization (HMO), every health alliance, can have a representative sample of health risks, even if they are all prohibited from denying or discontinuing membership on the basis of existing or predicted costs of service. There are natural communities, related, for example, to location, employment or school and university affiliations. They are bound to have quite different distributions of individuals by age, occupation, environment, life style and other characteristics related to risks of ill health.

Even so, the principle of community rating could be implemented. The risks facing a given insurer can be rated from the characteristics of the clientele. On the basis of the deviation of the rating from that of a national representative sample, the insurer would either pay or receive an annual 'risk equalization payment'. These payments would balance out in total. They would be based on advance (*ex ante*) risk assessments. If insurers were charged or paid on the basis of their actual (*ex post*) experience, they would have no incentives to control costs. The same statistical sophistication that now guides insurers in selecting risks and setting differential premiums, a highly developed calculus, would be used to determine the formulae for risk-equalization payments.

MORAL HAZARD AND COST CONTROL

Universal coverage would extend the already prevalent institution of 'third-party payment' for medical services. The 'moral hazard' involved deprives patients and providers – physicians, hospitals, pharmacists and pharmaceutical companies, laboratories, and so on – of incentives to hold costs down by eschewing procedures of low expected marginal benefit. If someone else is going to pay, why take any chances? For this reason many existing and proposed plans involve co-payments, like the deductibles in home-owners' and automobile insurance policies. They may not be worth the trouble. They cannot be big enough to overcome moral hazard among the upper quartiles of the income distribution. For patients in the bottom quartile, they are all too likely to be an incentive to avoid needed visits to the doctor and needed treatments, often with expensive consequences for the patient and for society at later times.

CAN MARKET COMPETITION DISCIPLINE COSTS?

It's hard to imagine how anyone who faces honestly the implications of universal coverage can expect that ordinary market competition can keep costs down in this industry in economics textbook fashion. That is why economists invading the field have sought to contrive institutions for 'managed competition' – among providers for the custom of insurers and among insurers for the custom of group or individual buyers. The idea of health alliances is to give the ultimate customers more clout by combining them into big group buyers – less managed competition than managed monopsony. But these devices necessarily bring with them bureaucratic surveillance, kibitzing of physicians and hospitals, some fee-setting and indeed some rationing.

A deeper and subtler form of moral hazard is that guarantee of no-questions-asked treatment dulls incentives to adopt and maintain healthy life styles. Smokers, drinkers, drug abusers, over-eaters, habitués of careless sex – make your own list – should we charge them extra for health insurance before they need help and can't pay, or give them fair advance notice that they will not be treated for infirmities resulting from their own behaviour? Too often there is no way to detect hazardous behaviour until it is too late and no foolproof way to distinguish between misbehaviour and bad luck. Probably the best we can do is to tax products hazardous to health and use the proceeds not only for delivering services to alleviate their consequences but also for programmes of education and prevention, reinforcing the considerable non-financial incentives for non-self-destructive life styles.

In any case, the commodities bought and sold in this industry are unlikely material for those informed consumer choices on which we rely for competitive discipline in other markets. Consumers cannot know enough about the products they are buying – or someone else is buying for them. They are not in a position to do comparison shopping. They are in the market irregularly, usually under unique circumstances. Often money, even the patient's own money, is no object. The provider is not just a seller but the customer's trusted expert counsellor.

'BAUMOL'S LAW' AND THE RISE IN RELATIVE COSTS OF MEDICAL CARE

Why are medical costs rising faster than other prices, and faster than population and GDP? One answer is that they aren't, that conventional numbers exaggerate medical price inflation and understate the growth in the quantity and quality of services delivered per visit to the doctor or day spent in the hospital. Spectacular progress has surely been made in many aspects of medicine. It would be nice to see more of its fruits show up in statistics of mortality, morbidity and public health, especially in comparison with countries that spend smaller amounts both absolutely and relative to GDP.

The increasing cost of medical care is a manifestation of a general phenomenon. Although it is an obvious point well known in economics from time immemorial, Senator Daniel Patrick Moynihan recently learned it from William Baumol, a professor at Princeton and NYU, and Moynihan baptized it 'Baumol's Law', a convenient enough label. Baumol's Law says that in a progressive economy the costs of products that rely heavily on personal services rise relative to other prices. Technical progress in manufacturing, transport, communications, utilities and agriculture typically saves labour and relies on new machinery and equipment. Wages rise as a result, and competition for labour compels the higher wages to be paid throughout the economy, for example in schools and universities where 1900 vintage technology and equipment are still employed. Despite all its new high-tech procedures, medical care is still a labour-intensive activity. It's quite reasonable for a society to choose to direct some of the fruits of technical progress in some industries to maintaining or increasing its consumption of the services of industries that did not share such labour-saving advances. Given the spectacular increase in output per farmer since 1900, we would have been crazy to eat it all rather than shifting the children of Minnesota wheat farmers into arts, computers, recreation, tourism and, yes, medical care. If society doesn't want to spend increasing *shares* of its income on labour-intensive products like universities and medical care, it will have to be content with consuming absolutely less of such products.

Baumol's Law is a particularly thorny problem when those 'backward' activities are provided through government budgets, as they frequently are to a disproportionate degree. Politics focuses on the overall ratios of government outlays and tax revenues to GDP or taxpayers' incomes. If it is a political crime for these ratios to increase, then resources will not be made available to meet the increased relative prices of government services and transfers.

In the debate on health care reform, it is difficult to keep politicians, pundits and public focused on the nation's overall health care budget, combining what goes through governments and what does not, rather than worrying just about what outlays are counted in government budgets and what charges are scored as taxes rather than insurance premiums.

Like me, you have doubtless heard George Will and many other critics of the Clintons' health care reform plan refer to it as socialism, an expansion of the size of government unprecedented in the United States. This might be true, and not necessarily bad, if the Clintons were planning to put all the physicians in the country on government payrolls and take over ownership of all the hospitals, and in other respects actually realize the old American Medical Association nightmare of socialised medicine. But buying goods and services from private enterprises is not socialism in that sense; nor is transferring funds to private individuals so that they can buy goods and services, nor, even, is mandating private businesses to provide insurance to employees and facilitating such arrangements by tax incentives and subsidies. The republic has survived, and capitalism has survived, the public roles in social security, Medicare and Medicaid.

I don't want to exaggerate the role of Baumol's Law in medical care. For one thing, wages have scarcely been rising in the United States these past two decades, especially for the unskilled workers medical facilities employ in abundance. Increased costs reflect the increased use of highly educated and highly paid specialists and of advanced technology and equipment, presumably to the benefit of patients. However, competition appears to work sometimes in bizarre and perverse ways in this industry. For example, superfluous hospitals do not die or fade away. They modernize to survive, adding expensive equipment and services, duplicating underutilized facilities nearby. This is a syndrome known to economists as monopolistic competition with trivial product differentiation, typified by four gas stations on one corner. It's clear that free market competition is not going to discipline costs in this situation. It will take a bit of overall budget control to prevent uneconomic duplication and achieve efficient utilization of high-tech medicine.

CAN PRICE CONTROLS WORK?

In early 1994 some 500 economists subscribed to a well-publicized statement objecting to imposing price controls on medical services. They rounded up the usual arguments – the failures and disasters attributed to price controls from the Emperor Diocletian and the fall of Rome to the ill-fated controls of oil prices in this country at the time of the OPEC embargo and price-gouging in 1973–74. The economists' manifesto said nothing at all about prices in the health care industry or about the handicaps that free markets face in this industry, as I outlined them above. Perhaps the signatories don't know that we already have price controls, notably Medicare's setting of the fees they will pay. According to Joe White of the Brookings Institution such ceilings are prevalent throughout the world, and they work. So, in suitable circumstances, do limits on overall budgets. I was not particularly proud of members of my profession who signed the statement, and especially not of those among them who were designers and advocates of 'managed competition', itself a contrivance to control costs in the same way Medicare does, by creating and deploying market power.

EMPLOYER MANDATES VS. INDIVIDUAL MANDATES

In implementing the basic principle of universal coverage, at the same time an entitlement and a mandate, the major issue is between an individual-based and an employer-based system. The Administration proposes employer mandates. Since employers are already the locus of most health insurance, making their responsibilities compulsory seemed the least disruptive way of moving to a universal system and the least politically painful way of financing it. I believe, however, that sticking permanently to an employment-based system is a great mistake. The several current revolts against employer mandates suggest that they may also be a political mistake, endangering the crucial goal of reform, universal coverage. Apparently the Administration has not succeeded in keeping employer-mandated payments of insurance premiums out of the federal budget and free of the label 'taxes'. The Clintons might do better not to make employer mandates a symbol of their legislative success and a test of loyalty to their cause.

Employer-based medical insurance is a historical accident – a path that no designer would choose now if given a clean slate. During World War II, trade unions and employers circumvented federal wage ceilings by negotiating medical fringe benefits. Their popularity and generosity boomed after the War, as Congress sheltered them from personal income and social security taxes.

Much of the Administration's 1342-page proposal is devoted to expedients intended to mitigate difficulties and anomalies intrinsic in employer mandates. It's an endless and hopeless task. Some families, even among the non-elderly, have no employed members; some have two or several, usually with different employers. Many employees work part-time; some have more than one job. Americans frequently change jobs, employers, work locations, places – even states – of residence. The stereotypical family with one breadwinner attached to the same employer from youth to retirement is more and more obsolete.

Under the Clinton's plan, responsibilities for paying a family's premiums would generally be divided among several sources – various employers, governments, supplementary insurers and the family itself – in proportions varying from year to year and indeed from month to month. Keeping track of these liabilities would involve enormous paperwork and administrative hassle, contrary to Mrs Clinton's claim that an employer mandate decentralizes the system and eliminates the need to track individuals.

Nor would the Clintons' system be fair in either of the usual two senses of equity. Vertical equity demands that public subsidies, direct or via employers, be a larger share of premiums and of income the poorer the family. Horizontal equity requires that families' subsidies be the same if their incomes are the same. In the Clinton's plan, subsidies depend more on the size of employers' payrolls than on the individual family's ability to pay. Their plan is also full of bad incentives for both employers – don't hire workers with dependents – and individuals – best to work for big companies with generous health plans exempted from the standard rules.

It's individuals who get sick and need medical services. It's individuals and families whose ability to pay is the proper criterion of equity. It's individuals who must be guaranteed coverage. So it's individuals who must be required to have insurance. Let employers help pay the employees' premiums if they wish, but count those payments as incomes taxable to the employees. Treat self-employed in exactly the same way.

Bill Clinton properly made a big thing of his goal that every individual would have a national health card that would be perfectly portable, honoured in case of need throughout the land. Social security and Medicare are universal entitlements and mandates for individuals, and those cards are perfectly portable and honoured throughout the land. Those individual-based systems work, very economically too; the Clintons and Congress should learn from the precedents.

THE GRAETZ–TOBIN PLAN – 'FEDMED'

In February Michael Graetz, a Yale law professor with experience in the US Treasury 1990–92, and I sketched a reform proposal in a *New York Times* Op-ed article advocating universal coverage enforced by individual mandate. Our plan is directed at the population not now covered by Medicare, essentially people under 65. (It is not that Medicare needs no changes. The agenda would include coverage for catastrophic illness; provision for long-term care outside hospitals; higher fees for Part B, scaled to ability to pay. But those matters don't have to be solved this year.) Individuals would be required to buy insurance promising at least a national standard package of services, the same as contemplated in the Administration proposal. The federal government would help lower-income individuals and families pay the premiums.

People could buy this insurance wherever they choose; it would be up to states to make sure that carriers actually can and do deliver the standard package and others offered. However, the central institution of the plan would be a Medicare spin-off, which we call 'Fedmed'. A similar institution is envisaged by Congressman Stark's bill and other proposals in Congress, sometimes called Medicare B. Our Fedmed would set actuarially fair premiums such that it would break even overall every year. In addition to offering the required standard package, Fedmed might offer more inclusive packages, for example the choices available under the Federal Employees Health Insurance System.

One of Fedmed's initial tasks would be to enrol the currently uninsured and the acute care clients of Medicaid, which would be wound down. But other individuals could join Fedmed if they wished, and any of Fedmed's members could move to other insurers during annual re-enrolment periods. Community rating, with the help of risk-equalization payments, would apply to the private competitors of Fedmed.

Those provisions would protect Fedmed from becoming the last-resort receptacle for bad risks. As in Medicare itself, people could choose their own clinics, HMOs, physicians and other providers. A fee-for-service version of the basic package might cost a bit more. Like Medicare, Fedmed would have low administrative costs and would wield enough clout to limit payments to providers. But Fedmed need not be a monopoly; its competition would be sufficient discipline to make its private competitors offer good value, without the need for much else in the way of price and cost controls.

Our proposal dispenses with the Clintons' bureaucratic layer of health alliances between the ultimate consumers and the insurance carriers or HMOs, or combination insurers and providers.

Equitable Premiums and Subsidies

Federal subsidies to individuals and families would take the form of refundable tax credits, 'vouchers', excuse the expression, payable to Fedmed or other certified insurers. For poverty or near-poverty persons, below an income threshold, the subsidies would cover the whole premium of the basic package. No individual or family would be out of pocket more than 8 or 10 per cent of income above the threshold. That is, if the premium exceeds that amount, the government will pay the difference. Most people – about the same population that is not above the 28 per cent marginal income tax bracket – will get some help. More affluent people will pay the whole premiums themselves. This system is direct, simple and fair. It avoids unnecessary channelling of funds through ordinary taxes into outlays for health services. It does not make health services for the whole population a burden on general taxpayers, disconnected from the health insurance the taxpayers receive.

Table 26.1 reports calculations for four alternative plans.

Where will the money come from? From discontinuing Medicaid acute care ($75 billion a year in 1999). From eliminating the exclusion of employer-paid health care fringe benefits from employee taxable income and earnings ($100 billion in 1999). From new cigarette taxes and whatever other sources the Clintons intend to get the $100 billion a year in 1999 they will need for their subsidies to employers and low-income people.

The biggest political obstacle would be the elimination of the current tax exclusion, an indefensible subsidy disproportionately of benefit to higher-income brackets. Our subsidies would make this up for persons not above the 28 per cent marginal income tax bracket. Moreover, these reforms all can and should be phased in gradually. The Clintons' solicitude for existing institutions and interests is understandable. But they should not be frozen permanently into the health care system of the next century.

Opportunities for fundamental reform of institutions come rarely and must not be wasted in incrementalist politics as usual. The President and Congress have a historic opportunity comparable to the enactments of social security in 1935 and Medicare in 1965, and indeed a much more difficult challenge because it is remaking existing institutions, not just creating new ones.

Above all, President and Congress must not compromise away or long delay universal coverage, the unifying purpose of the whole crusade. Michael Graetz and I believe our proposal is the best way to fulfil that basic promise.

Table 26.1   Characteristics of plan, assumptions and estimates for 1999

	# I	# II	# II	# IV
Net cost of basic package to family is $0 for per cap. inc. below threshold of	$3,500	$5,000	$6,500	$7,500
Equivalent threshold in 1992	$2,944	$4,206	$5,468	$6,309
Net per cap cost. to family not to exceed x% of (per cap. inc. minus threshold). x is:	10.0	8.0	9.0	6.0
Full premium for basic package per person assumed	$1,750	$1,750	$2,250	$1,550
Equivalent premium in 92$	$1,197	$1,197	$1,539	$1,060
Population growth 1992–99 (%/yr)	1.25	1.25	1.25	1.25
Per cap. real inc growth (%/yr)	1.50	1.50	1.50	1.50
General inflation 1992–99 (%/yr)	2.50	2.50	2.50	2.50
Excess med. infl. (%/yr)	3.00	3.00	3.00	3.00
TOTAL COST TO GOVT IN 1999 ($ billion)	$153	$206	$313	$231
Approx marg. cost. of extra $100 premium in 1999 ($ billion)	$17	$20	$21	$21
Lowest non-subsidized income four-person family	$84,000	$107,500	$126,000	$133,333
28% of four-person family premium	$1,960	$1,960	$2,520	$1,736
Income at which plan subsidy equals 28% of premium	$64,400	$83,000	$98,000	$104,400
Top income of 28% bracket	$100,000	$100,000	$100,000	$100,000

Index